Refiguring ENGLISH STUDIES

Refiguring English Studies provides a forum for scholarship on English studies as a discipline, a profession, and a vocation. To that end, the series publishes historical work that considers the ways in which English studies has constructed itself and its objects of study; investigations of the relationships among its constituent parts as conceived in both disciplinary and institutional terms; and examinations of the role the discipline has played or should play in the larger society and public policy. In addition, the series seeks to feature studies that, by their form or focus, challenge our notions about how the written "work" of English can or should be done and to feature writings that represent the professional lives of the discipline's members in both traditional and nontraditional settings. The series also includes scholarship that considers the discipline's possible futures or that draws upon work in other disciplines to shed light on developments in English studies.

Volumes in the Series

John Staunton, *Deranging English/Education: Teacher Inquiry, Literary Studies, and Hybrid Visions of "English" for 21st Century Schools* (2008)

Laurie Grobman, *Multicultural Hybridity: Transforming American Literary Scholarship and Pedagogy* (2007)

Bruce McComiskey, editor, *English Studies: An Introduction to the Discipline(s)* (2006)

Ray Misson and Wendy Morgan, *Critical Literacy and the Aesthetic: Transforming the English Classroom* (2006)

Linda S. Bergmann and Edith M. Baker, editors, *Composition and/or Literature: The End(s) of Education* (2006)

Shari J. Stenberg, *Professing and Pedagogy: Learning the Teaching of English* (2005)

Robert P. Yagelski and Scott A. Leonard, editors, *The Relevance of English: Teaching That Matters in Students' Lives* (2002)

Chris W. Gallagher, *Radical Departures: Composition and Progressive Pedagogy* (2002)

Derek Owens, *Composition and Sustainability: Teaching for a Threatened Generation* (2001)

Amy Lee, *Composing Critical Pedagogies: Teaching Writing as Revision* (2000)

Anne J. Herrington and Marcia Curtis, *Persons in Process: Four Stories of Writing and Personal Development in College* (2000)

Charles M. Anderson and Marian M. MacCurdy, editors, *Writing and Healing: Toward an Informed Practice* (2000)

Stephen Parks, *Class Politics: The Movement for the Students' Right to Their Own Language* (2000)

Stephen M. North, with Barbara A. Chepaitis, David Coogan, Lâle Davidson, Ron MacLean, Cindy L. Parrish, Jonathan Post, and Beth Weatherby, *Refiguring the Ph.D. in English Studies: Writing, Doctoral Education, and the Fusion-Based Curriculum* (2000)

Bruce Horner and Min-Zhan Lu, *Representing the "Other": Basic Writers and the Teaching of Basic Writing* (1999)

Michael Blitz and C. Mark Hurlbert, *Letters for the Living: Teaching Writing in a Violent Age* (1998)

Jane Maher, *Mina P. Shaughnessy: Her Life and Work* (1997)

Robin Varnum, *Fencing with Words: A History of Writing Instruction at Amherst College during the Era of Theodore Baird, 1938–1966* (1996)

James A. Berlin, *Rhetorics, Poetics, and Cultures: Refiguring College English Studies* (1996)

Jed Rasula, *The American Poetry Wax Museum: Reality Effects, 1940–1990* (1995)

David B. Downing, editor, *Changing Classroom Practices: Resources for Literary and Cultural Studies* (1994)

Undergraduate Research in English Studies

LAURIE GROBMAN

Pennsylvania State University, Berks

JOYCE KINKEAD

Utah State University

National Council of Teachers of English

1111 W. Kenyon Road, Urbana, Illinois 61801-1096

Copy Editor: JAS Group
Production Editor: Carol Roehm
Interior Design: Jenny Jensen Greenleaf
Cover Design: Frank Cucciare
Cover Image: iStockphoto.com/Atropat

NCTE Stock Number: 55585

ISSN 1073-9637

It is the policy of NCTE in its journals and other publications to provide a forum for the open discussion of ideas concerning the content and the teaching of English and the language arts. Publicity accorded to any particular point of view does not imply endorsement by the Executive Committee, the Board of Directors, or the membership at large, except in announcements of policy, where such endorsement is clearly specified.

Every effort has been made to provide current URLs and email addresses, but because of the rapidly changing nature of the Web, some sites and addresses may no longer be accessible.

Library of Congress Cataloging-in-Publication Data

Grobman, Laurie, 1962–
Undergraduate research in English studies / Laurie Grobman, Joyce Kinkead.
p. cm.
Includes bibliographical references and index.
ISBN 978-0-8141-5558-5 ((pbk.))
1. English language—Study and teaching (Higher) 2. English language—Writing—Study and teaching (Higher) 3. English language—Written English—Study and teaching (Higher) I. Kinkead, Joyce A., 1954– II. Title.
PE1065.G784 2010
428.0071'173—dc19

2009043837

Contents

IV Case Studies across the Discipline of English

Literature

Composition and Rhetoric

Acknowledgments

It is the unknown that excites the ardor of scholars, who, in the known alone, would shrivel up with boredom.

—Wallace Stevens

As this volume will no doubt attest, we are passionate about undergraduate research and scholarship. We are grateful to the contributors, who join us in this ardor with stories and theoretical perspectives about their work with student scholars. We thank the anonymous peer reviewers, Bonny Graham, Kurt Austin, and everyone else at NCTE who gave support and assistance. Michael Spooner also offered valuable feedback and insight. Likewise, at each of our institutions, we credit our colleagues and leaders for their ongoing support; in particular, Brent C. Miller, vice president for research at Utah State University, has been noteworthy for his unflagging enthusiasm for undergraduate research.

Natalie Marie Hatch, undergraduate researcher in the Department of English at Utah State University, provided invaluable assistance with the references. Natalie is but one instance of a student who brings to her studies a zeal for inquiry. We celebrate undergraduates who bring to their studies that same enthusiasm and commitment.

LG
JK

Introduction
Illuminating Undergraduate Research in English

LAURIE GROBMAN
Pennsylvania State University, Berks

JOYCE KINKEAD
Utah State University

According to the Council on Undergraduate Research (CUR), "undergraduate research is an inquiry or investigation conducted by an undergraduate that makes an original, intellectual, or creative contribution to the field" (*About CUR*). Such student research is *distinct from the ubiquitous research paper*. Undergraduate research involves students as apprentices, collaborators, or independent scholars in critical investigations using fieldwork and discipline-specific methodologies under the sponsorship of faculty mentors. Students engaged in genuine research gain an insider's understanding of field-specific debates, develop relevant skills and insights for future careers and graduate study, and most important, contribute their voices to creating knowledge through the research process. Thus, student research, like faculty research, aims to fill a gap in the knowledge base, and assuming it succeeds, is disseminated and shared—locally, regionally, nationally, or internationally. Undergraduate research in the liberal arts, particularly, has its roots in both the nineteenth-century seminar and honors education. While the thesis is the final product in that latter forum, the current curricular movement emphasizes even more strongly the contribution of knowledge through dissemination, typically more public than a thesis archived in the honors office.

Undergraduate Research in English Studies aims to mobilize the profession to further participate in undergraduate research.

By *English studies*, we mean the wealth of fields within English, including writing studies, literary studies, creative writing, English education, folklore, American studies, linguistics, and cultural studies. We believe there are islands of excellence around the nation and the world where undergraduate research in English has taken hold. This collection shares exemplary practices in writing and literary studies and seeks to spread them widely. Although the movement may be fragmented at the moment, we are clearly on the cusp of implementation in all subfields of English throughout our various institutions.

This volume provides models, but is also a clarion call for the integration of undergraduate research in English studies. As David DeVries (2001) claims, humanities teacher-scholars need to find ways to "persuade all of our colleagues and peers that research is just as vital, just as sustaining, for the humanities and their students as it is for the natural and social sciences" and to recognize "the inestimable value of independent research in the intellectual and professional growth of young scholars" (155). *Undergraduate Research in English Studies* combines theory and practice, laying the groundwork for further practice and inquiry. The research performed by undergraduates highlighted in this collection, we believe, will inspire and lead colleagues to consider similar approaches.

Why is undergraduate research slow to grab hold in the humanities, particularly in English studies? Our suspicion is that we as faculty have not articulated to our students the methodology of inquiry in our fields except as injunctions in our classrooms to "write a paper." Though the scientific method is transparent, that is not always the case in the humanities. We may not always agree on a process of inquiry; some might even call the discipline fragmented. And certainly some theoretical literature is quite dense for undergraduates. As faculty, we need to articulate our methodology, define appropriate tasks for students, and ask for authentic scholarship. What happens in humanistic inquiry? It is actually quite similar to other disciplines and may be outlined as follows: the identification of and acquisition of a disciplinary or interdisciplinary methodology; the setting out of a concrete investigative problem; the carrying out of the actual project; and finally, the dispersing or sharing of a new scholar's discoveries with his or her peers—a step often missing in undergraduate educational programs. How often do we unpack this methodology in our classrooms for our students? Do we assume too much prior knowledge on their part? Are we committed to inducting them into the club of scholars, asking important questions and investigating the answers? Do we ask them to share their discoveries more widely?

It is our hope that undergraduate research may help shape the future of the discipline of English studies and the profession. Ronald Dotterer (2002), former president of the National Conferences on Undergraduate Research (NCUR), proposes that undergraduate research offers "a new 'vision' that scholarship and teaching may not be as separable as conventionally thought or practiced" (81). Ernest L. Boyer suggests the same in *Scholarship Reconsidered* (1990). Many scholars have noted and discussed, from varying perspectives, the division between what we do as teachers and as scholars. Undergraduate research brings together our passions for teaching and for research. It is one site for realizing the "synergy between teaching and scholarship" called for in the white paper "Student Learning and Faculty Research" (Teagle Working Group 3).

We have titled this introduction "Illuminating Undergraduate Research," as we like the concept of *illuminating*. It first came to mind inspired by one of our contributors, an undergraduate who described studying an illuminated manuscript. In many ways, illuminated manuscripts serve as the origin for what we do as scholars of texts, and also are a source of literacy. We wish in this volume to illuminate student research by revealing its historical origins, providing informative and instructive models, addressing its challenges, and shedding light on the possibilities for future directions.

The History of Undergraduate Research as a National Movement

Undergraduate research, an educational movement and comprehensive curricular innovation, is "the pedagogy for the twenty-first century," according to the *Joint Statement of Principles* composed by the Council on Undergraduate Research (CUR) and NCUR (2005). The undergraduate research movement has been fueled by CUR, NCUR, the Boyer Commission report *Reinventing Undergraduate Education* (1998), and its resulting action organization, the Reinvention Center. Originally, the scientific community initiated a focus on undergraduate research for several reasons, including reports of the scientific illiteracy of American students in the 1990s, as well as the media's and public's questioning of research universities' attention to undergraduate education. The movement has spread to all areas of academe, including the humanities.

Twenty years before the groundbreaking Boyer Commission report, CUR was established by a group of chemists from private liberal arts colleges to provide support to *faculty*. According to CUR, "faculty members enhance their teaching and contribution to society by remaining active in research and by involving undergraduates in research" (*About CUR*). While founded in the sciences, CUR has expanded in its thirty-year history to include all disciplines and all types of institutions. At this writing, it has nearly 3,000 individual members and almost 500 institutional members. A signature event for CUR is its annual Posters on the Hill, at which colleges and universities share undergraduate research posters with members of Congress. A biennial conference offers faculty the opportunity to meet and discuss undergraduate research broadly as well as in the context of particular disciplines, including an Arts and Humanities division. CUR's publishing arm includes a quarterly periodical, edited collections, and monographs.

Founded in 1987, NCUR is an annual meeting where undergraduates present their research, scholarship, and creative products. Its mission is to "promote undergraduate research, scholarship, and creative activity done in partnership with faculty or other mentors as a vital component of higher education" (*About CUR*). Attended by more than 2,000 students annually, NCUR provides plenary sessions, poster sessions, oral presentations, and performances. Realizing their mutual interests as advocates for undergraduate research, these two important organizations—CUR and NCUR—voted to merge, effective in 2010.

A third organization, the Reinvention Center, grew out of the benchmark Boyer Commission report. Although directed at research universities, the report offers ten points to improve undergraduate education, recommendations that could be applied to any institution—and have. A prime one is "to make research-based learning the standard." As the report notes, "Undergraduate education [. . .] requires renewed emphasis on a point strongly made by John Dewey almost a century ago: learning is based on discovery guided by mentoring rather than on the transmission of information. Inherent in inquiry-based learning is an element of reciprocity: faculty can learn from students as students are learning from faculty" (23).

Educational researcher George Kuh, notably through his work on the National Survey of Student Engagement (NSSE), has identified undergraduate research as one of a few certifiable high-impact educational practices. The role of the mentor and the opportunity for authentic publication or implementation are key. The results include greater satisfaction with the undergraduate experience. Colleagues in the United Kingdom and Australia, convinced by their experiences and research, advocate for undergraduate research for all (Healey and Jenkins 2009).

The Times They Are a-Changin'

First-year students doing original research? Humanities research presented in poster format? Undergraduates as coauthors with faculty? The times they are a-changin', but at a rather sluggish pace. Although the undergraduate research movement has gained notable ground throughout the academy, Dotterer noted in 2002 that "[h]umanities departments have been the slowest to participate" (83). Signs indicate that this is changing for the humanities, and in particular for English studies. At the 2007 CUR Posters on the Hill event, in which undergraduates shared their research with Congress, a humanities poster was selected for the first time in the history of the event. Likewise, CUR has created a new division dedicated to the humanities and arts. The 2008 NCUR received the highest number ever of abstracts in English and allied areas, trumping chemistry submissions.

Similarly, scholarship on undergraduate research and the humanities is on the upswing. Several published articles focus on the benefits, obstacles, and challenges for undergraduate research in the humanities and call for humanities instructors to find ways to engage students in this important curricular movement (see Bost 1992–1993; DeVries 2001; McDorman 2004; Rogers 2003; Wilson 2003; Schilt and Gilbert 2008).

Scholar-teachers in the humanities have questioned the compatibility of undergraduate research and the humanities, pointing out that unlike research in the sciences, the "kind [of] scholarship for which [humanities scholars] are rewarded" is "essentially non-collaborative" and "trivializes student involvement" (Rogers 2003, 132). As a result, the majority of humanities scholar-teachers advocating undergraduate research stress, as did Daniel Rogers's collaborations between faculty and students, "plac[ing] our undergraduates at the center of our research endeavors as co-researchers" and "view[ing] ourselves as co-learners" (Rogers 2003, 133). Todd McDorman (2004) suggests three different models of involving undergraduates in faculty research: (1) faculty-driven collaboration, in which faculty have primary responsibility and students "supply meaningful contributions in the construction of the final product" (39); (2) faculty mentoring, which he describes as a *reciprocal process* whereby faculty and students work in tandem on their own research but provide meaningful feedback for one another; and (3) student-driven collaboration, where the student is the lead author and final decision-maker, while the faculty member guides, critiques, and suggests (42). Responding to these calls for models that imitate the sciences, Laurie Grobman (2007) suggests that contributive research in the humanities may, *but need not*, follow the models of the sciences, citing significant undergraduate research achievements in what she calls the *independent model*, where faculty members mentor and guide the student's project.

In addition to national organizations such as CUR, NCUR, and National Collegiate Honors Council, federal and state humanities organizations can be change agents in how undergraduate research in the humanities is viewed. In 2009 the Utah Humanities Council inaugurated a new fellowship competition for students, establishing opportunities for both undergraduates and graduates to receive support for their independent research. We urge the National Endowment for the Humanities (NEH) to offer support to students, such as a summer seminar for undergraduates. Naomi Yavneh at the University of South Florida offered an NEH-styled seminar that gave participants a stipend and engaged them in research with an expectation of dissemination. Although such research experiences for undergraduates are available in the sciences, particularly through the good work of the National Science Foundation (NSF), unfortunately, similar paid research-intensive experiences for students of the humanities are rare, which speaks to the value placed on humanistic inquiry.

The English profession is moving toward conversations about how undergraduate research applies in our own discipline, and scholarship on undergraduate research in English studies is emerging. In an essay in *Developing and Sustaining a Research-Supportive Curriculum* (2007), Kinkead addresses specifically ways in which lower-division courses in composition could provide a foundation for research-based learning, particularly in introducing students to principles of Responsible Conduct of Research (RCR). In the writing major, significant articles point to an increasing emphasis on undergraduate research. Dominic DelliCarpini (2007) notes that at York College of Pennsylvania, students in an undergraduate professional writing major "became interested in the back story, in our shoptalk—i.e., in the scholarly and theoretical bases of our discipline" (15). Several of these students produced scholarship that was presented at professional conferences and published in undergraduate journals. Amy Robillard (2006), in *College English*, suggests that undergraduate research has the potential to transform how compositionists conduct research. In a September 2009 article in *College Composition and Communication* (CCC), Grobman argues that by viewing undergraduate research production and authorship along a continuum of scholarly authority, student scholars obtain *authorship* and *authority* through research experiences. In literary studies, Larry K. Uffelman (1995), a professor of English, describes his successful collaborative research project with undergraduates in Victorian literature. Jeanne Moskal and Shannon R. Wooden's coedited collection, *Teaching British Women Writers, 1750–1900* (2005), includes several chapters describing undergraduate research on noncanonical women writers from the Romantic era. The articles cited above provide an early foundation in scholarly inquiry upon which to build.

Models and Mentoring

As the chapters in *Undergraduate Research in English Studies* illustrate, English studies faculty encourage various models of undergraduate research, including students conducting their own original research with faculty *as mentors*, and students conducting original research as co- or assistant researchers, with faculty functioning *simultaneously as collaborators and mentors*, following the model of the sciences. We believe that multiple models, with the many shapes they take, are valid and valuable, and that our collection can only begin to imagine the possibilities. Whatever model is chosen, the instructor must make transparent the ethical dimensions of the partnership.

Therefore, we also believe that mentorship is crucial to all models of undergraduate research. The research on mentorship suggests that a strong faculty mentor significantly enhances a student's undergraduate research experience (Guterman 2007). Leo Gafney's (2005) study of successful mentoring in the sciences and Robert Beer and Corine Myers's (1995) flexible contract outlining the partners' goals, timetable, and procedures offer suggestions for developing these relationships. Aaron Monte (2001) gives students a set of general guidelines outlining his expectations for them and their many responsibilities as researchers in his chemistry lab. The EUREKA (Enhancing Undergraduate Research Experience, Knowledge, and Access) program at the University of Texas–Austin stresses the importance of a research advisor (Schilt and Gilbert 2008, 52–55).

In this collection, we initiate discussions of mentoring in English studies. David Elder and Joonna Smitherman Trapp show how the process of mentoring can be mutually beneficial and rewarding, and that mentoring may be more about collaboration and friendship than a transfer of knowledge from mentor to mentee. Margaret Earley Whitt and her undergraduate assistant, Matthew Henningsen, explain how they came together to create an anthology of short stories about AIDS as a result of an institutional summer grant. Their successful partnership, which they negotiated in-process lacking any real models, replicates the dominant model of undergraduate research in the sciences. Drawing on educational research on nontraditional students, Jane Greer expands the conversation surrounding undergraduate research in English studies to include nontraditional students, and explores how mentorship of adult students places additional demands on—and offers additional rewards to—faculty members.

Conducting Research Responsibly

Mentorship of undergraduate research in its various forms and models carries with it significant ethical implications. Kinkead (2007), advocating for the centrality of writing programs in undergraduate research programs across the curriculum, argues, "A required writing course that focuses on research is the natural site for introducing Responsible Conduct of Research" (203). Shachter's "Responsible Conduct in Research Instruction in Undergraduate Research Programs" (2007) in the Karukstis and Elgren volume, while based in the sciences, has significant implications for promoting RCR in English studies. Students in literary studies typically have an undergraduate course in literary theory and practice; yet even these long-standing courses will need to adapt to issues that arise when undergraduates collaborate with faculty and attempt to disseminate their single- or coauthored scholarship, such as submission practices and authorship credit. Faculty themselves may not be familiar with the broader definitions of research ethics that extend beyond plagiarism. Ethical issues will be increasingly important and even mandated. NSF has begun requiring RCR training for students involved in funded grants. Although some might consider instruction in integrity and ethics in research yet one more bureaucratic burden, in actuality, we owe our students and society at large education in these sensitive areas, to help them understand just what responsible research entails. In the final analysis, this instruction is humanistic in origin: ethics.

Two chapters in *Undergraduate Research in English Studies* bring the discipline's attention to RCR. Deaver Traywick outlines the major issues that faculty research mentors should address with all undergraduate researchers pursuing human-participant research in composition and communication studies. Issues covered include designing meaningful research that adheres to ethical standards; using online human subjects protection training; navigating local institutional review board (IRB) procedures; and reporting findings in ways that conform to IRB protocol. Jaqueline McLeod Rogers outlines a research methodology course designed to provide a capstone experience for students finishing their undergraduate degree in writing (although it could be modified to suit the interests of students at earlier stages of degree work).

Disseminating Undergraduate Research in English Studies

Undergraduates in English studies have several opportunities to disseminate their research, both in print and at conferences. Over its twenty-two-year history, NCUR has featured hundreds of presentations from literary studies, composition and rhetoric, creative writing, English education, and linguistics. In 1985, Professors Mikel Vause and Michael Meyer of Weber State University (Ogden, Utah) initiated the National Undergraduate Literature Conference. Sigma Tau Delta, the International English Honor Society, hosts an annual convention inviting all members to submit critical essays, creative nonfiction, original poetry, fiction, drama, screenplays, or panel proposals. Another students-only meeting is the Undergraduate Conference in Medieval and Early Modern Studies at Moravian College (Bethlehem, Pennsylvania), which started in 2006. On a regional level, Virginia Military Institute's Department of English and Fine Arts has hosted an annual undergraduate research conference.

On-campus celebrations of undergraduate research, scholarship, and creative activity are widespread and enable students to share their work. In this volume, Ted Hovet describes the ins and outs of Western Kentucky University English department's Undergraduate Conference on Literature, Language, and Culture for its English majors, modeled after a typical academic conference. Among Hovet's most important aims is to demonstrate that "local" efforts can spur students to success on a larger stage. Equally important is the unintentional but vital consequence of this undergraduate conference for the Department of English: it gives the department a chance to promote itself and its students to a wider public. Chapters by Hovet, Christie Fox, and Laura Gray-Rosendale suggest that poster presentations are fast becoming common forms of dissemination at undergraduate conferences, enabling a greater number of students to participate and share their work.

Perhaps the earliest concerted effort to publish the work of undergraduates in English studies is *Writing Lab Newsletter*, founded by Muriel Harris, which published its first "Tutor's Corner" (now called "Tutor's Column") in 1984. *Young Scholars in Writing*, appearing in 2003, is an international, undergraduate research journal written for and by undergraduate students involved in rhetoric and composition. It has published on such topics as rhetorical analyses of political speeches, comedy acts, and literary texts; studies of peer tutoring; explorations of women's rhetoric; and investigations of online environments.

The Oswald Review, published since 1999, includes refereed articles primarily in literary studies. The *Pittsburgh Undergraduate Review* (*PUR*) publishes research articles written by students, the majority in the humanities, arts, and social sciences. In 1984, the University of Texas–El Paso honors program began publishing *The National Honors Report* (Gingerich 1985, 20–21). Several campuses have undergraduate research journals that are general to the university (for example, University of North Texas's *The Eagle Feather*) or specific to departments (for example, Utah State University's *Scribendi*). In this volume, Marta Figlerowicz, an undergraduate at Harvard University, argues that students in literary studies should pursue in-depth research projects aimed at professional publication, even though their chances for publication may be slim. Figlerowicz traces her four major research projects to date, including a recent publication in the prestigious *New Literary History*.

We believe that opportunities for students to publish their undergraduate research in English will continue to increase—and not just opportunities for students from elite institutions. The high-impact nature of undergraduate research as an educational experience bodes well for its pervasive entry in English studies at two-year colleges, comprehensive colleges, land-grant colleges, and branch campuses as well as Ivy Leagues. That range of institutional types is apparent in this volume. We also recommend that faculty mentors and English department administrators increase their role in encouraging and teaching students about dissemination opportunities for undergraduate research at local, regional, and national levels.

Sites of Undergraduate Research in the English Curriculum

There are many places in the curriculum in which undergraduate research in English studies does and should occur. To maintain a manageable scope and length, this volume focuses on writing and rhetoric and literary studies, although many chapters describe projects and curricula that overlap with other subfields of English, such as English education, cultural studies, and linguistics. Undergraduate research is also taking place in creative writing and folklore. This collection is a call to broaden undergraduate research possibilities in all areas of English.

Writing and Rhetoric

Undergraduate research in writing and rhetoric is steadily increasing. Not surprisingly, scholars in composition and rhetoric are exploring the research of undergraduates in the first-year writing program. Douglas Downs and Elizabeth Wardle's (2007) "Teaching about Writing, Righting Misconceptions" suggests that students in first-year writing classes are able to contribute disciplinary insights about writing itself if given the proper scaffolding. Downs and Wardle extend their analysis in their chapter in this volume, describing their efforts to engage first-year students in writing-related empirical research, discussing the goals of such projects, examining the benefits and drawbacks, and suggesting some theoretical conceptions for understanding the project of first-year research.

One of the most prominent types of undergraduate research is in the teaching of writing, especially related to writing center tutors and writing fellows programs. In this volume DelliCarpini and Cynthia Crimmins describe ways that writing centers can act as spaces for the development of undergraduate research projects. The authors focus on the ways in which the experiential element of a peer-tutoring course has led their students to move from *praxis* to *gnosis*, from the practical work of teaching and tutoring writing to an interest in the scholarship surrounding that work.

The possibilities for undergraduate research projects in writing studies are numerous. In this collection, Gray-Rosendale offers a case study of undergraduate research in a senior-level seminar course on how rhetoric is used in memoirs. Brian J. McNely argues that programs and departments of rhetoric, writing, technical communication, and related fields should focus first and foremost on curricular change to foster meaningful undergraduate research, change which is inculcated at our institution by the development of rhetoric and writing courses that study rhetoric and writing itself.

Literary Criticism

Literary criticism also offers undergraduate research opportunities. As the array of conferences and journals attests, students are conducting literary criticism as independent scholars, following the model of their faculty. In addition to Figlerowicz's chapter, Hovet's chapter includes examples of undergraduate literary scholars. We have also found that students working as independent scholars will likely have an easier time finding a gap in knowledge if they study archival and noncanonical texts.

In this collection, several chapters reflect on and theorize innovative faculty-student collaborations in literary research. D. Heyward Brock, James M. Dean, McKay Jenkins, Kevin Kerrane, Matthew Kinservik, and Christopher Penna demonstrate how they "conspire" in the learning and writing process to produce high-quality, researched essays while approximating the best features of scientific collaboration. Each supervises student partners in topics related to his or her current research. Christine F. Cooper-Rompato, Evelyn Funda, Joyce Kinkead, and undergraduates

Amanda "Mannie" Marinello and Scarlet Fronk describe the experiences of two research fellows who engage in scholarship from the outset of their undergraduate careers. Cooper-Rompato and Scarlet, a first-year English major, detail their work on an illuminated manuscript in medieval studies; and Funda and Mannie explain how Funda mentored Mannie on research about Willa Cather, which led the student to explore and "own" similar themes with J. M. Barrie.

Further Implications of Undergraduate Research in English Studies

Beyond the major issues already described—models and mentoring, instruction in responsible research, sites of undergraduate research, and dissemination possibilities—we raise here several implications of undergraduate research and English studies that emanate from our contributors' chapters. We stress that research, reflection, and critique of these issues is vital to realizing the potential of undergraduate research in English studies. The afterword suggests several future-forward issues to consider.

Student Learning

Generally, research proposes some important benefits to students. As active meaning-makers in a scholarly community, students "develop ownership" of the discipline (Lancy 2003, 88) and apply knowledge gained in the classroom to questions and problems needing answers. In so doing, they improve and refine their research, writing, and revision skills, and undergo the frustrations and exhilaration we all feel as researchers. Students also learn and practice different forms of collaboration. Undergraduate research promotes creativity and alternative ways of thinking, develops students' critical reading and critical thinking skills, and sharpens their ability to analyze, interpret, and synthesize.

The relationships students develop with faculty mentors have been shown to have positive effects on retention, student achievement, and student satisfaction (Malachowski 1999; see also Wilson 2003). Undergraduate research stimulates intellectual curiosity and encourages students to pursue graduate school and further research opportunities (Hathaway, Nagda, and Gregerman 2002.) Elaine Seymour, Anne-Barrie Hunter, Sandra L. Laursen, and Tracee DeAntoni (2004), in their initial report of a three-year study of four liberal arts colleges in eight science disciplines, found that 91 percent of students involved in their study referenced positive gains from the undergraduate research experience. In a later study, Hunter, Laursen, and Seymour (2007) found that faculty and their students generally agree on the nature, range, and extent of students' undergraduate research gains.

The contributors to this volume, directly or indirectly, affirm the consensus in undergraduate research circles that students benefit in myriad ways. They confirm that students develop their facility at inquiry and problem solving through the focused mentorship provided by faculty. The students suggest that these experiences provide more authenticity and make them feel like members of an exciting field. They also seem to be on a path to further research through graduate studies. Moreover, we hope these chapters are the stepping-stones for continued research on what *and* how students best learn through undergraduate research in English studies.

Accessibility

Yet, who are the students who enjoy these benefits? Philosophically, undergraduate research is accessible to all students. Our collection illustrates that genuine student research is not reserved for elite students, nor for elite institutions. Departments of English studies must, if they have not already, address the issues of faculty time, institutional conditions, roles, and rewards to ensure student access, and to make the extraordinary ordinary.

We believe that all students must have equal access to undergraduate research. What this means in practice is that we must make efforts to level the playing field so that all students, regardless of socioeconomic or ethnic/racial background or gender, are given these opportunities. Undergraduate research can occur in any number of sites in English studies: a course in the sequence of a program, an honors course, an independent study, a capstone research seminar, and even in lower-division course work. Faculty, administrators, and students should advocate for scholarships and grants that support undergraduate research. Students conducting archival research, for instance, may require funds to travel to collections. In this volume, Amanda Marinello describes her research in Scottish libraries following an inquiry into J. M. Barrie's personal albums that was funded by a university grant. In addition, departments must include opportunities about undergraduate research in the field in public sites such as departmental webpages. These pages should feature exemplary models of other students who have engaged in research, scholarship, and creative activity. Such venues will improve access and participation. In brief, students need access to information as well as opportunity.

To improve access to undergraduate research, we must take into account issues pertinent to students of color and students from low socioeconomic status. Several studies in disciplines other than English studies have begun this work, and we should follow suit. For example, Angela Johnson (2007) found that female students of color in the sciences more often than not were discouraged by their undergraduate research experiences (810). But John Ishiyama (2007) reports that African American students participating in the McNair program at Truman State University are much more likely than white first-generation college students from low incomes to emphasize psychological benefits from the research experience and to describe a successful mentor as personally supportive. In their study of the Undergraduate Research Opportunity Program (UROP) at the University of Michigan, Sandra Gregerman, Jennifer Lerner, William von Hippel, John Jonides, and Biren Nagda (1998) report increased retention rates for African American students, especially African American males whose academic performance was below the median for their ethnic/racial group. Additionally, the researchers found positive trends for Hispanic and white students who participated in UROP during their sophomore year (66; see also Gregerman 1999.) The CUR publication *Broadening Participation in Undergraduate Research* (Boyd and Wesemann 2008) focuses on undergraduate research programs that reach out to underrepresented ethnic and racial minorities, students with disabilities, females, students of low socioeconomic status, first- and second-year students, and others not traditionally involved in the development of new knowledge.

Finally, undergraduate research scholars and practitioners are thinking seriously about undergraduate research in lower-division courses, not just in the major. Linda Rueckert, editor of the fall 2008 *Council on Undergraduate Research Quarterly*'s (*CURQ*) special issue, "Undergraduate Research: An Early Start," states that "it might be possible to introduce students to research earlier" (4). In the same issue, Brent Cejda and Nancy Hensel report on an NSF grant–funded initiative undertaken by CUR and the National Council on Advanced Technological Education (NCIA) on student research at community colleges. Cejda and Hensel state that most participants in the study desire "more" undergraduate research at community colleges, even though the obstacles to undergraduate research at community colleges are substantial (10). Joseph Grabowski, Margaret Heely, and Jacob Brindley describe the successes of the First Experiences in Research program at the University of Pittsburgh, which engages first-year students in faculty research in the humanities, social sciences, and natural sciences.

Issues of Collaboration and Authorship

Among the most interesting and complicated issues arising from the proliferation of undergraduate research in its various models are authorship and collaboration. For example, Jenn Fishman, Andrea Lunsford, Beth McGregor, and Mark Otuteye's "Performing Writing, Performing Literacy" (2005), which received the 2006 Richard Braddock Award for Best Article in CCC, is written largely in the collective "we" of teacher-scholars Fishman and Lunsford, while undergraduates McGregor and Otuteye's separate sections in the middle of the article are text versions of their presentations at the Conference on College Composition and Communication (CCCC) Convention in New York City in 2003, "where they both described and enacted writing performances" (234). Based on the first two years of a five-year Stanford Study of Student Writing, Fishman and colleagues' article links student writing to theories and practices of performance, such as spoken-word poetry and radio broadcasting (226). Yet the article constitutes a complex, and unusual, kind of coauthorship, primarily because the students are positioned as *both* "study participants" and "coauthors" (224).

Scholarship on authorship in diverse disciplines is a good place for us to begin to unravel these issues for faculty-student research partnerships. Kami Day and Michele Eodice (2001) distinguish *co-writing*, that is, "face-to-face, word-by-word text production," from *coauthoring*, "working together—topic and idea generation, research, talk, possible co-writing, decisions about how the final product will look, etc., on a writing project" (121–22). In their study of six coauthoring faculty academic teams, most did some combination of coauthoring and co-writing (131). In contrast, in the sciences, as John Trimbur and Lundy A. Braun's (1992) study of multiple authorship demonstrates, authorship may have little to do with writing and a lot to do with "the processes of negotiation by which recognition is allocated" (21), usually "along 'hierarchical' lines" (22).

What will we expect from student-faculty scholarly collaborations in our own discipline? How will we assign authorship? Will students who help with the research but not the writing be included as authors (as in the sciences)? As more essays are produced by collaborations between faculty and students, models and practices of these partnerships will emerge (see Grobman, "The Student Scholar" [2009], for further discussion of collaboration and authorship in undergraduate research). Given the many collaborative variations possible in joint faculty-student undergraduate research, our discipline will need to work toward consensus regarding authorship credit.

Faculty Reward System

We acknowledge that faculty members, particularly those on the tenure track at research universities, are rewarded for authoring scholarship and research, not necessarily for writing about how research may be done with their students, or for coauthoring an article. Essays and chapters that may be viewed as pedagogical in nature may not carry the same weight for merit, tenure, or promotion as does original research. Even so, issues of tenure and merit are highly dependent on the nature of the institution. For many fields in English studies, single-authored original scholarship is the standard. In a faculty review, mentoring of students most likely does count as part of teaching and learning. There may be more openness in some subfields to multi-authored, collaborative works, more typical of a social sciences or education model. In addition, many institutions have adopted the *scholarship of teaching* model, advocated by Boyer (1990), that rewards pedagogical scholarship. This is especially appropriate to institutions that enroll primarily undergraduates or are comprehensive institutions. Post-tenure faculty may also find tremendous satisfaction in working with undergraduates, sharing in their achievements. Finally, we note that many institutions market themselves through student success stories. A mentor of undergraduate researchers may very likely be a stellar candidate for the Carnegie Foundation U.S. Professors of the Year Program. In brief, it will be important to analyze the mission of the institution and its roles and rewards structure—and perhaps to revisit that language. In the sciences, faculty may welcome additional pairs of hands to assist with research projects. The same may be true for humanities faculty. Witness the enormous assistance that Henningsen provided Whitt (see Chapter 2). The bottom line is that institutional support and funding for such activities are more prevalent in the sciences than in the humanities, although evidence abounds that humanities students are increasingly included in undergraduate research grants and other awards. Faculty members are right to ask about roles and rewards, for it is only when mentorship of students—undergraduates or graduates—is codified that they can be sure that such activity truly counts in decisions on merit, tenure, and promotion. We are heartened by Cooper-Rompato's comment in Chapter 9 that her department head tapped her for mentoring an undergraduate researcher because "it would look good in her tenure file." Perhaps her experience indicates a sea change toward what Carolyn Ash Merkel (2003) calls a "culture of undergraduate research" (42), evidenced by its being embedded in the educational experience: faculty know about it and encourage it; administration supports it with resources; and students know the opportunities exist and how to take advantage. Our hope is that *Undergraduate Research in English Studies* will begin to codify undergraduate research in English studies as an important teaching activity for faculty that will be equitably accounted for in faculty promotion and tenure decisions.

Benefits to the Discipline(s) of English Studies

No doubt, the current status of English studies in higher education is in flux. Inside and outside the academy, constituents are demanding assessment and accountability, evidence that what students learn in their English courses and majors will transfer to on-the-job readiness. Like Reed Wilson (2003), we believe that undergraduate research is one means for humanists to promote the value of what we do to the public at large, including our students, who are the future taxpayers, philanthropists, and parents (79). How wonderful if our students can articulate that importance for us, understanding the value of humanistic inquiry *because* they have been makers of knowledge in the field. In our view, *value* is broadly conceived, and the varied scholarship our undergraduates do and can produce exemplifies this diversity. Yes, we are boosters of undergraduate research, but we also understand the barriers—both cultural and institutional—that hamper the adoption of this high-impact educational experience.

The authors of these chapters contribute to the conversation on the increasing emphasis on interdisciplinary approaches to teaching and scholarship. They suggest, and also describe, the power of inquiry and its effect not only upon the students, but upon their mentors. Please join us in this conversation about an emerging movement in English that draws on developments in fields other than our own, and also creates new ways to engage students in meaningful and authentic scholarly work that contributes to what we know about English studies.

References

Beer, Robert H., and Corine Myers. 1995. Guidelines for the Supervision of Undergraduate Research. *Journal of Chemical Education* 72 (8): 721.

Bost, D. 1992–1993. Seven Obstacles to Undergraduate Research in the Humanities (and Seven Solutions). *CUR Newsletter* 13 (1): 35–40.

Boyd, Mary K., and Jodi L. Wesemann, eds. 2008. *Broadening Participation in Undergraduate Research: Fostering Excellence and Enhancing the Impact.* Washington, DC: Council on Undergraduate Research.

Boyer Commission on Educating Undergraduates in the Research University, Shirley Strum Kenny (chair). 1998. *Reinventing Undergraduate Education: A Blueprint for America's Research Universities.* Stony Brook: State University of New York.

Boyer, Ernest L. 1990. *Scholarship Reconsidered: Priorities of the Professoriate.* Carnegie Foundation for the Advancement of Teaching. Princeton, NJ: Princeton University Press.

Council on Undergraduate Research and National Conferences on Undergraduate Research. 2005. *Joint Statement of Principles in Support of Undergraduate Research, Scholarship, and Creative Activities.* http://www.cur.org/SummitPosition.html.

Council on Undergraduate Research. *About CUR.* http://www.cur.org/about.html.

Day, Kami, and Michele Eodice. 2001. *(First Person)²: A Study of Co-Authoring in the Academy.* Logan: Utah State University Press.

DelliCarpini, Dominic. 2007. Re-writing the Humanities: The Writing Major's Effect upon Undergraduate Studies in English Departments. *Composition Studies* 35 (1): 15–36.

DeVries, David. N. 2001. Undergraduate Research in the Humanities: An Oxymoron? *CUR Quarterly* 21 (4): 153–55.

Dotterer, Ronald L. 2002. Student-Faculty Collaborations, Undergraduate Research, and Collaboration as an Administrative Model. *New Directions for Teaching and Learning,* 90 (Summer): 81–89.

Downs, Douglas, and Elizabeth Wardle. 2007. Teaching about Writing, Righting Misconceptions: (Re)Envisioning "First-Year Composition" as "Introduction to Writing Studies." *College Composition and Communication* 58 (4): 552–84.

Fishman, Jenn, Andrea Lunsford, Beth McGregor, and Mark Otuteye. 2005. Performing Writing, Performing Literacy. *College Composition and Communication* 57 (2): 224–52.

Gafney, Leo. 2005. The Role of the Research Mentor/Teacher. *Journal of College Science Teaching* 34 (4): 52–56.

Gingerich, Willard. 1985. On Publishing an Honors Journal. *The National Honors Report* 6 (1): 20–21.

Gregerman, Sandra R. 1999. Improving the Academic Success of Diverse Students through Undergraduate Research. *CUR Quarterly* 20 (2): 54–59.

Gregerman, Sandra R., Jennifer S. Lerner, William von Hippel, John Jonides, and Biren A. Nagda. 1998. Undergraduate Student-Faculty Research Partnerships Affect Student Retention. *Review of Higher Education* 22 (1): 55–72.

Grobman, Laurie. 2007. Affirming the Independent Researcher Model: Undergraduate Research in the Humanities. *CUR Quarterly* 28 (1): 23–28.

———. 2009. The Student Scholar: (Re)Negotiating Authorship and Authority. *College Composition and Communication* 61(1):178.

Guterman, Lila. 2007. What Good Is Undergraduate Research, Anyway? *Chronicle of Higher Education*, August 17.

Hathaway, Russel S., Biren A. Nagda, and Sandra R. Gregerman. 2002. The Relationship of Undergraduate Research Participation to Graduate and Professional Education Pursuit: An Empirical Study. *Journal of College Student Development* 43 (5): 614–31.

Healey, Mick, and Alan A. Jenkins. 2009. *Developing Undergraduate Research and Inquiry*. Heslington, York, England: Higher Education Academy.

Hunter, Anne-Barrie, Sandra L. Laursen, and Elaine Seymour. 2007. Becoming a Scientist: The Role of Undergraduate Research in Students' Cognitive, Personal and Professional Development. *Science Education* 91 (1): 36–74.

Ishiyama, John. 2007. Expectations and Perceptions of Undergraduate Research Mentoring: Comparing First Generation, Low Income White/Caucasian and African American Students. *College Student Journal* 41 (3): 540–49.

Johnson, Angela C. 2007. Unintended Consequences: How Science Professors Discourage Women of Color. *Science Education* 91 (5): 805–21.

Karukstis, Kerry K., and Timothy E. Elgren, eds. 2007. *Developing and*

Sustaining a Research-Supportive Curriculum: A Compendium of Successful Practices. Washington, DC: Council on Undergraduate Research.

Kinkead, Joyce. 2003a. Learning through Inquiry: An Overview of Undergraduate Research. In *Valuing and Supporting Undergraduate Research*, ed. Joyce Kinkead, 5–17. San Francisco: Jossey-Bass.

Kinkead, Joyce. ed. 2003b *Valuing and Supporting Undergraduate Research.* New Directions in Teaching and Learning. San Francisco: Jossey-Bass.

———. 2007. How Writing Programs Support Undergraduate Research. In Karukstis and Elgren 2007, 195–208.

Kuh, George D. 2008. *High-Impact Educational Practices: What They Are, Who Has Access to Them, and Why They Matter.* Washington, DC: Association of American Colleges and Universities.

Lancy, David F. 2003. What One Faculty Member Does to Promote Undergraduate Research. In Kinkead 2003b, 87–92.

Malachowski, Mitchell. 1999. Promoting Undergraduate Research in Non-Science Areas at Predominantly Undergraduate Institutions. *CUR Quarterly* 19 (3): 126–30.

McDorman, Todd. 2004. Promoting Undergraduate Research in the Humanities: Three Collaborative Approaches. *CUR Quarterly* 25 (1): 39–42.

Merkel, Carolyn Ash. 2003. Undergraduate Research at the Research Universities. In Kinkead 2003b, 39–53.

Monte, Aaron. 2001. Mentor Expectations and Student Responsibilities in Undergraduate Research. *CUR Quarterly* 22 (2): 66–71.

Moskal, Jeanne, and Shannon R. Wooden, eds. 2005. *Teaching British Women Writers, 1750–1900.* New York: Peter Lang.

Robillard, Amy E. 2006. Young Scholars Affecting Composition: A Challenge to Disciplinary Citation Practices. *College English* 68 (3): 253–70.

Rogers, V. Daniel. 2003. Surviving the "Culture Shock" of Undergraduate Research in the Humanities. *CUR Quarterly* 23 (3): 132–35.

Rueckert, Linda. 2008. Undergraduate Research in the First Two Years. *CUR Quarterly* 29 (1): 4.

Schilt, Paige, and Lucia Albino Gilbert. 2008. Undergraduate Research in the Humanities: Transforming Expectations at a Research University. *CUR Quarterly* 28 (4): 51–55.

Seymour, Elaine, Anne-Barrie Hunter, Sandra L. Laursen, and Tracee DeAntoni. 2004. Establishing the Benefits of Research Experiences for Undergraduates in the Sciences: First Findings from a Three-Year Study. *Science Education* 88 (4): 493–534.

Shachter, Amy M. 2007. Responsible Conduct in Research Instruction in Undergraduate Research Programs. In Karukstis and Elgren 2007, 209–39.

Teagle Working Group. Student Learning and Faculty Research: Connecting Teaching and Scholarship. American Council of Learned Societies. Apr. 2007.

Trimbur, John, and Lundy A. Braun. 1992. Laboratory Life and the Determination of Authorship. In *New Visions of Collaborative Writing*, ed. Janis Forman. Portsmouth: Boynton/Cook. 19–36.

Uffelman, Larry K. 1995. Victorian Periodicals: Research Opportunities for Faculty-Undergraduate Research. *CUR Quarterly* 15 (4): 207–8.

Wilson, Reed. 2003. Researching "Undergraduate Research" in the Humanities. *Modern Language Studies* 33 (1/2): 74–79.

I

Mentoring Undergraduate Researchers in English Studies

Mentoring is a brain to pick, an ear to listen, and a push in the right direction.

—John C. Crosby

Chapter One

Mentor as Method: Faculty Mentor Roles and Undergraduate Scholarship

David Elder
Texas Christian University

Joonna Smitherman Trapp
Northwestern College

> *To say that hierarchy is inevitable is not to say that any particular hierarchy is inevitable; the crumbling of hierarchies is as true a fact about them as their formation. [. . .] And it reminds us, on hearing talk of equality, to ask ourselves, without so much as questioning the possibility that things might be otherwise: "Just how does the hierarchic principle work in this particular scheme of equality?"*
>
> —Kenneth Burke, *Rhetoric of Motives*

David's Story

"Warning! Do not wait until the last minute to do these!" I saw those words printed at the bottom of my final assignment sheet for the culminating class of a writing and rhetoric degree, and I heeded them for the first time in my college career. The assignment was for Joonna Trapp's History and Theory of Rhetoric class that I took as a second-semester junior. This dual assignment required me to "analyze an admirable rhetor or rhetorician" and "identify an ethical or theoretical problem or question." I decided that the single longer paper option would be best after choosing comedian

Chris Rock as my admirable rhetor. I watched Chris Rock stand-up routines and read theoretical articles about epideictic rhetoric and its function in a community, and then connected the two by giving examples of the theory I found in Rock's comedy.

That was my research method—read, listen, read, write, in a point-by-point "here's what I found in Chris Rock that corresponds to epideictic theory" manner. I remember receiving a B and being relatively content with that grade; however, Joonna was not. She thought that the idea behind the paper was much more original than its presentation—it was actual undergraduate research. She liked that I had blended primary and secondary research, but the way I had connected the two needed some work. However, the semester was over, so I didn't think there was much else to do. I knew that I would need to revise the paper to be a better writing sample for graduate school, but I was content to just leave it over the summer and return to it in the fall when I got back into a school rhythm. Luckily for me, Joonna was a good friend and mentor and pushed me even further by mentioning the journal *Young Scholars in Writing*. She told me that with some work, my paper would make a good article for publication. She wrote many comments on the paper, asked me to revise it over the summer, and promised that we'd get back together in the fall to discuss the changes I'd made and see where it needed to go from there.

Joonna's comments encouraged me to see Rock's stand-up as a case study for epideictic research, and to tease out the qualities found in Rock's comedy that fit and modified current epideictic theory, to theorize how current conceptions of epideictic may be changed or challenged because of Rock's unique use of it. She pushed me into a way of thinking about research that had not been taught in my other classes—she asked me to be *a part* of the scholarly conversation rather than just a reporter of it. And she did this very subtly. I didn't even know that my writing was changing from reporting to research until Joonna had already spun the cocoon around me, forcing me to either reformulate my writing into research or let it die.

After I revised the paper, I sent it to *Young Scholars*. I got very positive feedback and was asked to go through two revision cycles. I was disheartened by this news, but Joonna seemed excited (for which I secretly resented her). She told me that this was a great opportunity to do valuable research for the field, and was quite normal for the publishing process. Most significant, she said that she would help me every step of the way. We met regularly for the next month, making changes and reading through my rewrites. The ten versions of the article on my computer—all very different—could not have been written without Joonna. She helped me work through ideas, taking time out of her already busy schedule, and most important, she infused in me a developing sense of research methodology.

This was a valuable process for me as a student on my way to graduate school, especially because the publication assisted me in the graduate fellowship I received. I think I would have done well in graduate school without this process, but finding out how to do *real* research while still an undergraduate gave me a chance to understand the kind of work I would be expected to do. I learned how to fuse primary and secondary sources in an intelligent way, and I learned how to converse with a field and make original contributions to it.

I was lucky to have a mentor who valued undergraduate research and who was (and continues to be) a good friend. Without this friendship, I doubt the mentoring process would have been possible, institutionally or personally. As is the case with any collaborative effort, mentoring takes a lot of time. Joonna and I had forged a mentor-friend relationship over the course of my three years in college, and most of that was outside of class, in conferences or during her office hours (which were often extended because I just wouldn't leave). Because of the nature of the *Young Scholars* journal, I was the credited author, but I have always had the sense that Joonna was my coauthor.

Joonna's Story

One of the more surprising changes for me as a teacher, in moving from my graduate work at a large institution to a small institution, was involvement with students. "Getting into the lives of our students" is the expectation of incoming faculty at the small (1,300 students) midwestern private college in the liberal arts tradition at which I took my first full-time job. Opportunities to see the interests, abilities, and dreams of the students are a reality. Students are often in faculty homes as visitors and permanent houseguests. We see them at church, and are served by them in our local restaurants. They wait on us in the coffeehouses, and we contract them to work in our yards. More important, we share our lives together in this small town by standing on the street, just visiting in an opportune moment—and in the halls, after class, in the offices and libraries, conversation and real lifetime friendships develop.

Not surprisingly, these friendships develop, as many friendships do, around common interests. David Elder was a first-year student in my College Writing class who brought from his high school experience a deep hatred for writing. However, he discovered that first year of college that he actually loved to write. And so we began to build a relationship that had as its base a friendship with common interests: history, humor, writing, and stories of good and bad teaching in both of our pasts.

The day that David stormed into my office, threw his books on my desk and proclaimed, "I finally know what I want to do with my life—I want to be you!" was quite the shocker. As he continued, I learned that he had fallen in love with writing and thinking about writing, and he wanted to work with young writers so that he could help them learn to love writing. We laughed, told stories about his first-year experiences with writing, and set about planning how to make graduate study in English a possibility for him. As a mentor, I had to get him to focus on his ultimate goal of becoming a teacher of composition in an English department. I explained to him the various kinds of positions at colleges and high schools and the training each position required. I also explained tenure, salary norms, and the kinds of programs of study available. After about three hours of conversation in which we explored vocation, his future plans for marriage and family, and his own attitudes about leaving his family located in the same town as our college, David left with a list of tasks to accomplish over the next week. I gave him a series of questions to ponder, including what he wanted to teach and his attitude toward the various subfields of English. He also had a research assignment: to find five schools with programs that drew his attention. He brought his ideas to me a week later, and after another long conversation, we mapped out a vocational plan. He had a year left at his undergraduate school and developed the following goals for that time: (1) do some work in the writing center as a part of his preparation for graduate school; (2) work diligently at his remaining classes to bring his GPA up as far as possible; (3) begin preparing for the GRE; and finally, (4) secure a publication of original research, or at least try. Striving toward a published research article would help David see if he could find joy in graduate work. It would also give him an impressive writing sample to send with his application.

Mentoring of undergraduate research has the strongest influence on the student when it is connected in deep and meaningful ways to personhood and vocational dreams. David found himself wanting something, maybe for the first time in his life, that gave him drive and direction. Though the research project was connected to the other goals of the vocational plan, it was part of his new life, his new possibility—who he was going to be. Setting our feet on this path meant that we would be in each other's lives for quite a while as true collaborators, friends, supporters, judges, and fellow writers. David's commitment went beyond writing an original essay and seeing it through to publication. Much work lay ahead—researching suitable graduate programs, planning for true vocation, writing and revising the personal statement, developing a curriculum vitae, and gathering recommendation letters.

The project David expanded when he finished the History and Theory of Rhetoric class was fresh and new, and felt like David. He connected the assignment to his own quirky sense of humor and off-beat view of life, and to some interesting class discussions on race, miscommunication, and rhetorical theory. Working on the rhetoric of Chris Rock allowed him to blend some primary research on Rock's performances—many of which would be readily available in interviews, recordings, and biographies—with theory and reviews. It was the kind of project, because of its narrowness and specificity, which would work quite well as undergraduate research.

David was a mentor's dream—a student comes to you and asks for your help and advice. At times such as these, we should eagerly jump on the speeding train and enjoy the ride. What a blast it was working with such energy and creativity! The mentor is energized by the student. The act of research and writing (and ultimately being rewarded for that work) makes the new, confident person.

All students are different, yet looking back, I see a similar dynamic with another former student. My research assistant, Sarah Nytroe, helped me put together a summer research trip to archives around the South. We took the research we performed that summer to a conference together, and it became the basis of Sarah's dissertation in American history while she studied at Boston College. In her email correspondence with me on August 18, 2008, Sarah had this to say about the mentoring experience: "As I undertook intellectual projects in my undergraduate education, my mentor was there to continually push me to think more deeply about historical issues and questions, to recognize the value of my own ideas, and to recognize the importance of cultivating positive and affirmative relationships with students."

David and Joonna: The Value of Undergraduate Research and the Mentoring Relationship

David is convinced that Joonna taught him many things about research methodologies, which he needed, badly. But Joonna can point to new insights she gleaned from the relationship. The *Young Scholars* article argued for a new conception of epideictic rhetoric, and for David to write the article, he had to research epideictic extensively. He became an undergraduate research expert on the topic of epideictic rhetoric, and through reading and coaching his drafts, Joonna learned new ideas about epideictic rhetoric in popular culture, which she had not encountered before and which she could add to her teaching repertoire. Mentor and student taught each other and collaborated on original research, and even though the official relationship carried notions of hierarchy, Joonna's tenured status in the institution and David's undergraduate status did not prohibit these two from working as friends to find a way, as Kenneth Burke (1969) suggests in the epigraph to this chapter, to make the hierarchic nature of the academic relationship fit into the more congenial relationship of equality as friends.

Certainly this is not a new idea, for Nathaniel Hawthorne speaks to the value of working together as friends in *The Marble Faun* (1850): "It is a delicious sort of mutual aid, when the uniting of two sympathetic, yet dissimilar intelligences is brought to bear upon a poem by reading it aloud, or upon a picture or statue by viewing it in each other's company. Even if not a word of criticism be uttered, the insight of either party is wonderfully deepened, and the comprehension broadened; so that the inner mystery of a work of genius, hidden from one, will often reveal itself to two" (18.2). We don't mean to imply that boundaries should not exist in a mentor relationship, or even that it's often the case that the mentee has much more to gain (academically) from the relationship than does the mentor. In fact, we would argue that David needed Joonna in this academic situation much more than she needed him. But mentoring is not just about conveying knowledge. We both experienced effective collaboration with a lifelong friend—a relationship so beneficial that it has even created the opportunity of writing this chapter, and we suspect it will create many more opportunities for writing and speaking together. In essence, this model of friendship-based collaboration represents collegiality in research in the academy.

We are also convinced that the spiritual exists in such a relationship, regardless of whether the parties involved are religious people. Of course, articles, books, professional organizations, and conference presentations arguing for increased scholarly attention to the spiritual side of education can be controversial. We appreciate the definition by Jon C. Dalton and Pamela Crosby (2006), editors of the *Journal of College and Character*, that equates "the inward search or quest for personal meaning, purpose, and authenticity" (1) with spirituality. Perhaps nearly all of us can agree that education is about student growth, and certainly about the impact of education on the inner lives of the students, on how they reflect upon themselves as individuals, as citizens of the world, as community members, as caretakers of the environment and a host of other roles that require being reflective, engaged, and humane people. Dalton and Crosby further write, "Educational and student development efforts that ignore students' spirituality, i.e., how they make internal connections to the defining beliefs and purposes in their lives, will inevitably be less effective since they do not reach that part of students' lives where things really matter" (1).

Mentoring that "really matters" must be the kind of mentoring that makes these connections, and the student and the mentor are ultimately changed: the beliefs and purposes of lives forever altered. Noreen O'Connor (2008) notes that leaders in the undergraduate research movement claim that "research experiences can have a transformative effect on undergraduate students" (par. 4), but we believe the list she provides, while accurate, fails to get at the deeper transformations. Undergraduate research can introduce students to primary texts and materials, give students a real opportunity to "test hypotheses and intellectual models," and help students "contextualize and communicate objectives, approaches, analyses, and conclusions" (qtd. in O'Connor, par. 4). But undergraduate research gives the student the opportunity to do all these things in the presence of someone who *cares*, someone who cares to know and consider the values and beliefs of the student and how those are formed.

The O'Connor article further quotes an undergraduate research leader who claims that such research allows students to consider hard issues "on a more sophisticated level" (qtd. in O'Connor, par. 6) In our experience, the level of consideration moves past intellectual sophistication into ethical concerns, morality, and cultural values—places where the student researcher is forming and shaping a value system that will guide him or her for the rest of a career. David's work on Chris Rock made him think long and hard about racism, the role language plays in creating it and challenging it, and his own place in that conversation as an educated white man. And Sarah's work forced her to rethink her own inherited notions of what constituted the South, and the response of an oppressed society to history. Both of these projects took the students to places inside themselves that perhaps they had not visited before. Our vision of mentoring is reminiscent of the relationship between religious leaders and their pupils in the Middle Ages—often in cathedral schools, but also in the day-to-day relationships of clergy and their friends.

In a book about the history of Western schooling, Marcia Colish (1997) conflates the terms *mentor* and *spiritual advisor* when writing about St. Jerome's friendships (22). Friendship was the basis of a mentor relationship for Jerome; this shows the sacred relationship between master and tutor focused not only on the transmission of knowledge, but also on the dialogue that occurred between the two. We want to argue that this deeply spiritual aspect of mentoring is carried on in good mentor relationships today. It is also one of the reasons that good mentoring is so hard to find, and possibly one of the reasons that mentoring is seen as a "master" role.

What we have outlined in this chapter as a good mentor relationship is difficult to achieve. It requires both mentor and mentee to be vulnerable, which is especially difficult for the mentor because of the sometimes unquestioned hierarchies involved in any relationship between professor and student. Giving the mentee partial control of what happens during a mentoring relationship requires sacrifices that are usually unrecognized by the institution. Holding on to a traditional mastering notion of the mentor would allow much more time for activities and scholarship that are more often acknowledged by departments. Grobman and Kinkead argue in this collection's introduction that faculty must be rewarded for mentoring undergraduate research; Joonna found out on a recent job search that more and more institutions are calling for evidence of undergraduate mentoring. These are steps in the right direction if we want to see more faculty and students cultivate the kind of healthy mentoring relationship that we experienced.

The highly regarded Donald L. Finkel and his collaborator, William Ray Arney (1995), bravely discuss the friendship they had in their collaboration in these terms: "Finally, it needs to be understood that the friendship, the collaboration, the respect, and the love between the two colleagues is not going to end when their common course concludes. There is no way to predict what will become of it" (197). Likewise, we would like to name our collaboration together as a spiritual enterprise of great value, and continue by naming it friendship, respect, and even love. And where it ends is also not predictable. But we suspect that such deep and abiding work together will not only multiply in continued work together, but find new forms as Joonna continues to mentor students in her care, and David, as a soon-to-be newly minted PhD, discovers that his interactions with students will require him to also give of himself in deep and meaningful ways. If such relationships were the norm for education, the end could be quite predictable.

References

Burke, Kenneth. [1950] 1969. *A Rhetoric of Motives*. Berkeley: University of California Press.

Colish, Marcia L. 1997. *Medieval Foundations of the Western Intellectual Tradition, 400–1400*. New Haven, CT: Yale University Press.

Dalton, Jon C., and Pamela Crosby. 2006. The Neglected Inner Lives of College Students. *Journal of College and Character* 7 (8):1–2.

Finkel, Donald L., and William Ray Arney. 1995. *Educating for Freedom: The Paradox of Pedagogy*. New Brunswick, NJ: Rutgers University Press.

Hawthorne. Nathaniel. 1850. *The Marble Faun*. Boston: Houghton Mifflin.

O'Connor, Noreen. 2008. Undergraduate Research: Not Just for Research Universities. *AAC&U News*, April. http://www.aacu.org/aacu_news/aacunews08/april08/feature.cfm.

Chapter Two

Partners in Scholarship: The Making of an Anthology

Margaret Earley Whitt
University of Denver

Matthew Henningsen
University of Denver, Class of 2008

The Partnership Begins: Margaret

In the spring term, when we begin to wrap up our academic year and all things converge to give new meaning to the word *busy*, Matthew dropped by my office to see if I had a project with which he might assist over the summer months. When he told me of his desire to apply for a Partners in Scholarship (PinS) grant, how much time he could give to my project, and how much he would be paid by the school, I immediately thought to myself, "I can get paid assistance to help me with literary research? This has never happened to me in my life! How could I *not* come up with a project?" I asked him to check back with me in a week.

Our university gives students the opportunity to apply for PinS grants, which pay $12 per hour for up to 37.5 hours per week for ten weeks, to assist faculty on their research projects during the summer—an institutional investment of about $4,500 per grant. The grants are competitive and especially popular within departments in the social science and natural science divisions; they are less sought after by arts and humanities students. As it turned out, Matthew was the only English major to apply for a summer PinS. I learned later that it is not unusual for humanities students and faculty to be unaware of the possibilities of partnerships. Support for research assistants in the humanities is rare. Although

Matthew was the instigator of our partnership, our project, when under way, took the form of a faculty-driven collaboration (McDorman 2004). This chapter illuminates, through alternating voices of faculty and student, how we initiated a project to compile an anthology of short stories, and what we discovered about such faculty-student collaborations in the process.

When Matthew contacted me a week later, I asked him if he would be interested in locating short stories about AIDS. I recently had edited *Short Stories of the Civil Rights Movement* (2006) and had given only the most casual thought to preparing a similar anthology called *Short Stories about AIDS*, one that would show how characters respond to those with AIDS—an anthology that would help us to read history through short fiction. I was particularly interested in what fiction can tell us about AIDS in the early days—the decade of the 1980s.

Different from literary anthologies that purport to deliver a survey of a country's literary showcase, theme- or subject-related story anthologies provide their own challenges. For example, the *Norton Anthology of English Literature*, as it continues through revisions and new editions, has issues about weight, length, and size. However, an anthology more focused in time and topic finds a closer analogy to a nation's survey, as David Damrosch (2001) puts it, in trying to be both a "mirror of its host culture [. . . and] a window into the culture" (211).

But before any theme- or subject-related story anthology can be shaped, it is essential to know what stories exist. Reading widely, then, is the first step. It was clear that discernible tasks existed that Matthew could undertake as a research assistant. I would need Matthew to find stories about AIDS, read through them, and evaluate them. Stories taken from index listings might or might not be about AIDS, even when AIDS is the subject heading. When I first spoke to Matthew about this project, I had not actually started my own research. I had no knowledge of how many stories existed, so I prepared him for the possibility that he might find very few.

The genesis of this anthology occurred in the fall of 2006, when I taught a class called The Cost of Freedom: Reading History through Short Fiction. My plan was to look at the most important events of the last half of the twentieth century for which lives were the cost of securing various kinds of freedom. The three events I selected each offered a different kind of freedom. What were we ready to sacrifice for it? What were we willing to pay? I selected the civil rights movement, the Vietnam War, and the advent of AIDS. I used my own anthology for the Civil Rights Movement, Tim O'Brien's *The Things They Carried* (1990), and Bruce Franklin's edited volume of *The Vietnam War in American Stories, Songs, and Poems* (1996) for Vietnam, but stories about AIDS were the most difficult to find. I located two single-authored texts—one about women with AIDS, and one about men with AIDS, the latter out of print. I read randomly, and found four more stories that showed how writers portray people with AIDS and those who care about them. I knew only that an anthology of stories about AIDS did not currently exist, so the idea for the collection was lying dormant in the back of my mind. Matthew's inquiry brought that idea to the forefront.

Literary collections became available for the first time in the eighteenth century, when genres were sorted into anthologies, "volumes that contain material selected self-consciously for consistency and quality, usually long after the individual pieces within had first been published" and miscellanies, which contained new material, published for the first time (Benedict 2003, 231). By this historical definition, the AIDS collection that Matthew and I prepared was both anthology and miscellany, for I sought out stories from writers I knew personally to fill some noticeable gaps.

When Matthew received word that his application was one of a dozen grants funded across three divisions, he returned to my office for our first talk about the project. My instructions went like this: "Start with the *Short Story Index*. Begin in 1981 or 1982 and move toward the present day. In the *Index*, you'll find the stories listed in alphabetical order under *AIDS*, if they exist there at all. If you find no such listing, then start with the Susan Sontag story 'The Way We Live Now,' considered to be the first major story on the subject, published in the *New Yorker* [1986]. Let me know what you find, and don't be disappointed if you come up with slim results. Knowing there are only a few stories will be helpful information."

After the term ended, I left for my summer home in North Carolina, and Matthew departed for our university library. I had spent a year ghost writing a memoir for a civil rights activist, which had recently sold to a trade press, and I looked forward to beginning some important background reading about AIDS. If Matthew were successful in finding stories, I would need to be knowledgeable about the disease to write the introductions—to the book and for each section, whatever those sections might be. If Matthew found only a few stories, it would still be important to be familiar with such seminal texts as Randy Shilts's *And the Band Played On* (1987). AIDS had passed its quarter-century mark; millions of people still lived in harm's way. If there were only a few stories listed in the *Index*, I still believed that AIDS stories were out there somewhere.

Within the week, Matthew emailed me with news that answered my question about the number of AIDS stories in existence: he had discovered that the *Index* listed more than 200 such stories. Because we communicated frequently by email, actual distance between us would not be a concern in our working relationship. Matthew began the task of finding those stories, evaluating them, copying them, and sending them to me in North Carolina.

In their "Guidelines for the Supervision of Undergraduate Research" (1995), Robert Beer and Corine Myers suggest several points to consider. Matthew and I discussed the first two points: (1) the objective of the project and (2) the procedure by which we would achieve our goals. The authors also suggest a regular meeting time for an effective student-faculty relationship. Because distance separated us during the summer project, Matthew and I "met" online to communicate or discuss any concerns. Of course, Beer and Myers's advice grows out of experience in chemistry, which is not entirely applicable to scholarship in the humanities. From the outset, then, I had to consider the possible role of undergraduates in humanities research generally, and Matthew's role in the AIDS project specifically. I asked myself some questions, not just about the anthology project, but also about humanistic research more broadly.

- Can a student undertake some of the foundational work for a project, particularly the bibliographic area?
- Is there a piece of the project that an undergraduate might undertake?

- Does the student have a particular skill that the scholar does not, such as a foreign or classical language, that might contribute to the project? Or does the student have a skill in technology that would be helpful in design or delivery of the project, as in designing a webpage?
- When a student is involved in a faculty member's project, what credit will that student receive?

With the news that sufficient stories existed about AIDS, we commenced, setting out to not only meet our goals but to discover what it means to be involved in a student-faculty partnership.

Getting Started: Matthew

I first learned about the PinS program while looking into possible summer job opportunities. I knew that I wanted to go to graduate school, and I didn't want to engage in summer work that I thought would not benefit that goal. Therefore, I considered the various opportunities available at the University of Denver (DU) through the school's website and stumbled upon the PinS program. Because I had known Margaret for the entire time I had been an undergraduate, I naturally thought that our already established relationship could be easily applied to a summer research opportunity. I stopped by her office to discuss my idea to apply for a PinS grant.

Once it was clear that a project was feasible, I drafted the application. The actual process was simple and straightforward. I provided basic information about myself and the professor with whom I would be working. In addition, I described the project and related the benefits of such research to my own plans for graduate study in the humanities. Shortly thereafter, we received word that the grant had been approved. Margaret suggested that I start with the *Short Story Index*, a reference tool unfamiliar to me, so I entered Penrose Library at DU and went straight to a librarian for help. As I had found throughout my undergraduate career, the librarian pointed me in the right direction. The *Index* is, on average, published once every few years in both electronic and hard-copy form, and includes information on short stories that appear in print during a particular span of time. Although I am of the Internet generation, I prefer to work from a book, and I quickly found the collection within the reference section. In the *Index*, short stories are organized according to category and author names. For instance, I randomly grabbed the volume for the years 1994–1998 and skimmed through the pages until I found the category devoted to AIDS. I saw for that particular span of years nearly a hundred stories. It appeared that I would have plenty to occupy my time during the ten-week period of the grant.

In order to describe the method I used to locate a story in the *Index*, I will take as an example a work by Thomas Glave, titled "The Final Inning" (2000). To begin, I found the AIDS category within the *Index* devoted to the years 1999–2004, and I recorded all of those stories; one was "The Final Inning" by Glave. Using the same volume of the *Index*, I uncovered Glave's first name: Thomas. The *Index* is organized in such a way that under each category heading, only the last name and first initial of each author is listed. Also, the publication information for each story is not contained in the category sections. Therefore, it was necessary to refine my search within the *Index* by looking up each author individually.

Once I had found Glave's name, I learned that the story he had written was included in a collection of his works published in 2000. This information proved crucial because it gave me a beginning point from which to continue my research in the Penrose Library database. Using the library catalog, I typed Glave's name into the search engine under the heading Keyword. The results listed the books Glave had authored that were accessible through our university library. I scrolled down the computer screen and found a collection published in 2000 titled *Whose Song? And Other Stories*. When I clicked on the book, the table of contents appeared, and "The Final Inning" was one of the stories listed. The remainder of my work was relatively easy: I found the book on the library shelves and photocopied the selected story.

I use Glave's story as an example of the way I conducted the bulk, if not the entirety, of my research. Once I had found the *Short Story Index*, I discovered it to be comprehensive and exhaustive, listing every story that was either directly or indirectly concerned with AIDS. After discussing this with Margaret, she agreed that using the *Index* was the best possible avenue to pursue my research.

I started with the volume for the years 1994–1998. Once I had located short stories concerning AIDS within this volume, I moved backward in time. It became apparent within older volumes that the number of stories gradually began to decrease. Finally, I was able to locate the year when the first short stories on AIDS were published. As Margaret had suggested, 1986 was a benchmark year with publication of the Sontag story. In addition to Sontag's story, three other works of fiction were listed.

My search obviously moved forward in time as well. Once I had discovered the base year for the short stories, I researched newer volumes in order to determine if other years contained short stories. A trend began to develop. After 1986, the number of stories about AIDS slowly began to rise. Then, in the early 1990s, the numbers increased greatly, reaching at times well over fifty stories during certain years (as in the volume 1994–1998). This trend of an increasing number of short stories continued into the present 2007 volume of the *Index*.

Refining the Project: Margaret

I followed Matthew's lead, and randomly picked a story to begin reading when the stories arrived—in batches of a dozen or so every week to ten days. After reading the first one, I wrote a brief summary, catalogued the story by a topic that seemed relevant, such as "support services for those with AIDS," indicated the story's particular strengths, and moved on. I did not know if the next story I read might be another about support services, or if the one I had just read would be vastly different from all other stories. So I just kept reading and taking notes.

Occasionally I would read a story, go to sleep, and wake up the next day thinking about that particular story. Short stories often have a way of bleeding into each other; of losing any distinct voice; of fading quickly due to limited action, flat dull characters, clichéd lines, and predictable events. However, when a story lives on in my head, I might feel haunted by its characters. Such was the case with Thomas Glave's "The Final Inning." When I read this story, I knew instantly that I would use it. Just as "The Final Inning" was a cornerstone for Matthew, it became the same for me. I kept in the back of my mind a quest for stories that would play off the themes and content of Glave's story.

Faculty-student collaborations feature ongoing negotiations. Matthew sent several stories that were actually novellas, one with a sticky note indicating how much he had liked it. I reminded him that this was to be a collection of short stories, and that no matter how strong or compelling the longer piece was, it did not fit this collection. Also, I needed to remind Matthew that all stories listed in the *Short Story Index* under the AIDS heading might not be about AIDS. He would need to read the story to ensure that it was on topic. The *Index* sometimes makes mistakes. Also, early stories about AIDS might not actually mention AIDS anywhere in the text. Sontag's masterful piece is such an example.

Matthew's role in photocopying the stories was important because making clean copies helps with the scanning process. Photocopying stories from a bound volume of the *New Yorker*, for example, is not a good idea. Words get lost in the center crease. Each story had to be accompanied by a copy of the collection's title page and any other page that acknowledged another source for the right to publish the story in the collection.

Refining the Project: Matthew

Margaret emphasized the importance of finding the publication history. As I progressed in my research, I discovered that the hardest piece of information to find *was* the publication data for each story. The *Short Story Index* listed the area where a certain story first appeared, such as a magazine or a collection of stories. However, the *Index* never specified the exact issue and month of a story's first publication. This information was important to my research because without it, the stories, if chosen for placement in an anthology, could not be adequately acknowledged and cited. Further, the lack of publication information obviously was a challenge if I happened to be looking for a story that I could not locate through the Penrose database. For example, if I was trying to find a story within a particular magazine that I could access either electronically or in hard copy, it took a great deal of work if I didn't know the particular issue and volume. In fact, whenever I found myself in such a situation, I often had to abandon my efforts for the sake of time and because hundreds of other stories awaited my attention. I came to realize that scholars face this kind of stumbling block in any research project.

Many of the short stories were published in obscure places. The magazines for such stories, because of their limited print run, were never available through Penrose Library, and, if accessed through the Internet, did not provide links to archival volumes. Even after consulting the librarians at Penrose and discovering other avenues for obtaining the correct publication information, I ran into dead ends—some stories would remain mysteries to me. But I didn't want to risk losing a good story because of insufficient publication data, so I worked particularly hard on this matter. It occurred to me that scholars before us had faced the same dilemma, and that some stories may have been lost to generations simply because of a glitch. Margaret's goal to "save" short fiction had infected me.

Stumbling Blocks: Margaret

I don't think I fully understood the difficulty of locating full publication information on the stories until I started to search for the information myself—in the fall, when Matthew's grant had run its course, and I was on my own. During the summer, when a batch of stories had arrived and the publication information was not readily apparent, I was disappointed, but I realized that Matthew's decision to just keep finding more stories was correct. I trusted Matthew and assumed he had a good reason for not including the data.

Juggling Time: Matthew

Even though Margaret had made clear the importance of publication information, if I couldn't find the data quickly, I chose to find more stories. The proliferation of stories had an interesting effect on my research. Because of large numbers of stories written during certain years, I became somewhat selective, looking first at those written by the same author. For example, if a single author happened to write five short stories in a one-year time span, I tended to focus my attention initially on their retrieval. My logic was that if an author had written more than two stories, it was possible that he or she had published a collection of short stories wholly dedicated to the AIDS epidemic. As a result, I first looked for such stories and, more often than not, was correct that certain collections were largely concerned with the various aspects of the disease. Once I had researched authors who had written a number of short stories during a particular year, I often simply began to move alphabetically down the list of stories presented. I felt that I was moving from working as a research assistant to becoming a scholar engaged in making crucial decisions.

Decisions, Decisions, Decisions: Margaret

Matthew's decision to send me multiple stories by one author helped me to put the issue on the table early and make important choices about how to deal with these AIDS-directed writers. Seeing the stories offered yet another opportunity to consider the project as a whole. Now that it was clear there were so many stories about AIDS, did I really want to use more than one by any single author? It seemed even more pressing to know some autobiographical information about the author. Were the stories from the same collection? Was the whole collection about AIDS? When did whole collections about AIDS by one author start appearing? Were the stories similar in nature—for example, were all the stories about men who had contracted AIDS through gay sex? Or were the stories a variety—both men and women, gay and straight, drug users, or people with hemophilia? Did the characters all live in the same geographical area? As I began to read my way through multiple stories by the same author, I found recurring patterns.

Most single collections were thematically similar. One by Jameson Currier, now out of print in English, *Dancing on the Moon* (1993), contained stories about gay men who lived on the

East coast. These stories were later translated into French and appeared in France in 2005 as *Les Fantômes*. Another, by Paula Peterson, *Women in the Grove* (2004), contained only stories about women with AIDS, and most were set on the West coast, particularly in and around San Francisco. These two collections in particular helped me to decide that I did not want to use more than one story by any one author. I eventually chose to use neither Currier nor Peterson, but their work helped me to shape my thinking about the anthology itself.

Expanding Search Engines: Matthew

Midway into summer, I began to find it more difficult to locate story collections in Penrose. Margaret reminded me of Prospector, a local search engine. This resource is an interlibrary loan system that connects Penrose to a variety of universities throughout Colorado, and to other libraries in Denver. For instance, if I was unable to find a short story at DU, I could use Prospector to see if the story was housed at a different library, and have it in hand within a day or two. On average, I used Prospector for one out of every five stories. When I had to rely on Prospector, the results always made it possible for me to acquire a particular story. Without this interlibrary loan facility, I would have located far fewer stories.

Considering Search Alternatives: Margaret

Prospector was an easy suggestion, but eventually I worried that Matthew would exhaust his good fortune with this search engine. He would have to move on to interlibrary loan, perhaps using WorldCat, and get the needed books from out of state, which would take longer. I also sent him suggestions about specific authors: "Go find Randall Kenan's *Let the Dead Bury Their Dead* [1992], skim the stories, see if you find anything about AIDS, and let me know." This task was a shot in the dark. I had read two of the short stories from this collection; neither was about AIDS, but both contained gay characters. Then I suggested that

Matthew simply go to the bound volumes of the *New Yorker*, starting in 1986 and going through 1996, pull each one in turn off the shelf, and take a look at the short stories. I believed that he could get through ten years of the *New Yorker* in a half day's work. Although the *Short Story Index* is perhaps the best reference tool for locating short stories by subject matter, it often does not catalog stories until they have been collected in some kind of book. Stories that have been published only in magazines must be found by wide or random reading. Sometimes the best stories are located by sheer chance. Those of us who were scholars before the Internet know that simply browsing can be a good search strategy.

Fortunately, Matthew did not have to pursue any of these suggestions because Prospector never let him down. Because I was trying to become informed on the range of stories about AIDS, I had no preconceived ideas about what specifically I was looking for—or what he should be seeking. I took my lead from what he sent. I knew how to go about shaping the anthology, but that time had not yet come. As the summer neared its end, I wanted to make sure that I had stories representing AIDS in countries other than the United States or Great Britain. Was there any possible way, I wondered aloud in an email to Matthew, to preference stories by author's last name or story title that suggested something other than a Western offering? By this time, of over a hundred stories I had read about AIDS, only a few came from outside the United States. I had not read a single story set anywhere in Africa.

Earlier in the summer, after Matthew had alerted me to the long inventory of stories about AIDS in the *Short Story Index*, I began checking off those stories that Matthew had sent in a table of contents that I had copied from the *Index*. Together, he and I, aware of summer's passing, picked another dozen to move to the head of the line. He went in search of these, and before I returned to Denver, Matthew had located all of the stories on our priority list. These particular stories provided the international perspective I knew was necessary to tell a more complete story of AIDS.

Lessons Learned: Matthew

Throughout this three-month time period, I learned a great deal about the process of research. I made my way through all of the volumes of the *Short Story Index* and copied over a hundred stories, funded through Margaret's own pocketbook. I discovered that the act of research is never stable, that whatever avenue I happened to pursue, change was constant. And I had to adapt. During the challenging times (for instance, when I could no longer locate publication information through the paths of research I knew to be available), I asked for help either from the librarians or directly from Margaret. They were always able to point me in the right direction. In addition, my summer work presented a new method of research to which I had rarely before been exposed. Normally, I wrote papers based on my analysis of secondary sources and materials. However, with the PinS program, I was able to deal with the primary documents of the short stories.

Unexpectedly, I learned a great deal about AIDS as I read each of the stories. I gained new respect and admiration for people suffering from the disease, and came to more deeply understand the various effects of the illness—not only the physical, but also the social, psychological, and familial implications and impact of AIDS. Further, I was pleased that awareness of the disease has spread, evident by the number of stories published over the years. From the paltry few stories in 1986 to the hundreds in the first decade of the twenty-first century, more and more authors have been concerned with conveying to the public the various dimensions of AIDS.

I began an MA program in literature at Clark University in fall 2008. No doubt my involvement in the PinS program aided in my acceptance to Clark. My application was enhanced by a letter of support from Margaret, who gave specific details explaining why I would make an excellent graduate student. She was able to discuss not only my academic achievement but also my skill as an undergraduate researcher. I am one of the lucky few who have had such opportunities in the humanities. Additionally, my experience with the PinS program has proven valuable in the growth of my understanding of the nature of academic research. When I looked at possible graduate programs, I approached the process through the lens of an undergraduate researcher. I feel that I am better equipped now, and more knowledgeable about how to begin my own extended research projects in my area of interest. Also, I have become more aware of my ability to rely on the efforts of other people in order to make a project ultimately successful. In fact, I view my success over the summer months as having largely to do with the numerous avenues of research that were suggested by other people. Now, as I begin a new academic phase of my life, I value these lessons and I'm certain that they will contribute to my success.

To future undergraduate researchers, I recommend constant perseverance. The application and partnership with a professor was the easiest, least time-consuming part of the process. However, when work truly began and frustrations were constant, it would have been easy to simply move on to another source. Yet it was remarkable what I was able to find when I continued to research a particular story. Although many roads seemed permanently blocked, they never stayed blocked for long, and soon I had found dozens of stories that I normally would have missed because of my already limited amount of time. "Undergraduate research is an apprenticeship," according to Merkel and Baker (2002, 3). I certainly learned by doing, and I benefitted from Margaret's coaching and example. She gave me a window into the intellectual work of a scholar.

Lessons Learned: Margaret

As Merkel and Baker point out, "Summer projects allow students and mentors to immerse themselves in the research without the distractions and interruptions of courses and the other attendant activities the academic year brings. Research becomes the focus of attention" (7). Matthew and I worked together on this project in an organic way, but intensively. Based on my own previous work on an anthology, I defined concrete tasks that he could complete. However, even with that experience, there were still surprises as the topic shifted from civil rights to AIDS. I did not know ahead of time what organization the collection of AIDS stories would take. I had to trust that the stories themselves would lead me to define sections and arrangement. I was often led by Matthew's findings to certain obvious questions and directions that, on the outset, I could not have known. He was smart enough to know when to take my advice. When the materials, the looming deadline, and the count on the number of stories dictated otherwise, he was smart enough to ignore me—or to see my suggestions as not the best use of his time.

When I returned to campus in the fall, I was heavily laden with photocopied short stories. I counted the stories remaining on the *Short Story Index* master list, and went about finding another forty or fifty. In all, I read about 170 stories before I decided that I had an ample sense of the range, repetition, and varying themes. The notes I had taken gave way to new, more collective categories, which became section headings. Then I selected twenty-eight stories for the anthology—fourteen by women and fourteen by men—and divided the collection into five sections. The characters included young and old, male and female, and they were geographically, ethnically, and sexually diverse. The stories represented the range of the fictional depiction of those with AIDS. I'm not surprised that of the twenty-eight stories I selected for the final cut, Matthew brought nineteen to my attention; two more I solicited from writer friends, and the other seven were from my own fall reading.

I sent *Short Stories about AIDS: An Anthology* to a university press at the end of the 2007–2008 academic year. During this review process, I am sharing with Matthew the stages that a manuscript undergoes for consideration. Authorship is an important matter to clarify when faculty and students collaborate. As this was a new experience—working with an undergraduate research assistant—it was not entirely clear what Matthew's contribution might entail. Once a contract is assured, Matthew and I will discuss how he will receive credit for his work. At press time, our AIDS collection had been returned from my first choice of university press. The collection then went to a second press where it is under review.

As I think back now about how we worked together over those summer months, I was fortunate to work with a student whose integrity I never doubted, and in whom I had a great deal of trust. Having known Matthew for three years was helpful to our working relationship. When a humanities faculty member enters a partnership with a student, there are considerations for the mentor. Were I to advise my colleagues about how they might engage with undergraduate researchers, I would offer the following observations. The relationship between mentor and mentee is important, with responsibilities and expectations for each role. Discuss those roles deliberately. The mentor serves as a role model, and it is useful for faculty mentors to consider themselves as exemplars, analyzing their own practices and articulating the process. Initially, a student may serve an apprenticeship—learning by doing—but at some point, the undergraduate researcher will probably define an independent project. Allowing the relationship to evolve is essential. A good mentor is supportive, giving advice and counsel, particularly about graduate studies, and also helps the undergraduate researcher develop skills typical to the field (for example, working with primary documents, or using a microfilm reader). As Matthew pointed out, one of the responsibilities of a mentor is to provide letters of recommendation; these letters are especially valuable, as a faculty mentor has insight into specific details concerning the reason that this student is a good fit for graduate studies.

Working with Matthew has helped me learn how to work more effectively with a peer, which is the case on my current anthology project that focuses on coming-of-age stories. Because I was not already an expert on the literature of AIDS, my undergraduate research assistant helped shape my views. In many ways, Matthew's peers are the target audience for the finished text, so when he liked a story, I listened carefully. I remain grateful that I was introduced to the value of working with an undergraduate. Nurturing a young scholar proved a serendipitous reward that I had not expected but appreciated.

References

Beer, Robert H., and Corine Myers. 1995. Guidelines for the Supervision of Undergraduate Research. *Journal of Chemical Education* 72 (8): 721.

Benedict, Barbara M. 2003. The Paradox of the Anthology: Collecting and Difference in Eighteenth-Century Britain. *New Literary History* 34 (2): 231–56.

Currier, Jameson. 1993. *Dancing on the Moon: Short Stories about AIDS*. New York: Viking.

Damrosch, David. 2001. The Mirror and the Window: Reflections on Anthology Construction. *Pedagogy* 1 (1): 207–14.

Franklin, H. Bruce, ed. 1996. *The Vietnam War in American Stories, Songs, and Poems*. Boston: Bedford/St. Martin's.

Glave, Thomas. 2000. The Final Inning. In *Whose Song? And Other Stories*, 151–82. San Francisco: City Lights.

Kenan, Randall. 1992. *Let the Dead Bury Their Dead*. New York: Harcourt Brace.

McDorman, Todd. 2004. Promoting Undergraduate Research in the Humanities: Three Collaborative Approaches. *CUR Quarterly* 25 (1): 39–42.

Merkel, Carolyn Ash, and Shenda M. Baker. 2002. *How to Mentor Undergraduate Researchers: Elements of Mentoring Expectations Practical Information*. Washington, DC: Council on Undergraduate Research.

O'Brien, Tim. 1990. *The Things They Carried*. New York: Broadway Books.

Peterson, Paula W. 2004. *Women in the Grove*. Boston: Beacon Press.

Shilts, Randy. 1987. *And the Band Played On: Politics, People, and the AIDS Epidemic*. New York: St. Martin's.

Short Story Index. 1984–2007. New York: H. W. Wilson.

Sontag, Susan. 1986. The Way We Live Now. *New Yorker*, November 26.

Whitt, Margaret Earley, ed. 2006. *Short Stories of the Civil Rights Movement: An Anthology*. Athens: University of Georgia Press.

Chapter Three

Nontraditional Students as Undergraduate Researchers: Expanding Horizons for Adult Learners and Their Mentors

Jane Greer
University of Missouri–Kansas City

Too often, both the needs and the aptitudes of nontraditional students have been absent from discussions about the place of research in the undergraduate curriculum.[1] At best, proponents of undergraduate research have described a universal student as the beneficiary of inquiry-based learning opportunities.[2] This seemingly typical undergraduate student brings little or no previous experience or expertise to the research project that he or she might undertake, and can probably pursue that project with few distractions from life beyond the academy. At worst, nontraditional students are more deliberately excluded from professional conversations about the educational value of undergraduate research in English studies. Reed Wilson's essay in *Modern Language Studies* (2003) serves as a useful example. While touting the importance of undergraduate research, Wilson describes students as "mostly teenagers" having their first experience "away from home for an extended period of time" and suggests that they need to form a relationship with an adult mentor (77–78). If unexposed to a significant population of nontraditional students, Wilson and other similarly situated faculty members might wrongly presume that nontraditional students are too busy with jobs and families to pursue independent research projects; that they are more vocationally oriented and want to obtain a degree or credential as quickly and easily as possible; or that undergraduate research is appropriate only for students interested in preparing for graduate study, a goal that may not be part of the midlife career plans of some nontraditional students.

The invisibility of nontraditional students in discussions of undergraduate research needs to be addressed. Richard Kazis and his coauthors (2002) note in their report for the U.S. Department of Labor that 44 percent of postsecondary students in the United States are now over age twenty-four, up from 28 percent in 1970 (2, 7). Less stability in the job market and the continual need to develop new skills are realities of the volatile global economy, making it likely that an even greater number of nontraditional learners will seek postsecondary learning opportunities in the years to come. Such students, though, often find that "the traditional structure and organization of higher education pose significant barriers to access and, particularly, to persistence and success" (3). As I will argue in this chapter, a robust undergraduate research program in English studies can offer nontraditional students more flexible access to postsecondary education, and the challenges and rewards of undertaking substantive intellectual projects is often more appealing to adult learners than are lectures, small-group discussions, tests, term papers, and other established instructional methods.

The voices of nontraditional students can also enrich current thinking about the undergraduate research experience. How does the role of mentor change when a mentor works with adult learners? If nontraditional students choose, quite reasonably, not to pursue graduate studies, how can a faculty mentor support their ongoing academic work in spaces outside the university? How can a faculty mentor support and validate nontraditional students as they disseminate the results of their research both in traditional academic arenas (for example, conferences, symposia, and peer-reviewed journals) and in other venues with more diverse audiences? Conceptualizing undergraduate research solely in terms of the needs, experiences, abilities, and goals of traditional, eighteen- to twenty-two-year-old students can lead only to impoverished notions of teaching, learning, and knowledge production.

Nontraditional Undergraduate Researchers: Working Portraits

Let me begin, then, by introducing some nontraditional students who have completed undergraduate research projects in English studies.[3] These students were all enrolled at the University of Missouri–Kansas City (UMKC), a public, metropolitan institution that serves more than 14,000 students. The average student age in 2005 was twenty-seven, and nearly one-third of the students pursue their degrees on a part-time basis. The students I describe in this chapter were enrolled in upper-level classes that were cross-listed in English and women's and gender studies, and I structured the courses so that students could engage with primary documents authored by girls and women. In order to produce a final research paper at the end of the semester, students moved through a series of scaffolded assignments: a "scavenger hunt" for primary resources in libraries and other repositories on campus and in the wider community; a project proposal; source analysis worksheets based on models created by the U.S. National Archives and Record Administration; an annotated bibliography of relevant secondary scholarship; readings of the work of established scholars as models; and, of course, multiple drafts and revisions based on feedback from classmates and from me.[4]

Kate S., the owner of a small commercial cleaning business, was in her late twenties when she decided to pursue a BA in English. I first met her in 2001 when she enrolled in my course on girls and print culture. A serious, thoughtful student, Kate was a favorite partner and group member for in-class activities—her classmates prized her analytical skills and the breadth of her knowledge about popular and canonical literature. Kate pursued the required archival research project on the writing of girls. While working on a preliminary class assignment on library resources, she located the microfilmed records of Beta Phi Theta Rho, a girls' club in Rolla, Missouri, during the middle decades of the twentieth century. For her class project, Kate studied the minute books kept by the club secretary. At the end of the semester, Kate approached me about whether she could continue working on her excellent final paper for independent study credit. Over the course of a subsequent semester, I recommended additional secondary sources for Kate to consult, talked through ideas with her, and responded to drafts of her still developing paper. Her project evolved into a nuanced argument about how keeping minute books served as an occasion for club girls to exercise power and create social hierarchies. Kate submitted her final paper to what was then a new publication—*Young Scholars in Writing*—and was thrilled to have her research published as the lead article in the inaugural issue. Kate graduated in 2004 and continues to run her cleaning business. She has considered pursuing an MFA, but has found that her interest in writing science fiction is generally frowned upon by the creative writing programs she has contacted. She continues to build an intellectually rich and rewarding life by serving as a reviewer for *Young Scholars*, working on a novel, attending university outreach programs, and participating in an informal study group with other UMKC students and alumni interested in issues of gender, literacy, and rhetoric.

Cynthia K., a divorced mother of two teenagers, was in her early forties when she decided to pursue the educational dreams she had put aside earlier in her life as she helped her now ex-husband earn his college degree. Using court-ordered spousal support to fund her education, Cynthia had earned an associate degree at a community college and transferred to a four-year university to pursue her bachelor's degree in English on a full-time basis. Warm and enthusiastic, Cynthia was a standout student in a junior-level course on women and rhetoric in 2003. For class, she wrote about disability and what she termed the "embodied spirituality" of Helen Keller's rhetoric, a project that carried even greater emotional valence for Cynthia when her mother was diagnosed with breast cancer. Cynthia continued studying the rhetoric of Helen Keller for her senior thesis, an optional capstone experience for English majors. Relying heavily on interlibrary loan, Cynthia was able to obtain a wide range of primary sources, including published editions of Keller's journals, letters, and speeches, along with several books authored by Keller that are now out of print. Cynthia tapped into scholarship from the emerging field of disability studies to help her interpret Keller's writings. When a call was issued for student presentations at the university's annual Undergraduate Research Symposium, Cynthia was eager to share her research with a wider audience. She crafted a ten-page version of her thirty-page thesis to present orally, and faculty members, fellow students, and friends were on hand to applaud her efforts. Cynthia is now teaching high school students and serving as English department chair at a local parochial school. She has earned her MA and also teaches online courses for other nontraditional students at the university.

Lauren P., a mother of six, worked part time as an executive assistant at a local community college to supplement the income of her husband's construction business. By forgoing full-time employment, Lauren could spend significant time with her daughter with special needs, Faith, and also pursue a bachelor's degree in English. Lauren enrolled in my class on girls and print culture, and the librarian in the special collections at our university library pointed her to the small, handwritten journal in which Nancy Holmes Corse recorded her daily life in Vermont in 1858 and 1859. Lauren's work on the Corse diary quickly became much more than a class project. She applied for and received a $1,250 grant from our university's undergraduate research program that allowed her to travel to New England to examine diaries and other documents penned by nineteenth-century girls. Accompanied by her oldest daughter, who has now developed her own interests in archival research, Lauren spent several days working in the archives at Smith College and at Harvard's Andover Theological Library.

Ultimately, Lauren authored an outstanding paper on the relationship between literacy and economic agency for young women like Corse. Lauren also tracked down Corse's descendants in Texas and engaged in a lively email exchange with them, eventually sending them a transcription of the diary and a copy of her final paper. Lauren went on to do a poster presentation for state legislators and other government officials during Undergraduate Research Day at the Capitol in Jefferson City, and to publish her research in *Young Scholars* (2005). She also worked with the staff in special collections at the university library to digitize the Corse diary.[5]

Lauren subsequently undertook another independent study project, this time working closer to home to investigate nineteenth-century female seminaries in Missouri. Lauren was awarded a smaller grant ($400) from the university's undergraduate research program to cover expenses as she visited local historic sites, sifted through uncatalogued holdings in the libraries of small liberal arts colleges in the area, and developed relationships with archivists and curators at county historical societies. Lauren again published her findings in a national, peer-reviewed journal for undergraduate research, and her work has become assigned reading in my class on women's rhetoric, along with the work of eminent scholars Shirley Wilson Logan, Susan Wells, and Carol Mattingly. Celebrating her many accomplishments, Lauren's entire family attended her graduation in May, 2005; she was forty-seven years old. Lauren earned a second bachelor's degree in history in 2008, an opportunity made possible when she left her job at the community college and accepted a new position as an executive assistant at UMKC.

Heather F. was in her late twenties and had just earned her associate degree when she matriculated at UMKC to pursue her BA in English. Though she had enrolled at a regional, four-year institution in rural Missouri immediately after graduating from high school, the serious illness and eventual death of a sibling had derailed Heather's initial progress toward a bachelor's degree. Eager and outspoken, Heather sat in the center of the front row in a large, junior-level survey course on American literature. Though her schedule did not permit her to take any of the more advanced courses I teach on rhetoric and the literacies of women and girls, Heather approached me about doing an undergraduate research project. Together we constructed the outlines of a project focused on the rhetorical practices of Juliette Low, the founder of the Girl Scouts. Heather obtained a $1,250 undergraduate research grant to fund a trip to Savannah, Georgia, and she spent five days working in the archives at the Georgia State Historical Society, where Low's papers are housed. After her productive archival research trip, though, Heather began to struggle with various personal and health issues. Still, she eventually was able to produce a very fine paper based on Low's rhetorical activism. She also made a strong oral presentation at the Undergraduate Research Symposium at UMKC. Heather is currently working for an investment company, proofreading and editing written correspondence regarding complex financial transactions.

While juggling jobs, families, relationships, illnesses, and other life challenges both large and small, Kate, Cynthia, Lauren, and Heather all embraced the opportunity to undertake their own substantive intellectual projects as undergraduate researchers. They located primary sources that had yet to receive scholarly attention; delved into archives; read widely to develop a sense of how their findings might enrich ongoing scholarly conversations; drafted and revised theses, presentations, and articles; disseminated their work in a variety of public forums; and received feedback from various audiences. Their experiences and accomplishments seem to be just what the Boyer Commission report (1998) imagined when it suggested that inquiry-based learning for undergraduates would produce "a particular kind of individual, one equipped with a spirit of inquiry and a zest for problem solving; one possessed of the skill in communication that is the hallmark of clear thinking as well as mastery of language; one informed by a rich and diverse experience. . . . [an] individual that will provide the scientific, technological, academic, political, and creative leadership for the next century" (13). In the working portraits of undergraduate researchers offered earlier, one can see how curious, problem-solving, clear-thinking, well-spoken academic and community leaders for the twenty-first century may well come from the ranks of nontraditional students. Indeed, as I will argue, undergraduate research opportunities may be a particularly suitable way both to meet the needs of nontraditional learners and to help them reach their full potential.

Adult Education and Undergraduate Research

Postsecondary educational institutions traditionally have been structured logistically to meet the needs of a student population that is just entering adulthood and is able to attend school full time with few familial or job-related demands. Classes meet several times a week at a central campus, and students are presumed to have flexible schedules that will allow them to meet in study groups and access the university libraries outside of class. Moreover, instruction in many college classrooms and lecture halls remains firmly entrenched in what Paulo Freire has so aptly termed the *banking concept* of education. Instructors authoritatively deposit knowledge in the youthful heads of students, who are positioned as passive recipients of their elders' wisdom. For nontraditional students, both the logistics of postsecondary education and the conventional pedagogies of a college classroom can be misfits. Undergraduate research can address both problems.

For Kate and Lauren, opportunities to pursue their research as independent study projects, for which they earned three credit hours, alleviated the need for them to be in a campus classroom on a weekly basis. We arranged to meet as they deemed necessary, often in the late afternoon or early evening to accommodate their work schedules and family needs. Email also served as a conduit for asking or answering questions, recommending readings, and circulating drafts with responses. Such scheduling flexibility can be tremendously important in ensuring that adult learners can successfully move toward their degrees. Kazis and his coauthors (2002) note that issues of accessibility and the scheduling of classes on nights and weekends was the second most popular reason that nontraditional students elected to enroll at particular postsecondary institutions, a concern that did not appear in the surveys of traditional students (43).

Kate and Lauren also were able to access libraries and repositories that were more convenient to them than the resources on the main campus. When she began her project on female seminaries, Lauren chose to investigate archives nearer her suburban home, rather than travel to the special collections department at the main library on the university's midtown campus. The reels of microfilm containing the meeting minutes of Beta Phi Theta Rho that served as the basis of Kate's undergraduate research project were held by the Western Historical Manuscript Collection, an underused repository where staff members happily make arrangements for researchers to use the collections in the evenings and on weekends. In terms of logistics, the autonomy that can come with an undergraduate research project is well suited to the needs of nontraditional students.

More important, though, are the ways in which such inquiry-based learning may better fit the intellectual aptitudes of nontraditional students. Since adult educator Malcolm Knowles (1970) popularized the term *andragogy* in opposition to *pedagogy* in the middle decades of the twentieth century, scholars and educators have worked to better define and understand the needs of more mature students. Rather than presume that teaching models and methods devised for working with children and youth are applicable for older students, andragogy focuses on the learning processes of adults. For Knowles and his intellectual descendants, adult learners are likely to be more self-directed; to bring a rich reservoir of experience to any learning situation; to integrate their learning with their social roles beyond the classroom; and to be less focused on simply knowing a subject, and more focused on the actions and performances that new knowledge will allow them to undertake.[6]

The research projects undertaken by Kate, Cynthia, Lauren, and Heather arose from work begun in traditional classrooms, but these students' abilities to manage their learning processes were most evident as they pursued intellectual projects they had devised. Setting her own pace, Cynthia moved through her reading of Keller's letters and speeches even as she attended her daughter's high school drill team performances and cared for her mother. Heather took the initiative to assemble her own impressive collection of secondary scholarship on girl scouting, including journal articles from the fields of history, women's studies, journalism, cultural studies, and literary criticism, even purchasing unpublished dissertations on scouting that were relevant to her study of Juliette Low.

Students like the ones I have described can bring their own experiences and expertise to bear on their research. It seems to me no coincidence that the four women whose intellectual work I have described here were committed to researching the lives of girls and women. Unlike many of the younger women I teach who are initially uncomfortable with or even disdainful of any "feminist" project, Heather, Lauren, Cynthia, and Kate threw themselves into their investigations of women's literacy practices and rhetorical performances. Having encountered sexism on the job, negotiated difficult compromises between work and family, and been sustained through good times and bad by the women in their own lives (grandmothers, mothers, aunts, sisters, daughters, friends, and lovers), these nontraditional female students were passionate about the projects of feminist historiography they undertook. Their life experiences positioned them to appreciate the importance of women's often unrecognized work in the world, and they relished opportunities to learn from their foremothers and to amplify female voices that had previously been silenced or marginalized.

These nontraditional undergraduate researchers also brought considerable expertise to their projects. As a businesswoman experienced in documenting her own professional activities and keeping records of client meetings, Kate brought a unique perspective to reading the minute books kept by girls in Rolla, Missouri, in the 1940s and 1950s. Lauren's previous efforts as a genealogic researcher tracking down her own ancestors made it possible for her to locate the descendants of Nancy Holmes Corse, and she was fully prepared for the painstaking work of transcription because she had run a secretarial services firm before the birth of her daughter, Faith. Given opportunities to define their own intellectual projects, students like Lauren, Kate, Cynthia, and Heather can bring to bear expertise they have developed in other contexts, and can use their experiences as leverage to move their research forward in productive—and sometimes wonderfully unanticipated—ways.

Nontraditional learners also carry their intellectual work back into the social roles they occupy outside the academy. As the daughter of a woman battling cancer, Cynthia found great solace in her study of Keller's struggles, and she shared her sense of hope with other families of cancer patients, passing along inspirational bracelets and handmade scarves as concrete expressions of encouragement. As the mother of five daughters, Lauren shared her research on diary writing with her family. In an email to me in 2005, she explained how her children and other family members were affected by her research:

> I encourage my children to write letters, with pen and pencil. [. . .] I'm going to propose to my sisters and daughters that we invest in several journals, which will be kept for about one week while we write in our family diary, then mail it on to the next family, who will keep it for one week and write in it. That way we always have one diary in our home, to read the entries of distant family members, write our own, then pass it on.

For nontraditional students, their undergraduate education may not occur during a brief, four- or five-year time span when they are relatively sequestered on a college campus. Instead, the educational experiences of adult learners are intertwined with jobs, PTA meetings, housekeeping, the demands and rewards of family life, and long-standing obligations to civic and religious organizations. It's not surprising that for nontraditional students, the boundaries between their roles as students and their roles as workers, parents, spouses, and community members are fluid, and their intellectual work is carried into the social roles they occupy beyond the academy.

The final way adult learners may differ from their more traditional counterparts centers on issues of performance. Many adult learners find it valuable to enact the intellectual work they undertake. From oral presentations at undergraduate research symposia, to poster presentations for state legislators, to publication in refereed journals, Kate, Cynthia, Lauren, and Heather, like other nontraditional students, have eagerly seized opportunities to do more than simply turn in a paper for a grade. Far from being too busy to take advantage of such performance opportunities, these adult learners sought out occasions that allowed them to demonstrate their capabilities as producers of knowledge and to share their research in professional venues. As experts on the minute-keeping practices of club girls or the rhetoric of Juliette Low, they moved well beyond the deferential role of undergraduate student and claimed the status of author/authority for themselves. With little interest in "busy work," Kate, Lauren, Cynthia, and Heather all took advantage of opportunities to perform their academic work in ways that bridged the gap between their status as subservient students in the classroom and their status as active agents—parents, workers, and community members—beyond the academy.

In sum, then, both logistically and pedagogically, undergraduate research experiences are well aligned with the needs and aptitudes of many nontraditional learners. The growing number of such students on college campuses and their diverse circumstances make it increasingly untenable to argue for the value of undergraduate research based on uninterrogated assumptions about the "typical" college student. To be sure, students like Heather,

Lauren, Cynthia, and Kate are not the teenagers in need of adult mentors described by Wilson. While undergraduate research projects may well be a particularly appropriate way for teachers to structure educational experiences for nontraditional learners, so too do adult learners have much to teach their teachers.

Mentors and Nontraditional Undergraduate Researchers: Expanding Horizons

Few discussions of undergraduate research fail to mention the importance of mentoring as an essential component of such inquiry-based learning. Mentorship is the first of four characteristics that Toufic Hakim (1998) uses to distinguish undergraduate research projects from more conventional assignments that require students to do research. Originality, acceptability (of research methods and techniques), and dissemination are the other three characteristics. Without a productive mentoring relationship, though, an undergraduate researcher is unlikely to be able to disseminate an original piece of scholarship using methodologies acceptable to wider professional audiences.

The faculty mentors of undergraduate researchers can be called upon to serve many functions: sharing their intellectual expertise; providing access to equipment, facilities, and institutional resources; directing students through bodies of published scholarship; helping students manage the research process; introducing students to professional contacts and integrating them into academic networks; serving as audience and responder for students' research and providing a professional assessment of their work; and calling students' attention to additional academic and professional opportunities (Lopatto 2003; Ishiyama 2007). For the undergraduate researchers interviewed by Hakim, mentors played a crucial role as students began their projects, helping to initiate them into their particular academic discipline. Mentors could then step back as students assumed "ownership of their discipline" (191).

For many undergraduate researchers, this disciplinary initiation offered by faculty mentors lays the groundwork for what will become lifelong career pursuits that include graduate and professional school. Such was the case for Cynthia, who chose to pursue an MA in literature. As I read and responded to drafts of Cynthia's undergraduate thesis, I was mindful of pointing out how the research and writing skills she was developing would serve her well in graduate seminars to come. We talked about the oral presentation she delivered at the Undergraduate Research Symposium as preparation for conference presentations she might deliver as a master's student, and for work as a graduate teaching assistant standing in front of a class of first-year writing students.

But mentoring nontraditional students places additional demands on—and offers additional rewards to—faculty members. Rather than prepare for a seamless transition to graduate school or a professional career, some nontraditional students must seek ways to integrate their burgeoning intellectual interests into the lives they already lead. For example, family ties make it unlikely that Kate or Lauren will leave the Kansas City area, and both women question the financial prudence of taking on additional debt to immerse themselves in graduate study at a local university. In a 2008 email to me, Lauren acknowledged that she had hoped to earn an MA by the time she turned fifty, but that her life had "taken a detour." My role as a faculty mentor thus expands to include helping students find ways to continue their intellectual work in our community.

Mentors for nontraditional students, then, need to be in tune with local research resources, such as the outreach programs of public libraries; county historical societies that may seek volunteers to engage in projects to preserve local history; and local chapters of professional organizations that may welcome "amateur" members. Through such community organizations, talented undergraduate researchers for whom graduate school is not an option can continue to develop their skills and put their considerable intellects to work in meaningful ways.

Helping to organize and facilitate a study group of former students and recent alumni with shared intellectual interests can be another powerful way for faculty mentors to serve as a sustaining force in the intellectual lives of nontraditional students. Both Kate and Lauren have participated in such a group focusing on issues of girls and literacy. Meeting roughly once a month, the group members agree to read and discuss scholarship in the nascent field of girls' studies; share and respond to drafts of texts they are composing for a variety of purposes; and attend public lectures together on relevant topics, evaluating the speakers afterward over coffee or cocktails. Such informally organized study groups are long-standing traditions, as women and members of other marginalized groups have historically used their creativity and energy to circumvent their exclusion from higher education and other intellectual opportunities.[7] The activities of the "Saturday Night Club" (Sicherman 1993) or the "Semi-Colon Club" (Tonkovich 1995) can serve as rich models for mentors seeking to help nontraditional students continue their intellectual development beyond the academy.

Faculty mentors working with nontraditional students will also need to envision more expansive horizons in terms of what constitutes a meaningful dissemination of research. The undergraduate researchers described in this chapter delivered oral presentations to audiences of peers, faculty, and community members; prepared posters for display in the state capitol and discussed their research with state legislators; and published their work in peer-reviewed national journals. Laudable accomplishments to be sure. But they also disseminated their work in ways less valued by the academy but just as impactful for the student and her audience. Several of the students I have discussed return regularly to campus to share their insights on archival research with students currently enrolled in my classes, or at campus-wide workshops designed to encourage students to consider undertaking undergraduate research projects. Making such presentations validates the expertise of students like Heather, Cynthia, Lauren, and Kate, who in turn serve as powerful role models for other students. Indeed, on course evaluations, students often list the brief presentations made by previous undergraduate researchers as some of the most compelling days they experience in my classes. For Lauren, perhaps the most remarkable way she disseminated her research involved the Texas descendants of Vermont diary writer Nancy Holmes Corse. In a 2005 email to me, Lauren described this part of her undergraduate research experience:

> The relatives have read the diary, and Shirley, the 80+-year-old granddaughter of [Nancy Holmes Corse], e-mailed (e-mailed!)

> to tell me how much she enjoyed it, and that [Corse] really did learn how to use periods, capitalization, etc. later in life. [. . .] The Texas relatives have never spoken with anyone in Vermont, until now. Shirley and her cousin get together and go over all the old family stories, look at documents, visit cemeteries, eat sandwiches, and laugh a lot. I asked her to adopt me. Technology is amazing; but it took an old weather-beaten, water-stained diary to connect me with a lot of interesting people.

Though Lauren's dissemination of her research to Shirley and other Corse descendants will have no place on a curriculum vitae or any other register of academic accomplishment, its very personal impact is no less significant. In mentoring undergraduate researchers in a variety of life circumstances, faculty members need to be attuned to such rare and wonderful opportunities to share in people's lives. Recognizing the multiple ways in which undergraduate research is disseminated better positions those of us in English studies to advocate for such programs with all types of students, with our colleagues, and with other constituencies inside and outside the university.

Expanded Horizons for Nontraditional Undergraduate Researchers and Their Mentors

As undergraduate researchers in English studies, Kate, Lauren, Heather, and Cynthia are certainly idiosyncratic. The portraits I have constructed of their lives and their academic work only begin to hint at the range of circumstances nontraditional students bring to the classroom and the potential work they might accomplish. Administrators and educators in postsecondary institutions can be sure, though, that more nontraditional students will be seeking the intellectual experiences that colleges and universities have to offer as postsecondary educational opportunities become "more critical for economic and labor market success" in the years ahead (Kazis et al., 4). Undergraduate research can serve as a significant way to make higher education more compatible with the needs and aptitudes of adult learners, even as these nontraditional students help faculty rethink their own roles as mentors. Just as nontraditional students bring their lives beyond the university to their academic experiences, so too might faculty mentors do well to consider how they might expand the horizons of their academic lives and stretch their work in productive new ways.

Notes

1. A capacious term, the *nontraditional* student can be defined in various ways depending on institutional context. The National Center for Educational Statistics (NCES) generally uses seven characteristics to classify undergraduate students as nontraditional: (1) deferring initial enrollment in postsecondary education beyond the twelve months after high school graduation; (2) attending college part time; (3) being financially self-sufficient; (4) working full time; (5) having dependents other than a spouse; (6) being a single parent; (7) having no high school diploma or GED (Choy 2002, 2–3). For NCES reporting purposes, any one of these characteristics places a student in the nontraditional category. Horn and Carroll (1996) have suggested, though, that it may be more appropriate to think of nontraditional status as a continuum (8–9). A new high school graduate who attends college part time while still living with his parents may be minimally nontraditional, while a single mother who enrolls in college for the first time at age forty-five, and attends classes only in the evening so she can maintain her full-time factory job, is highly nontraditional.

2. Important exceptions include John Ishiyama's (2007) work on the first-generation, low-income students and African American students who undertake undergraduate research projects; the scholarship of S. J. Langley-Turnbaugh, S. Locke, L. Cohen, and Nancy Lightbody (2007), who have described their experiences with undergraduate researchers with disabilities, including Attention Deficit Hyperactivity Disorder and hearing and visual impairments; the report of Daniel Wubah, Gail Gasparich, David Schaefer, David Brakke, Gina McDonald, and Daniel Downey (2000) on their efforts to use undergraduate research as a way to improve retention rates for minority students; and Sandra Gregerman's (1999) work on the relationship between undergraduate research and the academic success of diverse students at the University of Michigan.

3. Kate, Lauren, Cynthia, and Heather all reviewed and responded to several drafts of this chapter; they chose to be identified here by their first names and last initials. UMKC supports undergraduate research through its SEARCH program (Students Engaged in Artistic and Academic Research). Since 2000, SEARCH has distributed roughly $30,000 annually to undergraduate researchers in all disciplines. At the 2008

Undergraduate Research Symposium, sixty students presented their research, delivering papers orally, making poster presentations, displaying architectural models and artwork, and performing as dancers and musicians.

4. The worksheet from the U.S. National Archives and Records Administration and other resources on teaching students to work with primary materials is available at http://www.archives.gov.

5. The digitized diary of Nancy Holmes Corse can be accessed at http://library.umkc.edu.

6. For more on Knowles's concept of andragogy, its validity, and its impact on the field of adult education, see Jill Ellsworth (1992); André Grace (1996); and Daniel Pratt (1993, 1988).

7. See also the work of Anne Ruggles Gere (1997), Elizabeth McHenry (2002), and Katherine Adams (2001) for more on extracurricular study groups and their importance to women and other marginalized learners.

References

Adams, Katherine H. 2001. *A Group of Their Own: College Writing Courses and American Women Writers, 1880–1940*. Albany: State University of New York Press.

Boyer Commission on Educating Undergraduates in the Research University, Shirley Strum Kenny (chair). 1998. *Reinventing Undergraduate Education: A Blueprint for America's Research Universities*. Stony Brook: State University of New York.

Choy, Susan. 2002. *Nontraditional Undergraduates*. Washington, DC: U.S. Department of Education, National Center for Educational Statistics.

Ellsworth, Jill H. 1992. Adults' Learning: The Voices of Experience. *Journal of Adult Education* 21 (1): 24–34.

Freire, Paulo. 1996. *Pedagogy of the Oppressed*. New York: Continuum.

Gere, Anne Ruggles. 1997. *Intimate Practices: Literacy and Cultural Work in U.S. Women's Clubs, 1880–1920*. Urbana: University of Illinois Press.

Grace, André P. 1996. Striking a Critical Pose: Andragogy—Missing Links, Missing Values. *International Journal of Lifelong Education* 15 (5): 382–92.

Gregerman, Sandra R. 1999. Improving the Academic Success of Diverse Students through Undergraduate Research. *CUR Quarterly* 20 (2): 54–59.

Hakim, Toufic. 1998. Soft Assessment of Undergraduate Research: Reactions and Student Perspectives. *CUR Quarterly* 18 (4): 189–92.

Horn, Laura J., and C. Dennis Carroll. 1996. *Nontraditional Undergraduates: Trends in Enrollment from 1986 to 1992 and Persistence and Attainment Among 1989–90 Beginning Postsecondary Students*. Washington, DC: U.S. Department of Education, National Center for Educational Statistics.

Ishiyama, John. 2007. Expectations and Perceptions of Undergraduate Research Mentoring: Comparing First Generation, Low Income White/Caucasian and African American Students. *College Student Journal* 41 (3): 540–49.

Karukstis, Kerry K., and Timothy E. Elgren, eds. 2007. *Developing and Sustaining a Research-Supportive Curriculum: A Compendium of Successful Practices.* Washington, DC: Council on Undergraduate Research.

Kazis, Richard, Abigail Callahan, Chris Davidson, Annie McLeod, Brian Bosworth, Vickie Choitz, and John Hoops. 2007. *Adult Learners in Higher Education: Barriers to Success and Strategies to Improve Results*. Washington, DC: U.S. Department of Labor.

Knowles, Malcolm S. 1970. *The Modern Practice of Adult Education: Andragogy versus Pedagogy*. New York: Association Press.

Langley-Turnbaugh, S. J., S. Locke, L. Cohen, and Nancy Lightbody. 2007. Research Experiences for Undergraduates with Disabilities in Science, Technology, Engineering, and Mathematics Majors. In Karukstis and Elgren 2007, 529–40.

Lopatto, David. 2003. The Essential Features of Undergraduate Research. *CUR Quarterly* 23 (1): 139–42.

McHenry, Elizabeth. 2002. *Forgotten Readers: Recovering the Lost History of African American Literary Societies*. Durham, NC: Duke University Press.

Petrillo, Lauren. 2005. "I Suppose I Am My Own Girl Now": The Diary of Nancy Holmes Corse, Enosburg, Vermont, 1858–1859.

Young Scholars in Writing: Undergraduate Research in Writing and Rhetoric 3: 103–10.

Pratt, Daniel D. 1988. Andragogy as a Relational Construct. *Adult Education Quarterly* 38 (3): 160–81.

———. 1993. Andragogy After Twenty-Five Years. *New Directions for Adult and Continuing Education*, no. 57 (Spring): 15–23.

Sicherman, Barbara. 1993. Reading and Ambition: M. Carey Thomas and Female Heroism. *American Quarterly* 45 (1): 73–103.

Tonkovich, Nicole. 1995. Writing in Circles: Harriet Beecher Stowe, the Semi-Colon Club, and the Construction of Women's Authorship. In *Nineteenth-Century Women Learn to Write*, ed. Catherine Hobbs, 145–78. Charlottesville: University Press of Virginia.

Wilson, Reed. 2003. Researching "Undergraduate Research" in the Humanities. *Modern Language Studies* 33 (1/2): 74–79.

Wubah, Daniel A., Gail Gasparich, David Schaefer, David F. Brakke, Gina McDonald, and Daniel Downey. 2000. Retention of Minority Students through Research. *CUR Quarterly* 20 (3): 120–26.

II

Conducting Research Responsibly

There is nothing like looking, if you want to find something. You certainly usually find something, if you look, but it is not always quite the something you were after.

—J. R. R. Tolkien

Chapter Four

Preaching What We Practice: RCR Instruction for Undergraduate Researchers in Writing Studies

Deaver Traywick
Black Hills State University

Two important events in my professional life have generated an interest in research ethics and the responsible conduct of research (RCR): the first was a failure of sorts, the second a success. The failure occurred six years ago, when a piece of narrative nonfiction I wrote for an edited collection was rejected by the publisher's attorney because he felt I had not adequately protected the privacy of someone described in the piece. The narrative concerned a writing center client I had worked with daily for more than two years. Despite my efforts to protect this person's identity and despite the narrative nature of the piece, the publisher argued that the piece should have been submitted for institutional review board (IRB) approval. My IRB office disagreed, and I made a half-hearted attempt to defend the creative nonfiction genre in an email exchange. However, during this exchange I realized that I could have taken many more steps to protect my client's right to "participate" in my writing.

Partly based on this experience, I now pay very close attention to the ways in which my own students approach the ethical responsibilities of their research. Writing centers—as other chapters in this volume attest—are ideal environments for undergraduate research, and my own undergraduate consultants have successfully conducted research and presented it at regional and national conferences. The process of mentoring these students as they design, seek IRB approval for, and present their studies has been an enlightening and rewarding opportunity. Yet this opportunity also carries a significant responsibility: the charge to educate these students in the basics of ethical and responsible research.

Nonetheless, RCR instruction for undergraduate researchers has not been formalized at a disciplinary level. Research ethics may be taught in some composition methodology courses, but students often do not encounter these courses until they reach graduate school. At present no single authoritative source exists on teaching RCR to undergraduate composition researchers. For example, Nicholas Steneck's *ORI Introduction to the Responsible Conduct of Research* (2006), which is the nucleus of the U.S. Department of Health and Human Services Office of Research Integrity (ORI) RCR promotion, is "written primarily for researchers and research staff engaged in research supported by the Public Health Service" (xii), not for undergraduates. The National Academy of Science's booklet *On Being a Scientist* (2009) treats science broadly, but its language ("empirical objectivity of scientific claims" (65); "validity of experimental data" (40); and examples (nearly all laboratory-based); don't consistently apply to research in writing and teaching.

Similarly, although Amy Shachter (2007) develops Steneck's *Introduction* into an excellent course of RCR instruction for undergraduates in the sciences and social sciences, her focus does not allow her to specifically address the concerns of disciplines, such as composition, with diverse research practices. In fact, most formal RCR instruction still uses the language and conventions of the biomedical research for which it was first designed. And, as Shachter and *On Being a Scientist* (1995) note, much of RCR instruction still happens informally, through observation, as if novice researchers will absorb principles of responsible research from their mentors through osmosis. In some cases, as Barbara Schneider (2006) explains, composition specialists have divorced their professional commitment to conduct research responsibly from their responsibility to prepare student researchers to do the same. "Focusing on the ethics of our research," Schneider argues, leads the composition community to "bracket off the ethics of our teaching" (80).

This chapter seeks to close the distance between conducting ethical research and teaching ethical research by providing an outline of issues that undergraduate research mentors can follow to formalize their RCR instruction. It draws together numerous sources on RCR and RCR instruction in the biomedical and social sciences, including the formative *Nuremberg Code* (National Institutes of Health 1949) and *Belmont Report* (National Institutes of Health 1979), federal guides to RCR, and online RCR resources. However, I will present these resources in the context of the composition community's conversations about our own ethic, ultimately arguing for a new, discipline-specific approach to RCR instruction: an approach that recognizes and benefits from writing studies' deep and complex interdisciplinarity.

Background: RCR and Composition Studies

Several important factors have contributed to the paucity of RCR instruction in undergraduate composition programs. The first is composition's relatively late arrival in the arena of undergraduate research. In their introduction to this volume, Laurie Grobman and Joyce Kinkead trace the formal organization of the undergraduate research movement to the founding of the Council for Undergraduate Research (CUR) in 1978 and the National Conferences on Undergraduate Research (NCUR) in 1987. Yet, as the authors note, not until 2007 was a humanities poster included in CUR's showcase Posters on the Hill event.

Second, composition has emerged rather recently as an active participant in the discussion of RCR criteria and professional ethics codes. For example, Paul Anderson (1998) cites the large number of person-based studies in composition journals that appeared for decades before the discipline established its own RCR guidelines, and he despairs that some "prominent composition researchers" seem to be unaware of federal regulation of human-participant research or do not teach this regulation in their research methods courses (64).[1] As the timeline demonstrates, efforts to formalize ethical research guidelines in writing studies (first codified in the 2000 Conference on College Composition and Communication [CCCC] position statement *Guidelines for the Ethical Treatment of Students and Student Writing in Composition Studies*) have followed by many years—sometimes decades—federal legislation and formal codes in many other fields, including literature and language (see Figure 4.1).

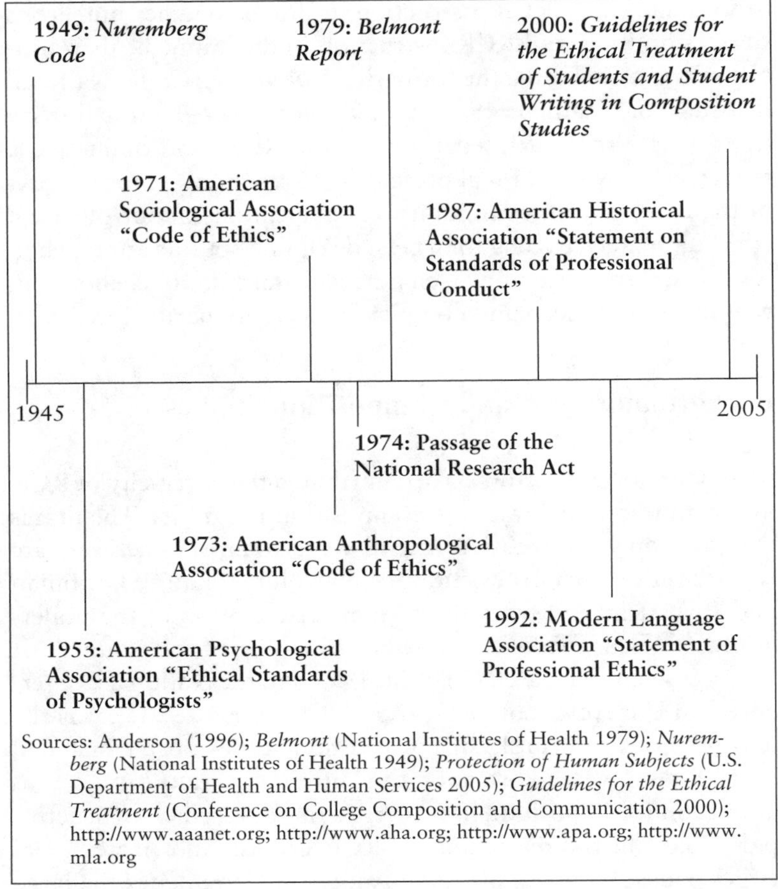

Sources: Anderson (1996); *Belmont* (National Institutes of Health 1979); *Nuremberg* (National Institutes of Health 1949); *Protection of Human Subjects* (U.S. Department of Health and Human Services 2005); *Guidelines for the Ethical Treatment* (Conference on College Composition and Communication 2000); http://www.aaanet.org; http://www.aha.org; http://www.apa.org; http://www.mla.org

FIGURE 4.1. *Milestones in formalizing research ethics.*

Not surprisingly, the composition community is also not at the forefront of RCR instruction. For nearly ten years, ORI has promoted a program identifying nine areas of RCR instruction:

1. data acquisition, management, sharing and ownership;
2. conflict of interest and commitment;
3. human subjects;
4. animal welfare;

5. research misconduct;
6. publication practices and responsible authorship;
7. mentor/trainee responsibilities;
8. peer review; and
9. collaborative science.

ORI's online educational resources are extensive and useful, although they rely primarily on the language and conventions of biomedical research. Likewise, there are numerous online courses in RCR from organizations and institutions invested in teaching responsible research, though few of them have specific modules for researchers in the humanities. (The Collaborative Institutional Training Initiative [CITI] program is the one notable exception.[2]) This relative ease of collecting RCR instructional materials for programs in science, and the absence of complementary materials for English studies, is an imbalance that requires a response from our community.

Finally, and surely most important, composition specialists have not designed a formal program in RCR instruction because the community is still defining the parameters of responsible research for itself. The CCCC *Guidelines* (revised in 2003 and retitled *CCCC Guidelines for the Ethical Conduct of Research in Composition Studies*) were first articulated largely in response to Anderson's 1996 and 1998 calls for standardizing the way writing researchers interacted with IRBs. Responses to the *Guidelines* have been many and varied since then. Janis Haswell, Maureen Hourigan, and Lulu C. H. Sun (2000) argued that the *Guidelines* were too restrictive, did not adequately account for the variety of research in composition, and relied too heavily on the social science and biomedical models. Ellen Cushman and Peter Mortensen (qtd. in Brooke and Goodburn 2003) responded that the *Guidelines* were not intended to address every research situation, and that they were a product of a particular historic moment in CCCC's development. Ellen Barton (2000) and Seth Kahn and Barton (2000), in a three-part exchange in the pages of *College Composition and Communication* (CCC), extended the debate to methodology, tussling over the ethics of empirical research methods that lack the reflexive, collaborative relationship between researcher and participant some consider essential. Heidi McKee (2003) revived the argument that IRB systems rooted in biomedical science are inappropriate for reviewing composition proposals, and called for separate IRBs to evaluate composition research. More recently, Schneider (2006) has shown how our commitment to responsible research does not always extend to our students whose research "is carried on in our names" (71). Will Banks and Michelle Eble (2007) have demonstrated how the complex relationship between writers and researchers in digital spaces, as well as the distinction between public and private writing, further complicates the CCCC *Guidelines*. Finally, Amy Robillard (2006) cleverly points out that when undergraduate researchers become published authors, as they do in the pages of *Young Scholars in Writing*, they challenge composition specialists' traditional practices of representing student writers as anonymous subjects of study.

The debate over just what constitutes RCR in writing studies is remarkable but understandable. Our discipline suffers from an identity crisis, one arising as its historical roots in the textual analysis of the humanities encounter recently acquired research methods "borrowed" from social science. As the characteristics of one discipline are "grafted" (Schneider 2006, 76) onto the other, complications inevitably develop. In this case, the textual analyst in us takes as the object of study a student-generated text, the very same text that social science methods indicate must be protected (and not objectified) at all costs. Consequently, I would argue, these interdisciplinary methods require not only a new interdisciplinary ethic (as many writers noted earlier have argued), but also an interdisciplinary way of teaching RCR.

The outline that follows is an effort to acknowledge the humanistic and scientific elements of our professional DNA, drawing on both of them in a blended approach to RCR instruction. The areas and issues I have chosen to highlight draw on the ORI nine areas of instruction that Shachter (2007) describes so well, the 2003 CCCC *Guidelines*, and several online RCR courses. Using the ORI areas to broaden the program's perspective and the CCCC *Guidelines* to focus it, this section will summarize several prominent areas that composition specialists should address with undergraduate researchers, with special attention to the protection of human research participants.

RCR Instruction in Composition Research

The following subheadings represent general areas of study for an RCR course in writing studies. They cannot describe or delineate every example of responsible conduct; they are intended to provide a starting place from which mentors of undergraduate researchers can begin to tailor an institutionally defined program of RCR education for their students.

History of Research Ethics

Although few formal RCR courses spend a great deal of time on the history of research ethics, nearly all RCR literature glosses the important points of the *Nuremberg Code* (National Institutes of Health 1949) and the *Belmont Report* (National Institutes of Health 1979). Given writing studies' foundation in humanistic inquiry, undergraduate researchers in composition should be receptive to studying this important history. (In fact, some students in composition may take an even greater interest in the history of research ethics than in the practice itself.) The *Nuremberg Code*, originating in the trials of Nazi physicians charged with conducting unethical and sometimes inhumane experiments on human subjects, consists of ten principles protecting the rights of all research subjects. The principles established include, in part, the subject's right to consent voluntarily to participate; the physician's responsibility to conduct research so as to "avoid all unnecessary physical and mental suffering and injury"; and the imperative that the research "yield fruitful results for the good of all society" (National Institutes of Health 1949).

However, several high-profile cases of post–*Nuremberg Code* research misconduct, including the Tuskegee syphilis experiments of 1932 to 1972 and widespread prescription of the experimental drug thalidomide in the 1950s and 1960s, prompted further action. The U.S. government finally established legal protection for all research participants with the 1974 passage of the National

Research Act, commonly referred to as 45 CFR 46 for its location in the Code of Federal Regulations (Anderson 1996; Banks and Eble 2007; U.S. Department of Health and Human Services 2005). That legislation established the National Commission for the Protection of Human Subjects of Biomedical and Behavioral Research, which issued the *Belmont Report* in 1979. This report establishes three broad and inviolate ethical principles of research: respect for all persons, beneficence, and justice. These three broad principles further lead to three applied requirements: (1) the requirement to obtain informed consent from participants; (2) the responsibility to perform risk/benefit assessment of all research; and (3) the charge to select subjects responsibly (National Institutes of Health 1979). The complete texts of both documents, as well as federal regulation 45 CFR 46, can be found at the website of the National Institutes of Health's (NIH) Office of Human Subject Research. Anderson (1996, 1998) and Banks and Eble (2007) both provide useful and succinct summaries of these documents' history and applications to research, as well as references to more comprehensive histories.[3]

Ethical Theory

In the young collection of literature on teaching RCR, there is scant support for providing formal instruction in ethical theory. Shachter (2007), for example, argues that given the limited time often afforded for RCR instructions, instructors should focus on "*everyday research ethics* [. . .] rather than *big ethical questions*" (211, Shachter's emphasis). Similarly, Kenneth Pimple (1995) argues that ethical theory is "not necessarily the place to begin" (4), especially for those many scholars not schooled as ethicists; he chooses instead a situation- or case-based approach. Santa Clara University's undergraduate research program Ethics in Science, which Shachter studies, bases its instruction not in traditional theory, but in thirty-two personal and professional values shared by responsible researchers (2007, 229–230). The National Academy of Science's *On Being a Scientist* (1995) also briefly addresses the intersection of personal values with scientific principles, but does not address ethical principles directly.

Recognizing again, however, the foundation of writing studies in humanistic inquiry, as well as the fact that students in English programs are often schooled in philosophy and critical theory, I suggest that instructors of RCR in our field pay more than lip service to ethical theory. Because of their educational background, composition students are more likely than students in the sciences to engage in a theoretical discussion, and they should be given at least a brief survey of applicable theory. As a starting point, Lucinda Peach's "An Introduction to Ethical Theory" (1995) gives a succinct and readable overview of consequentialist and deontological ethics, each in the context of decision making in scientific research. Another brief guide to ethical theory in the context of research ethics can be found at the University of California–San Diego's Resources for Research Ethics Education website (Resources for Research).

Methodology and Data Management

For many undergraduate researchers in writing studies, choosing a methodology that will best answer the research question is perhaps the first ethical choice they face.[4] This is also an area addressed in the *CCCC Guidelines* (2003) under the section titled "Maintaining Competence": "Composition specialists assure that they and their assistants are appropriately trained and prepared to conduct the studies they undertake. Training and preparation may include [. . .] study of relevant published research and methodological discussions" (par.1).

This demand for competence in methodological discussions can challenge any researcher, especially an undergraduate, because, as Barton (2000) observes, few disciplines engage in such "methodological and ethical diversity," ranging from "empirical investigation to humanistic inquiry" (409, 410). In an endnote, Barton lists some of the many studies undertaken by researchers in composition, but also objects to what she sees as a movement to classify some of these methods as more ethical than others. Peter Mortensen and Gesa Kirsch (1996), in particular, privilege methods that emphasize reflexive, collaborative encounters between researcher and writers above what Kahn, in a response to Barton, characterizes as traditional methods grounded in rational, empirical, and more distanced studies (Kahn and Barton 2000). For instructors of RCR in composition, the Kirsch/Mortensen/Barton/Kahn dialogue is a marker of the difficulty of establishing firm ethical guidelines in a discipline that draws from an interdisciplinary foundation. Few other fields will reflect so self-consciously on the ethical implications of choosing one methodology over another, and the fact that writing specialists do so is a trait of which undergraduate researchers should be aware.

On the practical side, students should be aware that acquiring data, whether by survey, interview, collection of writing samples, or institutional data mining, must conform to federal and IRB criteria for the protection of human subjects (see next section, "Protection of Human Participants and Compliance"). Managing collected data, especially maintaining its integrity and security, is an area in which undergraduates may need special training. Shachter (2007), for example, reminds mentors that undergraduates may not understand the strict privacy and nondisclosure regulations that accompany research notebooks and data; and she reminds mentors that undergraduates occasionally must be dissuaded of the "'bad habit' of selecting only 'good data'" for inclusion in their studies (212). Banks and Eble (2007), in another example, point out the difficulties of protecting data collected in digital spaces: anonymous surveys collected online, under the right circumstances, can be traced back to participants using Internet protocol addresses (34).

If undergraduate researchers or their mentors lack strong social science methodology training, responsibly gathering and analyzing data could present a challenge. To a certain extent, online RCR courses can provide some of this training; in other cases, undergraduates pursuing original research should be ready to consult researchers in educational and social science communities for additional instruction.

Protection of Human Participants and Compliance

On one hand, because our discipline is rooted in a fundamental respect for people, for their words and ideas, and for careful and critical introspection, protecting human participants should come naturally to writing scholars, whether professional, graduate, or undergraduate. Schneider (2006), for example, argues that writing specialists actually teach the ethics of textual scholarship—appropriate citation of sources, fair representations of others' work, reliance on ethical arguments—as well as anyone in the academy (81–82). On the other hand, we seem to lag when it comes to teaching the ethics of our scholarship rooted in the social sciences, especially regarding compliance with the federal regulation guaranteeing protections to human participants in research. The latter problem is probably a result of the former observation: writing specialists have, as Anderson (1998) indicates, probably assumed that RCR is an individual responsibility and an agreed-upon expectation of our work. That assumption, however, is simply wrong: researchers in composition studies, including myself, have not always provided sufficient protections to the participants in our research.

In composition's defense, most federal regulations and guidelines, arising in response to breaches of ethical practice in the biomedical and behavioral science, have been written to respond to practices in those fields. When guidelines written with biomedical research in mind are applied to composition research, the results are often ambiguous, contradictory, and dissatisfying. McKee (2003) provides the best examples, documenting her frustration as she submitted the same study for approval to eight different IRBs and received different responses from each, including many that applied biomedical standards to her composition proposal. Many of the responses to Anderson's 1998 call for disciplinary guidelines, including Haswell, Hourigan, and Sun's (2000), feared that compliance with federal statutes would unnecessarily restrict composition research, and Anderson himself warned against "blind adherence to a bureaucratically administered government policy" (1998, 72). Nonetheless, in the absence of discipline-specific regulation, composition specialists remain bound to the federal statutes. Next I describe the most prominent issues in human participant protection that RCR instructors should discuss with undergraduates.

Interacting with IRBs

Although research in writing studies traditionally has not been subjected to the same level of IRB oversight as research in the biomedical and behavioral sciences (though, arguably, it should have been), this is changing quickly. Even studies that researchers believe are exempt from IRB review are now required to seek an official exempt ruling from an IRB. In the section titled "Compliance with Policies, Regulations, and Laws," the *CCCC Guidelines* (2003) foreground compliance with all federal laws, including the regulation requiring IRB oversight of all research at institutions receiving federal research funding.[5] The *Guidelines* do allow composition specialists to "educate and negotiate concerning IRB requirements or restrictions that hamper research without increasing protection [. . .] of the persons studied" (par. 3) but educating IRBs dominated by medical or social science professionals, and swamped by submissions in those fields, could be challenging.

All undergraduate researchers should be aware of the criteria IRBs use in reviewing research proposals:

1. Risks to subjects are minimized.
2. Risks to subjects are reasonable in relation to anticipated benefits.
3. Selection of subjects is equitable.
4. Informed consent will be sought from each prospective subject or the subject's legally authorized representative.
5. Informed consent will be appropriately documented.
6. When appropriate, the research plan makes adequate provision for monitoring the data collected to ensure the safety of subjects.
7. When appropriate, there are adequate provisions to protect the privacy of subjects and to maintain the confidentiality of data. (U.S. Department of Health and Human Services 2005, n.p.)

Undergraduates should also be aware of the three levels of review: exempt, expedited, and full review. Many undergraduate research projects in writing studies may qualify for exempt or expedited review, but that determination can be made only by the local IRB.

On initial review, it may seem obvious that all research in composition should meet these seven review criteria. However, ambiguities and inconsistencies abound. For example, the definition of "risk" or harm to research participants is not fully articulated, and local IRBs may interpret the definition differently

(Anderson 1996; Banks and Eble 2007). For example, Banks and Eble point out that some medical research practices allowed by IRB would distress writing researchers, while writing research in gender and sexuality would seem "bizarre or vexing" for those outside our profession (37). Similarly, the requirement for "benefits" to participants, which may be easily defined in biomedical and laboratory sciences, is problematic to writing specialists; much of composition research does not provide this kind of easily measurable benefit to individuals or society. According to McKee (2003), one of the IRBs to which she submitted her proposal denied the review because her project did not provide "tangible benefits" (491). And retrospective research, more common in writing studies than in biomedical fields, is often prohibited by IRBs (Banks and Eble 2007). This restriction on retrospective work would, as several writers have pointed out, invalidate or restrict many significant works in writing studies, including Mike Rose's *Lives on the Boundary* (Anderson 1998; Haswell, Hourigan, and Sun 2000). In light of these ambiguities and disciplinary differences, it is particularly important that undergraduate researchers be prepared to communicate clearly the complexities of their research as they seek IRB approval.

Many online RCR education and training courses will adequately prepare undergraduate researchers for the rigors of the IRB submission process, even if most of these sites are designed for researchers in the biomedical and behavioral sciences. Undergraduate researchers in writing should plan to review or complete one or more of the courses. In fact, most IRBs now require completion of a training module, such as NIH's Protecting Human Research Participants tutorial or the CITI program, for any researcher seeking their approval.

Recruiting and Representing Students

Recruiting participants is an issue with special implications in writing studies. IRBs are charged with ensuring that selection of participants is equitable, and the fact that many composition specialists conduct research with their own classes complicates this requirement. The *CCCC Guidelines* (2003) do not forbid conducting studies with subordinates or a researcher's own students, but they do implore that researcher to take special care with those individuals (see "Obtaining Informed Consent" that follows). Writing studies that deal with other selected populations, such as prisoners or gay and lesbian writers, may come under additional scrutiny. IRBs will ask whether the research question and methodology require such limited populations, and undergraduate researchers should be prepared to articulate answers to such queries.

Fairly and responsibly representing student writers participating in research is another concern that composition specialists consider critically. For example, pseudonyms, once a standard tool for protecting student writers' identities in writing studies, are now considered by many to be inauthentic, disempowering, and even disrespectful. Bastian and Harkness (qtd. in Robillard 2006) point out the danger of writing studies that construct critical images of participants as poor or struggling writers, while Mortensen and Kirsch (1996) and Haswell, Hourigan, and Sun (2000) summarize additional ways that composition specialists privilege the researcher while othering the writers participating in their research. To counter this tendency, Haswell, Hourigan, and Sun outline three principles of ethical representation: (1) "use writing that I admire, that I want to acknowledge and celebrate"; (2) "maintain constant contact with the writer" while analyzing their texts and producing her own; and (3) allow writers opportunities to "respond in print to their published selves" (97). While the literature is wide-ranging and the perspectives diverse, undergraduate researchers should at least be introduced to the ways in which their subjectivity as researchers impacts the studies they design and carry out.

Obtaining Informed Consent

The *CCCC Guidelines* (2003) establish seven distinct pieces of information that composition specialists should communicate to individuals when seeking their participation in a research project.[6] Though these seven points may overlap with the informed consent requirements of any particular IRB, undergraduate researchers should understand that they are not inclusive of all IRB requirements, and federal law requires compliance with IRB protocols, not with the CCCC standards.

The *CCCC Guidelines* (2003) take special care in the section titled "Conducting Studies Involving Classes" to define the composition researcher's responsibility to this vulnerable population. Students who are participating in a class for a grade may not feel free to decline participation in any research study, whether conducted by their own instructor, another instructor, or an undergraduate researcher being mentored by an instructor (Anderson 1998; Schneider 2006). The *Guidelines* take care to protect those students by requiring researchers to explain in writing that, for example, "volunteering, declining to volunteer, or deciding to withdraw after volunteering will not affect a student's grade" (par. 1) and that all students in a class will receive the same attention and instruction regardless of their participation in the study. Despite these precautions, undergraduate researchers may not always realize how their role—as a research assistant, classmate, peer tutor, or just a friend—affects their research and other students' participation in a study. In preparation for IRB review, every effort should be made during RCR instruction to discuss the CCCC standards and to comply with them.

Using Unpublished Statements in Research

Another area of particular concern to composition specialists is the use of unpublished statements in research, whether those statements are written, spoken, or recorded in audio or video files. This issue could arise when student writing submitted as part of a course is included in a study (Anderson 1998) or when the selected writing is posted in a digital space, such as a discussion forum, website, or blog (Banks and Eble 2007). The *CCCC Guidelines* (2003) require composition specialists to obtain written permission to quote, paraphrase, or report any unpublished written statement or spoken statement *not* made in a public forum. The *Guidelines* also require written permission to display or use any photograph, video image, or audio recording of any individual. Additionally, composition specialists are charged with maintaining the highest standard of fairness in interpreting and representing these statements and recordings.

These standards—as well as broad interpretations of the *Belmont Report* (National Institutes of Health 1979) and IRB criteria—have called into question the use of all-encompassing "consent to quote from your work" forms still handed out to classes by some instructors (Anderson 1998, 82). On the other hand, defining writing in digital spaces as *public* or *private* remains a highly subjective exercise, so the *CCCC Guidelines* (2003) have not clarified researchers' responsibilities in these cases.

Authorship, Collaboration, and Mentor/Undergraduate Responsibilities

The issues in this section and the two following it are not directly addressed by the *CCCC Guidelines* (2003). However, they are important elements of RCR instruction at the ORI and in most online training courses.

Responsible authorship is a basic facet of RCR. It involves appropriate assignment of credit and responsibility for the contents of any publication, as well as acknowledgments for all individuals and institutions that assisted in or funded the research (Resources for Research). Authorship invokes social dimensions of status, prestige, and control, as well as ethical dimensions of veracity, transparency, and equity (Collaborative Institutional Training Initiative). At the very least, undergraduates should understand the process by which authorship is assigned to researchers, especially on collaborative projects, and they should understand the responsibility conveyed when researchers attach their names to published reports. Of course, responsible authorship also includes basic academic integrity: using sources fairly and citing those sources appropriately.

Although several descriptions of mentor/undergraduate researcher responsibilities can be found in publications such as *CUR Quarterly*, many of these still describe laboratory science experiences (Lopatto 2003; Monte 2001). At this point, most writing specialists working with undergraduates probably determine these responsibilities on a case-by-case basis, and examples of these relationships and responsibilities can be found elsewhere in this volume. For a general overview of the elements and expectations of mentoring, see Carolyn Ash Merkel and Shenda Baker's *How to Mentor Undergraduate Researchers* (2002).

Whether formally or informally, all mentors should be prepared to communicate to undergraduate researchers the expectations of the student's participation in a study. These expectations may vary widely: Merkel and Baker (2002) are careful to point out that undergraduates arrive at research opportunities with widely varying abilities and experiences, and expectations for summer projects should differ from those undertaken during the school term. Expectations will also vary depending on whether the student is conducting original research or functioning as a research assistant; some mentors will take a more hands-on approach, while others may expect only a consulting role. Mentors should also be prepared to allow for productive differences with their undergraduate researchers, and to let undergraduates make decisions whenever possible and appropriate (Collaborative Institutional Training Initiative). Before any project begins, both mentor and student should understand the portion of project design, IRB submission, data gathering, analysis, and reporting for which each is responsible. Defining these responsibilities early may seem overly cautious, but doing so can eliminate confusion and misunderstanding later. Other examples of mentor/undergraduate relationships and responsibilities specific to writing studies can be found in this volume.

Publication and Peer Review

All undergraduate researchers should be informed of the competitive nature of academic research publications and the role of peer review and the revision process in journal submission. Additionally, undergraduate researchers should understand the publication guidelines of any journal to which they may submit a manuscript (Resources for Research), and the responsibilities not to double-submit to journals, not to duplicate findings in multiple manuscripts, and not to fragment data unnecessarily in order to generate multiple publications from a single study (Collaborative Institutional Training Initiative; Resources for Research).

Although it is unlikely that undergraduate researchers will be offered opportunities to peer review, it is not impossible: several undergraduate research publications are peer reviewed by undergraduates (*Young Scholars in Writing*; *Impulse: An Undergraduate Journal for Neuroscience*; *International Journal of Exercise Science*; *Journal of Young Investigators*). At the least, RCR instructors should explain the role that peer review plays in ensuring the integrity of academic research, and the great responsibility that attends serving as a peer reviewer.

Research Misconduct

The National Science and Technology Council (NSTC) defines *research misconduct* as "fabrication, falsification, or plagiarism in proposing, performing, or reviewing research, or in reporting research results." The definition continues:

- Fabrication is making up data or results and recording or reporting them.
- Falsification is manipulating research materials, equipment, or processes, or changing or omitting data or results such that the research is not accurately represented in the research record.
- Plagiarism is the appropriation of another person's ideas, processes, results, or words without giving appropriate credit.
- Research misconduct does not include honest error or differences of opinion. (2008, par. 1)

This definition may suffice for the biomedical and laboratory sciences, but research in writing studies calls for a fuller definition. In a broad sense, research misconduct could include any action that intentionally and blatantly transgresses the principles of RCR listed previously. After all, pursuing a project without IRB approval or informed consent of participants, representing student writers in an unnecessarily negative light, and quoting an unpublished piece of writing without explicit permission of the author would not meet the NSTC definition of research misconduct, but could be considered research misconduct by other composition specialists.

In addition to learning how to recognize it, undergraduate researchers should be given clear instructions about what to do when they encounter research misconduct. Misconduct documenting and reporting requirements vary from institution to institution, so mentors should consult their local IRB or research office for guidelines. The National Academy of Science's *On Being a Scientist* (1995) suggests that those who witness misconduct consult a colleague or mentor before putting their complaint in writing. Undergraduates should be especially clear on options for documenting and reporting misconduct, because the misconduct may be perpetrated by their mentor. In light of this possibility, some courses and writers suggest including a lesson on dispute resolution in RCR education programs (Shachter 2007; Resources for Research).

Conclusion

It is certainly impossible to address all of the previous issues in less than a semester-long course. Given that mentorship of undergraduate research in writing studies is still most often a one-on-one activity undertaken in the interstices among teaching classes, pursuing other research, and serving our institutions, it is unlikely that any mentors will comprehensively teach these principles of RCR anytime soon.

However, recognizing what a daunting task RCR instruction is should not preclude us from doing everything we can to improve our "preaching" for undergraduate researchers. Our own research in the humanities and social sciences, Banks and Eble write, "already requires us to think rhetorically about risk and benefit and to make arguments about the social value of our work" (2007, 42). It seems a small but important step—and one fully in keeping with our discipline's emphasis on collaborative practices—to include our undergraduate researchers in that thinking and arguing.

Notes

1. In composition's defense, RCR instruction is still only moderately prevalent in the sciences, where undergraduate research got its start as a movement. Shachter (2007), in surveying 123 National Science Foundation-funded Research Experience for Undergraduates (REU) sites, reports that only 50 percent of sites included formal instruction in RCR. Descriptions of other undergraduate research programs that appear in *CUR Quarterly* (Lopatto 2003; Monte 2001) also do not address RCR instruction.

2. An extensive bibliography of RCR resources, including links to thirty-four training programs, can be found on the RCR education page of the U.S. Department of Health and Human Services Office of Research Integrity website (Responsible Conduct of Research).

3. Students of history may want to note that both the *Nuremberg Code* (National Institutes of Health 1949) and the *Belmont Report* (National Institutes of Health 1979) were commissioned in reaction to horrific lapses of ethical judgments on the part of Nazi (Nuremberg) and American (Belmont) scientists. It is an important point of study in itself that great leaps forward both in the history of research ethics and in the federal legislation accompanying them have come about not proactively—because scholars called for such codes—but retroactively, in response to great failures.

4. For more information on designing ethical writing studies, see Rogers's research methodology course outlined in this volume.

5. Researchers at institutions without IRBs should nonetheless seek approval for most studies through an IRB-regulated institution.

6. Prior to 2000, the National Council of Teachers of English (NCTE) maintained in-house "Consent to Participate in Research Study and to Publication of Results" and "Consent to Publication of Results of Research Study" forms for all NCTE journals (Anderson 1998). It is clear, however, that these consent forms alone do not satisfy IRB criteria found in the U.S. Code of Federal Regulations.

References

Anderson, Paul V. 1996. Ethics, Institutional Review Boards and the Use of Human Subjects in Composition Research. In *Ethics and*

Representation in Qualitative Studies of Literacy, ed. Gesa Kirsch and Peter Mortenson, 260–85. Urbana: NCTE.

———. 1998. Simple Gifts: Ethical Issues in the Conduct of Person-Based Composition Research. *College Composition and Communication* 49 (1): 63–89.

Banks, Will, and Michelle Eble. 2007. Digital Spaces, Online Environments, and Human Participant Research: Interfacing with Institutional Review Boards. In *Digital Writing Research: Technologies, Methodologies and Ethical Issues*, ed. Heidi A. McKee and Dànielle Nicole DeVoss, 27–47. Cresskill, NJ: Hampton Press.

Barton, Ellen. 2000. More Methodological Matters: Against Negative Argumentation. *College Composition and Communication* 51 (3): 399–416.

Brooke, Robert, and Amy Goodburn. 2003. The Ethics of Research and the CCCC Ethical Guidelines: An Electronic Interview with Ellen Cushman and Peter Mortensen. *Writing On the Edge* 13 (2): 7–20.

Collaborative Institutional Training Initiative. http://www.citiprogram.org.

Conference on College Composition and Communication. 2000. *Guidelines for the Ethical Treatment of Students and Student Writing in Composition Studies*. http://www.ncte.org/cccc/resources/positions/ethicaltreatmentstud.

———. 2003. *CCCC Guidelines for the Ethical Conduct of Research in Composition Studies*. http://www.ncte.org/cccc/resources/positions/ethicalconduct.

Haswell, Janis, Maureen Hourigan, and Lulu C. H. Sun. 2000. Affirming the Need for Continued Dialogue: Refining an Ethic of Students and Student Writing in Composition Studies. *Journal of Teaching Writing* 18 (1/2): 84–111.

Kahn, Seth, and Ellen Barton. 2000. Response to "More Methodological Matters: Against Negative Argumentation." *College Composition and Communication* 52 (2): 287–96.

Karukstis, Kerry K., and Timothy E. Elgren, eds. 2007. *Developing and Sustaining a Research-Supportive Curriculum: A Compendium of Successful Practices*. Washington, DC: Council on Undergraduate Research.

Lopatto, David. 2003. The Essential Features of Undergraduate Research. *CUR Quarterly* 23 (1): 139–42.

McKee, Heidi. 2003. Interchanges: Changing the Process of Institutional Review Board Compliance. *College Composition and Communication* 54 (3): 488–93.

Merkel, Carolyn Ash, and Shenda M. Baker. 2002. *How to Mentor Undergraduate Researchers: Elements of Mentoring Expectations, Practical Information.* Washington, DC: Council on Undergraduate Research.

Monte, Aaron. 2001. Mentor Expectations and Student Responsibilities in Undergraduate Research. *CUR Quarterly* 22 (2): 66–71.

Mortensen, Peter, and Gesa E. Kirsch, eds. 1996. *Ethics and Representation in Qualitative Studies of Literacy.* Urbana, IL: National Council of Teachers of English.

National Academy of Science. 1995. *On Being a Scientist: Responsible Conduct in Research.* 2nd ed. Washington, DC: National Academy Press.

———. 2009. *On Being a Scientist: Responsible Conduct in Research.* 3rd ed. Washington, DC: National Academy Press.

National Institutes of Health, Office of Human Subject Research. 1949. *Nuremberg Code.* http://ohsr.od.nih.gov/guidelines/nuremberg.html.

———. 1979. *The Belmont Report: Ethical Principles and Guidelines for the Protection of Human Subjects of Research.* http://ohsr.od.nih.gov/guidelines/belmont.html.

National Science and Technology Council. 2008. *Federal Policy on Research Misconduct.* http://www.ostp.gov/cs/federal_policy_on_research_misconduct.

Peach, Lucinda. 1995. An Introduction to Ethical Theory. In Penslar 1995, 13–26.

Penslar, Robin Levin, ed. 1995. Research Ethics: Cases and Materials. Bloomington: Indiana University Press.

Pimple, Kenneth. 1995. General Issues in Teaching Research Ethics. In Penslar 1995, 3–12.

Resources for Research Ethics Education. http://research-ethics.net.

Robillard, Amy E. 2006. *Young Scholars* Affecting Composition: A Challenge to Disciplinary Citation Practices. *College English* 68 (3): 253–70.

Schneider, Barbara. 2006. Ethical Research and Pedagogical Gaps. *College Composition and Communication* 58 (1): 70–88.

Shachter, Amy M. 2007. Responsible Conduct in Research Instruction in Undergraduate Research Programs. In Karukstis and Elgren 2007, 209–39.

Steneck, Nicholas H. 2006. *ORI Introduction to the Responsible Conduct of Research*. U.S. Department of Health and Human Services, Office of Research Integrity. http://ori.dhhs.gov/education/products/RCRintro.

U.S. Department of Health and Human Services, Office of Human Research Protections. 2005. *Protection of Human Subjects*. Code of Federal Regulations, Title 45, Part 46. http://www.hhs.gov/ohrp/humansubjects/guidance/45cfr46.htm.

U.S. Department of Health and Human Services, Office of Research Integrity. Responsible Conduct of Research (RCR). http://ori.dhhs.gov/education.

Chapter Five

An Undergraduate Research Methods Course in Rhetoric and Composition: A Model

Jaqueline McLeod Rogers
University of Winnipeg

When my department began offering a writing major in 2003, about six years ago, I offered to contribute a research methods course for students in the final year of their undergraduate degree work. I wanted to provide a course that would help them recognize the academy and knowledge itself as dynamic and tractable—things they might actually influence. Here we were: a newly minted Department of Rhetoric, built out of a writing program, a program itself grown as a breakaway unit from the English department, all in twenty years. To see such rapid change in my university was invigorating, particularly so because academic institutions are frequently characterized as fossilized and unexciting. I wanted to let students in on the excitement of seeing a discipline take shape.

Proposing a course to examine disciplinary formation seemed more staid than celebratory; proposing a course inviting students to engage in the research climate and conversation of our field seemed closer to the mark. But designing this course was no simple matter. I had to decide which research traditions to emphasize, and then whether to foreground practical engagement in project work over learning theory. I offer the model in this chapter as a flexible template. Although publications in our field provide some disciplinary precedent for my decision to build the course around ethnography, I admit to being drawn to this approach because of my long-term interest in narrative forms of scholarship. At every point of conceptualization—from topics to readings to assignments—individual instructors will want to think through their specific approach. A model like this provides a starting place, one likely to be particularly welcome to those teaching the course for the first time.

Choosing Ethnography from the Menu of Methods Used in the Field: Deciding What Students Need to Know and Do

The main question to consider when planning a research methods course for undergraduates in rhetoric and composition is what research-oriented work students have already done, and what they need to learn and do. A fair assumption is that they have practiced discourse analysis and written research essays. Most students still need more familiarity with empirical methods that come out of the social science tradition, methods to study human culture and communication in action. They need to learn through practice how to take a qualitative or descriptive approach. This kind of work is not only currently popular but also theoretically rich. Undergraduate students can conduct a qualitative study, and learn to recognize what this approach can accomplish, before moving on to pursue more advanced qualitative studies or quantitative questions that pose another form of complexity by requiring decisions about collecting and analyzing numeric data.

There is precedent for doing qualitative work before attempting to quantify, for this is the pattern by which many strands of actual research have been developed. For example, Ann Penrose (2002) points out that her quantitative study of retention in the population of first-generation university students emerged in response to questions raised by Mike Rose (1989) about the lives of poor and immigrant students in his auto-ethnographic *Lives on the Boundary*. Although Rose describes his own struggles with the educational system in meticulous and story-like detail, Penrose responds to one of the themes in his work by gathering data in response to several specific questions about first-generation student retention. In another case, in his book explaining ethnographic method, Harry Wolcott (1999) similarly observes that qualitative ethnographic studies—characteristically small-scale and uncontrolled—often prefigure broader social research studies, by "calling attention to problems seen in a broader context [. . .] or to helping others frame better questions for inquiry conducted on a larger scale" (74).

A good way to begin an undergraduate course in research is to have students examine several examples of quantitative studies, to define some of the conventional elements of this approach. Then they can examine samples of qualitative work to do the same, before moving on to compare the two approaches. They recognize immediately that the two texts look different—one more like story and the other like research report—and that to represent numerical data, writers usually rely on rhetorical strategies unlike those used by writers who describe empirical data. For example, differences are often apparent in styles of self-reference, quotation, attribution, and documentation, and in organizational features, such as use of headings and tables. Follow-up discussion can engage rhetorical questions about purpose, subject, and audience, to consider how these two forms of research accomplish different ends: quantitative usually answering a question or hypothesis, and qualitative cultivating insight.

There is no need to argue that one form is better than the other, a seesaw argument many researchers have abandoned in favor of the position that both approaches have their uses, and can be complementary, providing a lens for triangulation. Even advocates of increasing the presence of quantitative approaches in composition, such as George Hillocks (1992) and Cindy Johanek (2000), recognize that "both have validity under certain sets of conditions" (Hillocks 1992, 64). Most undergraduate students do not have sufficient background in research to engage in debating the merits of one approach over the other, and instead need to familiarize themselves with the broad contours of each approach to start understanding what each accomplishes. Moreover, defining how the two terms differ is a practical beginning in preparation for ethics checklists and proposal forms that often discriminate between these two terms.

In the early weeks of the course, students can achieve a clear overview of quantitative and qualitative approaches by reading the introductory chapters of several handbooks. Together, these chapters define quantitative or positivist approaches and qualitative or naturalist approaches, showcasing each in relation to history, uses, and new directions. For example, the Hillocks chapter (1992) defines both traditions, explaining differences and similarities. The introductory chapter in Martyn Hammersley and Paul Atkinson's *Ethnography* (2005) is particularly good at linking the two approaches and encouraging students to see that construction and interpretation affect knowing in the sciences as well as in the social sciences. Many students will be fascinated by the description these authors provide of how arguments by Thomas Kuhn unsettled the march of positivist research by revealing advances in this tradition to be more haphazard than systematic; even in the realm of science research, truth and fact are "interpreted differently by those working within different paradigms" (12), which means "that there is no theory-neutral observational foundation against which theories can be tested, and that judgments about the validity of any theories are never fully determined by any evidence" (11).

The point here is not only to define the two dominant and sometimes conflicting research models, but also to open up the epistemological assumptions accompanying each. Scientists have attempted to learn truths about things in the world through systematic investigation and measurement, and social scientists have attempted to understand and describe ever-dynamic human relations and systems. These differences in orientation aside, however, both traditions have been influenced by postmodern and feminist theories of representation and subjectivity. All researchers have had to acknowledge that subjectivity affects both knowing and telling—so that in the first place, our understanding is conditioned by our attachment to theory, and in the second place, the language we use to express our understandings is not value free.

To refine the focus on qualitative research, students can consult excerpts from Sharin Merriam and Associates (2002), and from Norman Denzin and Yvonna Lincoln (2003), drawn from handbooks considered standards in social science research. Merriam is good at describing the varieties of qualitative work and outlining the process, whereas Denzin and Lincoln are particularly good at giving historical developments and explaining "the crisis of representation" (25) as well as several other postmodern challenges that qualitative researchers currently face (28).

After introducing cross-disciplinary research terms and approaches, I begin focusing on ethnography, the particular qualitative approach that students practice in my course. To provide an example of the interplay between theory and method, I ask students to consider how ethnography differs depending on whether one is committed to *documenting* or *critiquing* culture. The reading by Hammersley and Atkinson (2005) provides theoretical underpinning for the first position, whereas Chapter 1, "Introduction to Critical Ethnography," from D. Soyini Madison (2005) explains the second. With some classes, I have discussed how feminist and narrative theories emphasize the role of the researcher in relation to the culture. With others, I have pointed out the need to examine linguistic and communicative cultural elements, to foreground rhetorical dimensions. The point students need to consider is that theory guides not only what the researcher sees, but also what he or she eventually distinguishes as the interesting patterns to write about.

Another way to take up the issue of how theory influences method is to assign three chapters from John Van Maanen's (1988) now classic study of writing ethnography, *Tales of the Field*. In his description of three evolving forms, Van Maanen suggests that time and trends in thinking influence how ethnographers write their reports. He provides three mini-ethnographies of police work to exemplify the three key styles: (1) realism, foregrounding the culture itself; (2) confessional, emphasizing the ethnographer; and (3) impressionism, depicting unfolding actions in a drama without authorial commentary. Students studying these three examples need to understand that more is at stake than picking a writing style to emulate. They need to recognize that how one writes about a culture establishes one's epistemological stance.

If students take a traditional approach by highlighting the culture itself—presenting it from multiple and detailed perspectives—they are endorsing a view of ethnographic method as a valid way of knowing and representing others. Alternately, if they work from a feminist position, they may be reluctant to render judgments about others; this standpoint leads to emphasizing their own identity in relation to the culture, and thus to writing a narrative auto-ethnography. The following observation by a feminist scholar links identity and knowing: "To the charges that the researcher brings her own biases [. . .] bias is a misplaced word. To the contrary these are resources and, if the researcher is sufficiently reflexive about her project, she can evoke these as resources to guide data gathering or creating and for understanding her own interpretation and behavior in the research" (qtd. in Bishop 1999, 119). Finally, if students are reluctant to interpret cultural interactions and prefer a documentary approach—recording conversations, gestures, and material artifacts—they adopt a postmodern posture of acknowledging the provisional and fleeting nature of knowing. The point need not be the superiority of a particular perspective, but how theoretical perspectives can influence method.[1]

Once definitions are in place, students can turn their attention to planning an ethnographic project that will engage them for the rest of the term. Choosing a culture to observe is the first challenge, for they need to pick one that is accessible and familiar to them, but not one in which they are so immersed that their ability to speak plainly is compromised. Having students tease out how the researcher's connection to those being studied affects what the researcher learns and says is a topic for front-end and return consideration. Writing a personal narrative at this early stage, while exploring one's connection to and interests in a group, can help students identify their connection, biases, and insights.

In my opinion, providing students with a variety of readings about ethnography is more effective than assigning any one of the current textbooks that showcase ethnographic method, for each of these texts has limitations. A strength of the popular text *FieldWorking* (Sunstein and Chiseri-Strater 2007) is that it guides students through the preparation of a term-length ethnographic study and prods them to be mindful of their relation to the group they study. It asks students to begin by considering issues around their status as insider/outsider (7–9), and to return periodically throughout the study to revise their thinking about who they are in relation to the group, adding a layer of complexity by introducing the term *positionality* (130–36). This approach encourages students to be aware of how perspectival changes affect what they observe and consider important. Yet because it sustains an introductory tone and takes up several basic writing matters, this book is probably better suited to first-year composition students.[2]

Other possible course texts present other kinds of problems. Wendy Bishop's (1999) *Ethnographic Writing Research* is directed toward guiding graduate students in education who study the teaching of writing, and Ian Cook and Mike Crang's (1995) *Doing Ethnographies* features extended examples of PhD projects. David Fetterman's (1998) handbook *Ethnography* is brief and well organized, but situates ethnography in the discipline of anthropology, and contains sections on collecting and analyzing data that emphasize content and statistical analysis.

The Research Project: Writing the Proposal and Seeking Ethics Approval

After spending the first weeks of class becoming acquainted with basic research terms and with ethnographic methodology, students need to prepare a proposal to study the discourse of a particular group or culture. It can be useful to define *discourse* as an inclusive term, referring to performative as well as linguistic elements. Although rhetoric and composition students might be expected to be particularly attuned to language-oriented elements, they can be encouraged to identify how visual and material elements (such as artifacts, body language, and costume) influence or enforce the discourse. Yet proposals need not be built around fully formed research questions. Instead of looking for answers to preformed questions and risking restricting what they see, students should approach the field looking for emergent questions and patterns. Many students find an open-ended approach intimidating, especially if key events and themes are slow to emerge. They can be reminded that reviewing their experience to identify patterns and key events is an essential part of the process of learning about the field.

Because proposal writing is new to many, providing a format with recommended headings like the following is useful: Project Summary (one-page summary including objectives, methods, procedures, significance, and benefits) and Project Description (scope, theory, objectives, scholarly significance and benefits, research methods, and work-plan). In-class workshops need to be scheduled to support proposal preparation, because most students have questions about how to describe key tasks in a time frame and how to account for the ethics of their proposed conduct. Every university has distinct policies governing the ethical conduct of research involving human subjects. Students need to become familiar with procedures to complete requisite forms. My university, for example, furnishes researchers with a lengthy checklist (more than twelve pages) that many students find daunting. Working in small groups in class helps them pay attention to what needs to be done. Our checklist calls for the submission of any instruments the researcher plans to use, so students need to draft consent forms and interview questions. Drafting these items can require another day of class instruction, for many students have difficulty adjusting their tone, especially to avoid sounding unintentionally arrogant. (Often they need to give up authoritative commands, such as "Your participation is required in study X, affiliated with institution Y," in favor of a more courteous and informative approach: "I am inviting you to participate in study X, which I am conducting as part of my coursework at institution Y.")

The process for obtaining ethical approval for student projects varies among institutions, so instructors need to clarify the requirements before the start of term. On my campus, classroom projects not intended for publication involving human subjects can be reviewed at the department level rather than by a university-wide board. Yet even this abridged process brings many pressures. The instructor needs to streamline this process with careful planning because students cannot begin conducting their research until they have secured ethical approval.

Even when committee members and students fulfill their obligations in a timely way, there are still frustrations. Committees change members on a yearly basis, and it is helpful to furnish them with information about what past committees have done. Students whose proposals are returned for some form of revision often become frustrated and even resentful, for without approval they are unable to go forward with their project. They should be encouraged to respect the approval process, and reassured that unexpected complications are part of conducting research with human subjects.

Fieldworking: Observing and Interviewing

While waiting for proposals to be approved, students can study two skills that they will need to practice during their fieldwork: note-taking and interviewing. With note-taking, three key aspects are emphasized. First, students should be aware of the importance of putting a date on everything they record. As notes accumulate to become a mass of papers, those without dates are a hindrance. Second, students need to be conscious of distinguishing what is actually out there from what they *think* about what they see. Two-column note-taking, recording objective reality in one column and subjective responses in the other, is one strategy. A third point students need to keep in mind is that people see things differently. To help make this more than a truism, students can watch several videos about ethnography, taking notes that they then share with the group listening for different points of emphasis. The film *Qualitative Research* (2006) contains a short and informative section on ethnography, indicating that differences among the notes students take are relatively subtle. To elicit more varied responses, instructors might show a film that is less straightforward and informative than most. Our library holds a copy of *Spirit of Ethnography* (1973), a film that generates a variety of responses because it is so dated as to be unintentionally comical.

Similarly, students can practice interviewing, exploring the difference between asking a set of predesigned questions and talking to an informant in an off-the-cuff way. When they use a script, students quickly recognize the difference between open and closed questions. The biggest challenge with interview material occurs at the transcription stage: Do researchers attempt to reproduce the interview conversation as it was spoken, or do they edit it to make informants more fluent? Should they use direct quotations or paraphrase the informant? If there are reasons to reproduce the speakers' voices, then the interview notes need to be thorough, but if students are editing responses, their notes can be less thorough. Another organizational point to emphasize is that details fade as the time increases between the actual interview and the transcription of what the informant said. To make student-researchers accountable, and to emphasize the link between notes and final report, it is wise to request as part of the assignment that students submit field notes, interview transcripts, and artifacts along with the final report.

Looking and seeing, taking notes, and asking questions are everyday activities, and some students may be inclined to think that there is no need to be made self-conscious about gestures that come "naturally." Instructors may head off this potential source of resistance by making good-natured reference to self-deprecating quips of practicing ethnographers—Van Maanen (1988) is one of several scholars who enjoy the element of parody that attaches so easily to those whose work is to observe others, and he provides this list of alternate ways to refer to ethnographers: "dull visitors," "meddlesome busybodies," "hopeless dummies," "social creeps," "anthrofoologists," "management spies," or "government dupes" (2). Yet acknowledging that this work is vulnerable to misunderstanding and parody should be followed by a reminder that observing, note-taking, and interviewing are research skills to be honed through practice and attention; the strength of these skills ultimately affects the plausibility and resonance of the final report. In-class exercises should be challenging enough to help students recognize that, far from being transparent, observing a culture and then determining how to represent it requires the researcher to be accountable for a series of choices.

A Unit on Online Ethnography: Netnography

Likely several students will elect to study an online community, conducting a *netnography*. Students observing a group on the Internet may save themselves the time-intensive burden of going somewhere to do their fieldwork, yet they are entering an area where conventions are sometimes complicated and unclear. Because this form of research raises many complex ethical issues, it can be useful for the whole class to discuss netnography in relation to ethics, looking for ways in which researchers working on the net face ethical dilemmas that both resemble and depart from those faced by other ethnographers. While students conducting netnographies will have cultivated expertise on this topic, all students can be informed and ready to participate in discussion if they complete assigned readings.

Ethical issues are still evolving in this relatively new area of study. For example, one student concluded that if she were simply going to visit a site to observe interaction among participants, and not solicit responses to specific questions or insert herself into the discussion to influence it, she could commence with her study without consent from the site manager. An ethics expert at my university supported her position, adding a cautionary warning that because ethical positions are still forming and in flux, the exercise of researcher ethos is pertinent.

Another student believed that any type of covert relationship to the group and site constituted stalking or creeping. As a long-term member of a chat group composed of adolescents exchanging advice (conducted using pseudonyms), she approached the manager, who at first denied her request to study the culture. He reminded her that questions of identity and authenticity had plagued the history of the group—leading to expulsion of errant members from the site. Just as the student was poised to find another group to examine, she was given permission, as long as she was willing to abide by several reasonable guidelines. Perhaps most important is that the student announced on the site her intention to collect information for her ethnography.

These projects have been remarkably successful, demonstrating the researcher's commitment to bring the group to life and to engage ethical practice. Whether they investigate controversial sites—like the Pro Ana website, a support group for those struggling to cope with anorexia—or investigate sites promoting more common cultural interests—for fans of classic rock music, particular events, or festivals, for example—researchers on the net should be aware that preserving conditions of anonymity and confidentiality is more difficult when mono- and dia-logue is a matter of public record, open to recovery by both readers and participants.

The Project: Writing the Final Report

Many students struggle with writing the ethnography, the final phase of the research process. Like all ethnographers, they struggle with deciding what to say—what to feature as the overriding theme, yes, but also what details to include and to leave out. Looking at models of projects completed by other students in previous classes is helpful, especially if these models have different strengths. It is less helpful to discuss models earlier in the process, before students struggle with the actual decisions and problems that arise in writing up results.

At the writing stage, they need to see a variety of examples, professional as well as student. They might select an entry from the *Journal of Contemporary Ethnography* to present and critique to the class, considering how it is structured (the author's stylistic and rhetorical choices) and whether it is effective (the way it responds to issues the author introduces, or develops insights into the culture). Here is a more complete list of questions students can consider that are aimed at helping them find solutions to problems they will face in the writing stage:

- How does the author introduce the topic (by describing the culture, the scene or place, or his or her relation to the culture)?
- Does the writer explain his or her cultural status as insider/outsider?
- Does the writer draw on or refer to past or recent personal experiences?
- Does the writer refer to other texts (about the culture? about ethnographic method?)
- Does the writer support observations by quoting informants or other experts?
- Is there a passage that exemplifies "thick description" (Geertz 1973)?
- Does the writer use headings to organize the presentation (if so, what is the connection between and among headings?)
- Is the voice colloquial (friendly, pitched close to the reader) or more formal (objective and distant, using a higher percentage of specialized language and denser sentences)?
- Would the approach be characterized as (a) self-oriented (emphasizing "me-in-this-culture," as in auto-ethnography or creative nonfiction) or (b) more concerned with representing the culture itself (aiming to serve academic ends by improving our understanding of a life or lives)?

The last question in the list goes to the heart of the decision students tackle as first-time ethnographers: whether to write in first person or to adopt a more objective, traditionally academic voice. Those who like creative writing usually gravitate toward a creative nonfiction narrative approach, and those who prefer academic writing to a more traditional report style. Though it makes sense for students to use their strongest voice, it is important at the same time to unsettle these choices by reminding students that they come with attendant assumptions. Earlier, I suggested that students should be guided in the opening weeks of the course to see that, more than an aesthetic question, the style of report a writer chooses is tied to his or her theoretical position. At this stage, students can engage or reengage the question of whether they identify with traditional, critical, feminist, or postmodernist theory, and how their theoretical affiliation influences their relation to the culture they have studied and the text they are writing. Are they committed to describing the culture to improve our understanding, to describing their struggle to know the culture, or to describing the culture as a changeable construction?

On a practical level, students should be familiarized with several skills attached to ethnographic writing. They should be reassured that most ethnographers feel overwhelmed by the data they amass, and that rather than attempt to represent everything, they should look for *key patterns* and *events*. They need to be mindful of triangulating the data they present, to convince the reader that their observations are drawn from several perspectives. They should think about including details to bring important scenes and contexts to life, using an approach Clifford Geertz (1973) termed *thick description* and usually writing in present tense. Perhaps the most helpful suggestions about these techniques are in Fetterman (1998, 92–101, 122–26).

Identifying Trouble Spots in the Course

There are several potential problems to avoid. Most obvious is that many students do not recognize that as a practicum, this course is unlike others in the undergraduate curriculum. Because the first few classes involve teacher presentation and class discussion to cultivate a shared understanding of research terms, students can be lulled into thinking that the course will continue in this familiar vein. But students should know on the first day that this class is different from others, and that they will learn primarily by doing and discussing. As other chapters in this collection indicate, the Boyer Commission report (1998) suggests that such approaches promote problem solving and independent thinking. Even with this clarification in place, there are still pedagogical challenges to promoting engagement and quelling resistance:

Keep course instruction relevant to the practicum element of project preparation.
Because students are all working on their own research assignments, they will not share the same problems. If the class meets twice a week, design the course so that one meeting involves directed instruction and the other allows for group discussion, individual presentations, or workshop. Even with this alternating pattern, students will still find that attention is given to research skills that may not be relevant to their project. For example, if the class is devoted to interview techniques, and if a student has designed a project with no interview component, it is likely that he or she will skip the class, or disconnect. Perhaps an attendance or participation policy could correct for this. Another option is to have an ongoing journal assignment that requires students to reflect on skills and principles discussed in class.

Prepare students to meet with disappointment and frustration as well as a sense of accomplishment.
Every term, several students are denied access to observing a group. Several have told me that they have verbal permission, yet when I press them to obtain signed letters of consent, they are surprised to be turned down. When this happens several weeks into the course, it disrupts their preparation and completion plans. Other common disappointments occur when informants cancel interviews, say contradictory things, or withhold "promised" materials, or when key events occur too early or too late to be included in the study. According to Bishop (1999), all ethnographers can take consolation in the phrase "If I only knew then what I know now." It helps to put this phrase on the board from

time to time and ask if it has become more resonant.

Remind students that recursion is central to this form of research. In their text *FieldWorking*, Bonnie Sunstein and Elizabeth Chiseri-Strater (2007) tell students to ask these three questions at every stage of project development: "What surprised me? (to track [. . .] assumptions) What intrigued me (to track [. . .] positions) What disturbed me? (to track [. . .] tensions)" (429).

Expect ethical considerations to arise for students at every turn, and thread the discussion of ethics into classes on a weekly basis. Early in the course, discussion of ethics tends to focus on the relation of the student-researcher to the culture: is one an insider or an outsider, and how does one's status affect what one may know and be able to access and learn? In the midst of doing fieldwork, issues arise when informants ask the researcher to overlook something seen or said, or otherwise attempt to influence or restrict the study, often in indirect ways. When the student writes the final report, he or she is hugely burdened with deciding how to depict the group in a way that is authentic to all participants, researcher and informants alike. Knowing that participants may read the final study increases this sense of burden, for, as Thomas Newkirk (1996) discusses in his article on ethics, the report needs to convey truth even if it is not always flattering or happy.

Expect some students to need a lot of one-on-one direction. Many students in this project-based course require intensive support, often looking for words of encouragement to help them see the project through a difficult phase. A seminar-sized class of about twelve to fifteen students is probably optimum. When I taught a class of only ten students, we would have benefited from hearing about a wider variety of projects; with a class of thirty-four students, we had so many projects underway that it was difficult to provide enough time for each student.

Some Final Classroom Considerations

In the last few classes, students become less group oriented, for they are anxious about completing their projects, and each is encountering different obstacles and challenges. My suggestion is that these classes can be used as an opportunity for students to begin framing responses to a final in-class reflection; with an impending assignment, they are more willing to participate in group discussion. Two areas in particular bear reflection. First, by mining their own experience as ethnographers, they can consider the strengths and weaknesses of ethnography as a way of telling about lives. Second, by tackling assigned readings about the position of ethnography in composition research, students can consider how ethnographic research is one of several ways of making knowledge in the field.

Disseminating Results: What Becomes of Research "Not Intended for Publication"?

The purpose of scholarly research is to extend disciplinary knowing, and the usual route is to find a venue for scholarly publication. Yet, because of the ethics approval process, the projects developed as a result of our classwork *cannot* be published. Any students committed from the outset to seeking publication follow different institutional review board (IRB) procedures. But for the majority who do not seek publication, there are several ways to extend the intellectual life of this research project.

Because ethnography is conducted in a social space, the researcher has a responsibility to be accountable to the people being studied. Often, documents used to secure ethical approval, such as consent forms, make overt reference to the responsibility of the researcher to "give" as well as "take"—to provide subjects of the study with some form of help or expertise. When students seek signed consent from an individual or representative to permit them to examine a culture, one of the paragraphs in the consent letter should ask if participants or subjects wish to receive a copy of the final report. Most people who agree to being observed in a study indicate that they want to see the final report. Some look forward to it as a source of insight into behaviors and connections they may have overlooked, while some more guardedly require a copy to ensure researcher accountability. Thus, the researcher writes the final report with a dual sense of purpose: first, to satisfy course requirements, and second, charged with ethical implications, to satisfy those at the center of the discussion. Although it is true that unpublished research remains outside disciplinary conversation and scrutiny, students nonetheless gain a sense of how research matters by the process of disseminating results within the community of those examined.

Like many preliminary ethnographies, these projects are valuable not only in themselves, but also in their potential to suggest future work. "Future research directions" is one of the points students can be asked to address in the final section of the ethnography. When engaged in conducting the study, many students will have encountered roadblocks and redirected their work for pragmatic reasons—learning in the process that making compromises is part of making ethnography. Even in broad, conceptual matters such as choosing a culture to study, some students will have been turned down unexpectedly, and learned that the group an ethnographer studies is often the "one he or she can get," if not quite the one envisioned. Rather than write the project as if coming to a bitter end, students should be encouraged to see what they might do, given the opportunity to extend or redirect their study. For those going on to graduate school, these plans may provide a focal point for extended research work.

Another possibility exists for disseminating results, this one requiring curricular planning. In a follow-up course designed to help students put together an e-journal featuring their ethnographies, students could develop e-publishing skills. To make this course more rigorous and to move beyond simply showcasing their completed reports, student-publishers might invite submissions from the general population of rhetoric and composition students, enacting the processes of making a call for submissions, vetting and editing.

By restricting publication possibilities, I do not mean to undermine what many students accomplish with these final reports, for many attain a professional quality. In addition to featuring sparkling prose and smart organization, many projects include artifacts and photographs, engaging visual as well as textual rhetoric. Besides introducing students to research methods well beyond the confines of the library, and requiring them to work independently to define a focus and gather data, assembling the final study engages creative and analytical thinking.

Notes

1. If a class is particularly interested in critical pedagogy, the point could be made that Van Maanen's (1988) third category—the imagistic or dramatic form—runs somewhat counter to current notions about the performative nature of social interaction and the role of research as an agent of change. Whereas Van Maanen captures the textual response of an ethnographer who despairs of knowing anything beyond perceptual reality, and therefore avoids the overlay of interpretive work, critical ethnography assumes the interested, embedded role of the ethnographer, who seeks to understand cultural gestures in order to critique and revise them. (See Clough [1992] and Madison [2005], if this is a theoretical approach you choose to feature.)

2. Adopting this text and using several supplementary readings may be a strong option for instructors who are facilitating an upper-level writing course for the first time and who want textual support.

References

Bishop, Wendy. 1999. *Ethnographic Writing Research: Writing It Down, Writing it Up and Reading It*. Portsmouth, NH: Heinemann.

Boyer Commission on Educating Undergraduates in the Research University, Shirley Strum Kenny (chair). 1998. *Reinventing Undergraduate Education: A Blueprint for America's Research Universities*. Stony Brook: State University of New York.

Clough, Patricia Ticineto. 1992. *The End(s) of Ethnography: From Realism to Social Criticism*. Newbury Park, CA: Sage.

Cook, Ian, and Mike Crang. 1995. *Doing Ethnographies*. London: Institute of British Geographers.

Denzin, Norman K., and Yvonna S. Lincoln. 2003. Introduction: The Discipline and Practice of Qualitative Research. In *The Landscape of Qualitative Research: Theories and Issues*. 2nd ed., ed. Norman K. Denzin and Yvonna S. Lincoln, 1–45. Thousand Oaks, CA: Sage.

Fetterman, David M. 1998. *Ethnography: Step by Step*. Thousand Oaks, CA: Sage.

Geertz, Clifford. 1973. Thick Description: Toward an Interpretive Theory of Culture. In *The Interpretation of Cultures: Selected Essays*, 3–30. New York: Basic Books.

Hammersley, Martyn and Paul Atkinson. 2005. *Ethnography: Principles in Practice*. 3rd ed. London: Routledge.

Hillocks, George, Jr. 1992. Reconciling the Qualitative and Quantitative. In *Multidisciplinary Perspectives on Literacy Research*, ed. Richard Beach, Judith L. Green, Michael L. Kamil and Timothy Shanahan, 57–65. Urbana, IL: National Conference on Research in English and National Council of Teachers of English.

Johanek, Cindy. 2000. *Composing Research: A Contextualist Paradigm for Rhetoric and Composition*. Logan: Utah State University Press.

Madison, D. Soyini. 2005. *Critical Ethnography: Method, Ethics, and Performance*. Thousand Oaks: Sage.

Merriam, Sharin B. and Associates. 2002. Introduction to Qualitative Research. In *Qualitative Research in Practice: Examples for Discussion and Analysis*, 3–17. San Francisco: Jossey-Bass.

Mortensen, Peter, and Gesa E. Kirsch, eds. 1996. *Ethics and Representation in Qualitative Studies of Literacy*. Urbana, IL: National Council of Teachers of English.

Newkirk, Thomas. 1996. Seduction and Betrayal in Qualitative Research. In Mortensen and Kirsch 1996, 3–16.

Penrose, Ann M. 2002. Academic Literacy Perceptions and Performance: Comparing First-Generation and Continuing-Generation College Students. *Research on the Teaching of English* 36 (4): 437–41.

Qualitative Research: Methods in the Social Sciences. 2006. DVD. Participants: Charlton D. McIlwain, Jo Ellen Fisherkeller, Rodney Benson, and Eric Dietrich. New York: Insight Media.

Rose, Mike. 1989. *Lives on the Boundary*. New York: Penguin.

Spirit of Ethnography. 1973. VHS. Produced and directed by O. Michael Watson. University Park: Pennsylvania State University, Penn State Media Sales.

Sunstein, Bonnie S., and Elizabeth Chiseri-Strater. 2007. *FieldWorking: Reading and Writing Research*. 3rd ed. Boston: Bedford/St. Martin's.

Van Maanen, John. 1988. *Tales of the Field: On Writing Ethnography*. Chicago: University of Chicago Press.

Wolcott, Harry F. 1999. *Ethnography: A Way of Seeing*. Walnut Creek, CA: AltaMira Press.

III

Disseminating Research and Scholarship

We have a habit in writing articles [. . .] to make the work as finished as possible, to cover up all the tracks, to not worry about the blind alleys or describe how you had the wrong idea first, and so on. So there isn't any place to publish, in a dignified manner, what you actually did in order to get to do the work.

—Richard Feynman, *Nobel Lecture for the Prize in Physics, December 11, 1965*

CHAPTER SIX

Creating an Academic Conference for English Majors

TED HOVET
Western Kentucky University

For the past seven years, the English department of Western Kentucky University (WKU) has held for its majors the Undergraduate Conference on Literature, Language, and Culture. This event, modeled after a typical academic conference, invites English majors to submit original essays on subjects within the broad field of English studies. It is scheduled for an afternoon late in the semester with students, faculty, and the general public invited to attend. This conference seeks to highlight the best analytical writing and research done by our students over the course of an academic year.

Establishing a departmental conference that promotes student writing provides important preprofessional experience for the participating students and establishes a high standard for student inquiry within English studies. The conference publicly recognizes what students have accomplished, and in doing so, raises the bar for future student work. At WKU, we also have used the conference as a means to provide professional training for our master's-level graduate students, who review the submissions, form the panels, and moderate the sessions. For faculty, the conference showcases the results of pedagogical practices of colleagues across the department, which, in turn, may inspire new assignments and more attention to student success beyond the classroom. The conference celebrates the diversity of subjects, interests, and approaches to scholarly writing among English majors, reflected in recent conference papers on topics from "Kerouac and Wordsworth: Enlightenment through the Journey in the Romantic Canon" to "Singing in the Reeve: An Analysis of Chaucer's Reeve," and from "'Goblin Market': Victorian Fairy Tale or Adult Erotica?" to "Boris and Natasha in Space: Science Fiction of the Cold War."

At a time when the value of literary studies may be questioned or even under attack, the conference also serves as a signature event to promote the accomplishments of our students, who produce research and other academic work of a professional quality and intellectual rigor on par with any other discipline. The many benefits of showcasing student accomplishments highlighted by David W. Chapman (2003) in his description of a university-wide student research conference apply at the departmental level as well. Indeed, through the strategic use of public relations, a departmental conference serves as a highly effective means of gaining the attention of a wider audience, including university administrators, families of students, and donors who have supported the department financially. Rebecca Moore Howard (2007), in an essay on the potential benefits of developing a writing major, provides a compelling model for a proactive use of public relations through "curricular activism" that "can seize the microphone, and the stage itself, to circulate informed, nuanced proactive visions of writing, of student writers, and of writing instruction" (42). The extracurricular activism of a student conference provides a literal stage and microphone that allows student writing to speak for itself, and demonstrates that the department takes an active role in supporting student success beyond the classroom.

Conference Goals

An undergraduate conference should begin by meeting the needs and interests of the home department, which will vary in different contexts and settings. When the WKU English department initiated our conference in 2001, my initial task as the principal organizer was to apply for a small budget through an internal university grant. The immediate benefit of the grant-writing process was that it required us to articulate specific goals for the conference. The first goal was to give undergraduate students an opportunity to share their best work in a public forum that models a setting that they are likely to experience as graduate students or professionals. The students who have papers selected for the conference receive the obvious benefits of an important professional experience and a significant honor to include in their academic résumé. We have since found that students participating in this conference have had success in getting papers accepted in regional and national conferences, as I will discuss further in the assessment section below.

The second goal was to enhance student learning beyond the classroom through a public demonstration of intellectual accomplishments by undergraduate English majors. This goal seeks to extend the benefits of the conference to the students who attend. The students in the audience witness firsthand the best critical and analytical work of their peers and the workings of an academic conference. Not surprisingly, many have found it inspiring to see their classmates in action. Of the fifteen students who read papers at the 2007 conference, ten had attended the conference in at least one previous year.

The final goal for the conference was to provide the English department with an opportunity to showcase for a wider audience the high quality and diverse range of our academic work. The conference serves as a way to build a stronger bond between the department and the students who are likely to be successful at the next level of their educational and professional pursuits. We plan to invite all past participants for the tenth anniversary conference in 2010, a way of keeping contact with these alumni and setting the stage, we hope, for future support. The conference enjoys strong support from the offices of the dean and provost, and other departments at the university have begun exploring hosting conferences of their own. With our conference well established, we make special invitations to those in the community who have contributed to the English department with donations and other services so that they can see the benefits of their support. Programs from past conferences have become a part of the recruiting material we provide to prospective students and their families. In short, we have found that the rewards of putting on an event that shows off the talents and creativity of our majors have been far-reaching, and we expect that the benefits will continue to increase.

Conference Planning and Logistics

Planning and logistics must be flexible enough to be adjusted to a variety of circumstances. The WKU conference consists of five panels with three papers each. We have scheduled the panels consecutively over about three hours on a Friday afternoon (on our campus, no classes are scheduled after 2:45 p.m. on Fridays) in a large auditorium-style classroom that seats about one hundred people. We have considered taking a longer period of time, and possibly moving the conference to a weekend, but we have concluded that a shorter time during the week ensures a greater number of attendees, as it fits better in the schedules of both participants and audience. Announcements of the time and date of the conference go out before the beginning of the semester, and many instructors place the conference on their course schedule and encourage students to attend. We have generally discouraged making attendance at the conference required or available for extra credit, as the best atmosphere is one in which everyone is there voluntarily. However, in some cases, such as the required senior seminar for graduating majors, participation in the conference (submitting and/or attending) can be worked in as a legitimate assignment to meet course goals designed to enhance students' preprofessional experiences.

Calls for submissions (CFS) go out at least two months before the scheduled date of the conference, with the deadline about a month in advance. The CFS asks for original analytical essays on any topic in English studies (creative writing is featured in other departmental events). The call targets all undergraduate English majors, reached through announcements in classes, posted fliers, and emails. We require students to submit full papers to ensure that all of the students selected have their work ready to go, though this does mean that reading through all of the submissions takes time (more below in the section on evaluating submissions). The conference organizer sends an email to students whose papers are selected, to congratulate them, inform them of the time of their panel, and request that they confirm their participation. This is followed by a formal letter of acceptance.

The panels are organized around common themes chosen by the graduate students who select the papers and also serve as moderators; the conference includes a diverse range of papers and panels. The majority of papers submitted are on topics within the fields of literary and cultural studies, though we welcome submissions in linguistics and rhetoric. The panels may focus on very specific themes centered around a single text, such as "Negotiating Cultural Waters: Postcolonial readings of *The Tempest*," or larger categories such as "Feminist Perspectives in British Literature." At times, a handful of papers do not fit logically with any of the others, in which case the graduate student reviewers have creatively formed catchall panels, such as "America Exposed: Literature, Documentary, Film" and, perhaps my favorite, "Differing Perspectives on Humanity: Freud, Jesus, and Vince McMahon."

To include as many papers as possible in the short time frame of the conference, we require students to strictly adhere to a ten-minute reading limit. In some cases, this means that students have to edit papers to fit this requirement (the CFS encourages essays that are between 1,000 and 1,500 words). That kind of revision process can itself be beneficial, and this limit also allows for the potential of a wider variety of papers to be included. However, longer works can be excerpted to fit within the constraints of this schedule. In two recent conferences, for instance, students have read selections from their senior honors thesis.

A ten-minute period is given at the end of each panel for questions and answers. This tends to be the part of the experience that most terrifies the student participants, who fear that the goal of the audience is to vigorously point out flaws in their arguments. Indeed, we did not include a discussion period in the first few conferences when just getting enough students eager to participate was still a challenge. In recent years these discussion periods have turned out to be lively and supportive, and the fear is rapidly fading. The graduate student moderators prepare at least one discussion question for each paper in the event that a participant doesn't get a query or comment from the audience, though this has rarely happened.

Taking into account the varying lengths of discussion, fifteen papers can be presented in a three-hour time slot. It is an intense three hours, and I would not want to expand it. Two years ago, the evaluators found it impossible to narrow the number of accepted papers to fifteen, so we held concurrent sessions in adjacent classrooms for one period of the conference, for a total of eighteen papers. I prefer the idea of consecutive panels so that everyone can hear every paper, but concurrent sessions are a viable option for expanding the number of participants. The total number of participants will vary depending on the size of the department and the goals of the conference. The acceptance rate for the conference at WKU has hovered between 25 percent and 33 percent, so those participating in the conference know that their selection has come from a highly competitive process. This also ensures that those who attend the conference, including audiences from outside the department, will experience consistently high-quality student work. We want everyone who sees or even hears about the conference—from first-year English majors to university administrators to families and potential donors—to come away with a strong impression of the excellent student work in our department.

Generating Submissions

The submissions received for the conference at WKU fall into three categories: required, solicited, and voluntary. Some classes in the department require students to submit a paper to the conference. This might be a writing assignment that the instructor includes as a matter of course for a given topic (such was the case the year that we had an entire panel on Sylvia Plath's bee poems, for instance), or it might be an assignment designed specifically for the conference. At least one instructor in the department makes the process of submitting a paper to the conference a topic in his or her writing course, covering the particular rhetorical situation of preparing a piece of prose for submission, and introducing students to the ins and outs of academic conference culture. Required submissions serve as a way to guarantee a certain number of participants and work best when students clearly understand how the submission process fits into the goals of the course, of the English major, and of the discipline at large. Requiring submissions also means that some students who would never submit on their own, even when solicited, have the experience of preparing a paper for formal evaluation and the chance of being selected.

Faculty members also solicit papers from students who have produced strong work appropriate for the conference. As conference organizer, I send an email at least once a semester reminding faculty to encourage students to submit their best work to the conference; this is especially important during the semester before the next conference, so that we can get submissions from the entire academic year. Students feel honored to be singled out in this way, and nearly all of them follow through with a submission. The first conference at WKU consisted entirely of solicited papers because we had anticipated that students would hesitate to commit to an event that was entirely unfamiliar to them, especially when they learned that the entire faculty was likely to attend. For that initial conference, I asked colleagues teaching four upper-division courses to encourage their top students to submit work, as I felt strongly that getting the conference off to a good start by featuring work by veteran students would provide a valuable foundation for the future of the conference. After a lot of persuasion, one no-show, and a near-fainting episode during one of the papers, that first conference turned out to be a great success. Since then we have been able to expand the number and increase the diversity of students who submit and participate. Even a handful of first-year students have presented their work—and two have had the honor of reading papers at the conference for four consecutive years.

Voluntary submissions come from students who have been informed of the conference through publicity or word-of-mouth and submit a paper on their own initiative. The number of voluntary submissions has steadily grown, counting for about one-fourth of submissions in 2007. To track submissions, the required submission cover page includes a place for students to indicate the nature of their submission: class requirement, recommendation of instructor, or open submission. The submission type plays no role when we consider whether to accept the paper, but has given us a good sense of the motivation for any submission. To me, the strongest indication of the conference's success rests in the growing interest of students who voluntarily participate.

Evaluating Submissions

In order to remove the burden of selection from faculty, I ask for volunteers from among our MA students; this has developed into one of the most productive and rewarding elements of the conference. The graduate student volunteers enjoy reading the submissions, and by participating from the start of the process, they have a stake in the conference's success. By forming the panels from among the selected papers and moderating those panels, the graduate students also gain professional experience in organizing an academic conference, and they learn about the work behind the scenes. The number of our MA students who have themselves given papers at regional and national conferences has greatly increased in the past few years. Though I can't make any claims for direct causality, because this has been part of a larger initiative by our graduate program, I'd like to think that their hands-on experience with the local conference makes them more comfortable and confident in their own conference experiences—exactly the same effect we feel it will have for the participating undergraduates as they continue their own development within the field of English studies. For departments lacking graduate students available for this role, other options for evaluators might be honors students, students who have given papers at previous conferences, or faculty. I suggest using students if possible, because when students can take credit for organizing a well-run conference, the event's value to the department increases.

Three graduate student readers evaluate each submission to the WKU conference. The submissions are anonymous (the cover page removed and names replaced with code numbers), and if a graduate student recognizes an author's work, he or she is asked to pass it on to other readers. The initial ranking of the papers is kept to a very simple three-point scale:

1. Excellent, very worthy of inclusion for the conference
2. Good, a possibility for the conference
3. Fair, not yet ready for the conference

We have tried to keep the criteria for these rankings flexible enough to account for the wide variety of writing found in English studies, which for this conference has ranged from creative nonfiction to formal research projects. We ask the readers to use the following criteria in their evaluation:

1. Clarity of argument
2. Strength and creativity of prose
3. Appropriate use of primary and secondary sources

In the past four years, when we have had a minimum of fifty submissions and as many as ninety, the scale and criteria have proved very effective for an initial vetting of the papers. A paper that receives a 1 rating from all three readers is automatically accepted. The most papers in any year that have received a 1 rating from all three readers is eight, and I have been consistently impressed with the tough, but fair, evaluations of the graduate student readers. The low number of papers that receive the highest possible rating means that some slots need to be filled with papers that received a combination of 1 and 2 ratings. We meet to discuss these papers, and some readers will strongly advocate for a paper they rated 1, while other readers who rated it lower will explain their reservations based on the criteria. Generally we can come to a consensus in this meeting, but if not, we put the papers in question back into the pool and ask additional readers to rate them, selecting the paper(s) with the best overall score.

The strongest disagreements tend to relate to the second category of the criteria. While some readers find great inspiration in a student who takes a "creative" approach to a literary analysis, others balk at the breaking of the conventions of academic writing. This leads to a lively and productive debate, and the interests and passions of the given reviewers in any one year will inevitably shape the final program. One year, for instance, the readers felt there were enough creatively unconventional papers of high quality to form a panel around this very issue, titled, "I Wrote This! Usurping Traditional Academic Writing."

To solicit graduate student readers, I visit the required Introduction to Graduate Studies course and explain the nature of the conference and the duties of the volunteers. I have never had a problem getting graduate student volunteers, and most who volunteer in their first year do so again in their second. Graduate students often ask about the conference even before I make my usual call for volunteers. I give all volunteers personal letters for their professional files, thanking them for their hard work and outlining in detail the specific duties they completed in helping to organize and run the conference.

Funding

As the description of the logistics should make clear, this conference need not generate many expenses. At WKU, we have been fortunate to receive a recurring $1,000 competitive grant from the office of the provost from a university-wide program that supports innovative ways to promote student excellence outside of the classroom. We have used the money from this grant for publicity, printing expenses, refreshments, and awards. Having some funds available to produce fliers for the conference helps to generate publicity, and as with any such event, there are plenty of copying expenses. While we strive to make the conference as comfortable and enjoyable as possible, it's also important to make it a formal event, and high-quality posters and programs contribute significantly. In the great university tradition of offering free food to enhance attendance, we use part of our budget to provide drinks and snacks. Refreshments contribute to the celebratory nature of the event and help all maintain good energy and stamina during three intensely engaging hours. The final part of the budget is reserved for awards for the student participants and graduate student volunteers. Although we have discussed the possibility of giving special awards to selected "best of conference" papers, so far we have maintained the practice of giving everyone who reads at the conference the same award, usually a gift certificate to a local book store, rather than single out individual papers for special recognition. In addition to the award, all participants get a certificate of participation signed by the department head and conference organizers.

Professional posters, refreshments, awards, and high-quality paper stock for programs and certificates are all nice. But by far the greatest value of funding is that it indicates institutional commitment to the event. To be able to state in all publicity that the event is sponsored by the Office of the Provost provides, in my view, an important "official" stamp of approval that enhances the event in intangible ways. When organizing or continuing such an event, institutional support might be found at the level of the department, college, or university. Perhaps even outside agencies or donors may be interested in helping to sponsor the event. In the past two years, the dean of the college has attended and opened the conference with remarks about the importance of this conference as a model for promoting student research and engagement.

Assessment: Creating Tradition and Demonstrating Value

The increasing emphasis on assessment in higher education has spread beyond the classroom to address ways in which a program enhances the value of students' experience through extracurricular opportunities. At WKU, we have been called on to track student engagement and to show how our department meets larger institutional goals as outlined in the university's Quality Enhancement Plan. Although it was not created for this purpose, the undergraduate literature conference at WKU has functioned as a key component of our department's efforts to meet these institutional initiatives. The conference demonstrates student excellence outside of the classroom to a public audience through an event that clearly provides important preprofessional training to the participants and the graduate student organizers.

The conference serves as a testimony to the department's commitment to student opportunities and success. We have tracked the raw number of submissions to the conference since its beginning, a number that increased from fifteen in the first year (all solicited) to a peak of ninety-one (at least 25 percent voluntary) in the sixth year. While the number of papers read at the program has remained steady at fifteen to eighteen, the rise in submissions demonstrates students' increasing interest, and gives even those who don't read at the conference the experience of preparing a piece of writing for evaluation outside of the usual classroom setting. Our assessment goal for the future is to increase the number of voluntary submissions. To that end, we have changed the submission requirement to allow a student to submit two papers if he or she is required to submit one for a class. For instance, if a student is in a Shakespeare class that requires all students to submit to the conference, but also has a paper from a film class that she would like to voluntarily submit, both will be allowed. No student, though, can have more than one paper accepted in any given year.

We have also tracked attendance at the conference, which has steadily increased from about thirty audience members in the first year to more than one hundred in the past two years. A majority of readers in the 2007 conference attended at least one previous conference, a clear measure of the value of simply attending the event. We are considering the possibility of having audience members complete a short survey indicating what they found most and least valuable about the event.

The number of undergraduate majors who participate in regional and national academic conferences has increased markedly since our local conference began. In 2004 we moved our conference from the spring semester to the fall semester to help our students prepare their work for submission to national conferences, most of which are in the spring. For some students, the local departmental conference serves as a rehearsal for a much larger stage. In 2007 and 2008, students who have first read papers at our conference have been accepted to the Midwest Undergraduate Film Conference at Notre Dame (two students), the Sigma Tau Delta International Convention (three students), and the National Popular Culture & American Culture Associations Conference in San Francisco (two students). In 2007, two student papers from our conference were also accepted at the National Undergraduate Literature Conference (NULC). With this track record, the department plans to more assertively encourage students to submit to national conferences, including the National Conferences on Undergraduate Research (NCUR). Although more than one factor contributes to the accomplishments of students at this level, we can assert that the local WKU conference plays a key role in preparing our students for success in academic and professional settings beyond campus. It conveys a message to students and faculty that dissemination of student work beyond the classroom is a key component of intellectual and professional life in our department.

Beyond any assessment formula, the most successful aspect of the conference, in my view, has been the establishment of a new departmental tradition that brings together students, faculty, and the larger community in a setting that manages to be both highly professional and a refreshing break from the usual classroom routine. The nerves of the readers run high, the intellectual energy of the papers is intense, and by the end of the day, the event becomes a genuine celebration of the achievements of our department. The students who read their academic work, the graduate students who organize the conference, the faculty who have mentored those involved, and the university that has committed support to this event all have a stake in its success and all reap its rewards. The conference serves as an excellent means to garner attention for our students, the department, and the discipline as a whole.

References

Chapman, David W. 2003. Undergraduate Research: Showcasing Young Scholars. *Chronicle of Higher Education*, September 12. http://chronicle.com/free/v50/i03/03b00501.htm.

Howard, Rebecca Moore. 2007. Curricular Activism: The Writing Major as Counterdiscourse. *Composition Studies* 35 (1): 41–52.

Chapter Seven

Making Long Shots: A Path toward Undergraduate Professional Publication

Marta Figlerowicz
Harvard University, Class of 2009

For undergraduates, the path toward producing a publishable piece of literary research is usually far more complex and difficult than they might expect, given the relative ease with which they can obtain a steady trickle of As and enthusiastic instructors' praise. Most prize-winning Harvard University English department essays circulate little further than the departmental archives. If shared at all, undergraduate research in the humanities usually makes itself apparent through local undergraduate publications and conferences, failing to reach a wider audience unless the student is obstinate enough to keep working on an idea until graduate school. Rather than constitute a voice heard beside those of their graduate school peers, resonant in both the preprofessional and professional academic worlds, undergraduates tend to be isolated on an archipelago of local islands of research activity, smaller and less organized than the activity of their counterparts in the experimental sciences (Wilson 2003, 74–75).

The reasons for this insufficient undergraduate presence in the broader community of literary scholars primarily reflect students' significant lack of experience. Undergraduate literary scholars can certainly show a wealth of innovative, enthusiastic analyses of the texts they are studying. However, professional research in the humanities is made meritorious not only by the quality of a single close reading, but of equal importance, by the breadth and depth of primary and secondary knowledge by which an author surrounds his or her analyses. Enthusiastic and eager as they are, undergraduates are only beginning their path in literary studies; they lack familiarity with much primary and secondary research related to their topics of choice. Moreover, even in the most rigorous courses, the undergraduate's main goal is to create an interesting and relevant literary argument, not necessarily a groundbreaking or unusual one. Indeed, as has been noted by Barbara Read, Becky Francis, and Jocelyn Robinson (2001), the constraints of classroom learning can often stultify students' potential for analytic originality (387–88). Given such limited expectations, and considering the fact that the time a student can allot to a term paper varies from two weeks to one month (the sole exception being the senior thesis), he or she can hardly hope to be able to produce research of any greater depth or specialization while completing regular coursework.

Nonetheless, my experiences and those of my peers have convinced me that undergraduates in literary studies should pursue in-depth research projects aimed at professional publication, even knowing that we may rarely be successful. We must find ways to bridge the gap between our inexperienced inventiveness and the rigor required of professional academic publications. As I trace my four major research projects to date, I will address three major factors that undergraduate researchers should consider as they move forward: (1) the availability of institutional support; (2) the mentor-mentee relationship; and (3) the student's need to persevere.

Undergraduate Research Opportunities at Harvard University

Harvard University provides three basic types of support for undergraduates trying to go beyond classroom requirements in their familiarity with the work of an academic. The first is the research assistantship, in which a student is apprenticed to a faculty member (Harvard Student Employment Office, *Faculty Aide*). Each year, about a dozen literary studies majors at Harvard find employment as part-time faculty aides or assistants to Harvard professors. In addition to being paid competitive salaries, these students are given the chance to observe and actively participate in the everyday course of research undertaken by a professional academic in their field of choice. A typical research assistant at Harvard will spend between eight and twenty hours a week at his or her job. Besides more mundane chores, such as organizing professors' personal libraries, students help their mentors during the many stages of preliminary research, and the drafting, editing, and publication of their books, talks, or papers. The assigned tasks vary in complexity, and tend to become more challenging and interesting as the student's relationship with a faculty member develops and the faculty member grows more confident in the student's skills. Tasks can range from photocopying articles and borrowing books from university libraries, through proofreading and fact-checking, to self-directed research in an assigned field and the building of annotated bibliographies and databases.

The second kind of research opportunity promoted at Harvard stems from the coursework students accomplish in their classes. At the end of a given semester, faculty members may suggest to the authors of particularly successful course papers that their work could potentially be turned into a publishable academic article. Faculty members then support students in polishing their original theses and redrafting their essays into a more academically rigorous format. Faculty become mentors, guiding and suggesting, but not imposing. This process may last between one and six months, depending on the degree to which a paper needs revision and the amount of time the student can devote to it.

The third means of furthering student research at Harvard is the provision of financial support—research and travel grants—for longer, more systematic projects that students must develop more independently, with varying degrees of faculty support and mentorship (Harvard Student Employment Office, *Harvard College Research Program*). Toward the end of each academic year and, to a lesser extent, at the beginning of each semester, Harvard allots significant funds to the pursuit of independent undergraduate research projects: in the academic year 2007–2008, this number exceeded $1,500,000 (Harvard Student Employment Office, *Facts* 2008). A portion of these funds are allotted to undergraduates pursuing projects in literary studies, either through meaningful travel or on-campus library research. This kind of research is often a natural continuation of the spontaneous faculty-student cooperation described previously, constituting a more structured development of what has proved to be both a promising and a time-consuming revision of a course paper. In other cases, the research is developed independently by the student, with considerably less faculty mentoring.

My experience as an undergraduate at Harvard has shown that a combination of these three research opportunities can allow a student to gain increasing skill and independence as a literary scholar—to the point of being published in professional academic journals. I have found these opportunities personally and professionally valuable, and feel that they have helped me grow as a prospective academic and as an individual.

Case Studies

Pursuing advanced research in literary studies can prove challenging, especially as it forces the student to adapt rapidly to a harsher and more competitive environment than that of college classes. Its success and value also greatly depend on the degree of openness and seriousness with which the student is treated by the faculty mentor. Though not all of my projects have been successful (as defined by publication), I finished each of them feeling more skillful and confident as a researcher. Taken together, my projects have provided fruitful research strategies I can repeat, a greater awareness of the difficulties I can expect to encounter, and methods I can use to respond to challenges. They have also increased my enthusiasm for academic research as an undergraduate and in my future.

While completing the four research projects I describe in this chapter, I was simultaneously working as a research assistant for an English department faculty member. Though my assistantship did not at any point coincide directly with my independent research projects, the skills that it helped me acquire—from conducting library and electronic resource research to summarizing and evaluating academic work—were consistently useful. In addition, observing how time-consuming it could be for my faculty mentor to fully prepare an article for print sobered me for the kind of work that lay in store for me. This realization, as it turned out, proved highly useful in all of my projects (see also Bauer and Bennett 2003).

An Unexpected Coauthorship

Perhaps the tensest experience for students on their way to professional publication is the fear that their independence as a researcher will be encroached upon by an elder mentor. This fear—justifiable or not, I find myself unable to tell—was the defining theme of a project on Yiddish and Polish comparative literature that I carried out from my first-year fall semester to my junior spring semester. On the one hand, this experience taught me some of the benefits of accepting faculty help in pursuing undergraduate research projects. On the other hand, it exposed me to the challenges of the relatively loose structure of this kind of endeavor—proving to me the importance of very clear boundaries and mutual agreements in any kind of faculty-student research cooperation.

A newcomer to Harvard University, I was overjoyed to learn that the first seminar in which I had enrolled yielded a term paper that my instructor thought was potentially publishable. With the help of my professor, I revised the paper, and two months after the course ended, I submitted it to a journal the professor had recommended. The journal responded with one substantive revision suggestion, asking that I provide more context for my decision to bring together the two literary figures I analyzed. I followed this advice to the best of my ability and resubmitted the manuscript.

The response I received two months later remained positive, but the journal's editor informed me that the manuscript required significant additional historical background in order to be accepted for publication. If I agreed, one of the reviewers would contribute this section. Without completely understanding the implications of this coauthorship, and wanting my paper to be published, I consented.

Over the next two years, I learned a lot about the questions surrounding coauthorship when one author is an undergraduate student and the other a professional. First, I had to shorten my piece to make room for my coauthor's contribution. Once his part was complete, we spent another three months fully integrating and polishing the two parts of the article. We communicated mostly via email (my coauthor works at another college), meeting in person two or three times to discuss the more general directions in which our article was heading. The article was published in 2007, with the two of us listed as coauthors.

I believe that the editorial staff of this journal had never before encountered such a situation and handled it as they thought they should. I am also convinced that the collaborative piece that my coauthor and I produced was more enriching for the general reader than the paper I had initially submitted as an independent author. Nonetheless, in retrospect, I am left with the deep conviction that, while faculty assistance should be sought and offered in student research projects, it is a potentially stressful experience for the collaborating undergraduate to an extent that the faculty member may not immediately recognize. An undergraduate has no experience of how much work, and what kind of work, preparing an article requires; nor is she usually able to assess the value and originality of the ideas she contributes. Whatever the intentions of the faculty collaborator—they may be of the very best sort—a research coauthorship that is not undertaken from the start, or whose rules are not clearly set, is confusing for the student in terms of authorship credit and fairness; and it creates difficulties if the student attempts to renegotiate any collaborative routines she opposes.

I concluded this project feeling that I would be much more comfortable if my faculty mentors acted as advisors rather than coauthors, even though this line can be blurred because collaboration takes many forms (see, for example, Elder and Trapp's chapter in this volume). This is the stance I took as I pursued three additional undergraduate research projects. Although this position tended to put much more responsibility on me, in making sure that my research was conducted properly, it also removed the strain of wondering how much credit my mentor would want for the work after helping me. This responsibility made my projects more laborious, but also ultimately more rewarding.

Renegotiating Research Goals

My second serious project proved both less palpably successful and more personally satisfying than the first. Though the original argument with which it began never reached a publishable form, it sprouted a side project to which I was able to devote myself with much greater motivation. This experience greatly improved my skills: I became more open and bolder in discussing and negotiating my plans with my faculty mentors. I also learned the benefits of decisiveness in pursuing the topics that interest me most.

In the fall of my sophomore year, I wrote a paper for a French literature class, which my professor encouraged me to try to publish. Working on this project would require considerable time and effort because my original paper lacked secondary research. Knowing that I would be unable to pursue this kind of work along with my regular classes, I persuaded my professor to recommend me for a few summer research grants. The funds I was awarded allowed me to spend the summer on Harvard campus conducting secondary research and rewriting my draft.

Toward the middle of the summer, when I had already produced a full-length article version of my original paper, I was struck by a philosophical theory in one of the books I studied. Fascinated by the questions the theory posed, I found my research interests diverging toward a more abstract critique of the philosophy of my primary sources, rather than the close readings I had been planning.

I tried to combine the two interests in the paper I was writing, but they proved far too divergent. I also attempted to discuss these philosophical issues with my faculty mentor, but—not being a specialist in this field—she was unable to help me. In addition, I soon found that the project into which I was attempting to digress was far too broad for an article-length endeavor. I was torn between what I felt to be a manageable, but far less interesting project, and a more fascinating idea, which threatened to be far more time-consuming than I could afford.

Faced with this dilemma, I made a choice that seemed risky at the time but that I do not regret. I developed my original project toward a form that I suspected would not be professionally publishable, but that was sufficiently well researched to gain the acceptance of my research grant committee. I then began to consult faculty members who specialized in the philosophies I was beginning to research. To my great joy, they were interested in the critiques I had developed and were eager to help me pursue them further. They also directed me to additional scholars, at Harvard and elsewhere in the United States and Europe, with whom I could consult in greater detail. Because most of the professors I contacted answered me with positive and encouraging feedback, I informed my original faculty mentor that I would most likely not continue to develop my paper in its present form. I informed her of the progress I had made on the new project that had sprouted. She accepted my decision, and left me to continue working with my new advisors.

I probably will continue to pursue this project on philosophy and literature; the research I still need to do just keeps expanding. I am very glad that I had the courage to jump into it instead of sticking to what had seemed a safer topic of inquiry. Working on this new project has given me more personal satisfaction and deepened my knowledge far more significantly than could have been the case with my original research plan. It has also allowed me to exchange views with prominent contemporary philosophers, and will—as I hope—culminate in a series of articles sometime during my graduate school years. In addition, the theoretical knowledge I have acquired has proved indispensable in my subsequent coursework and independent research, including the first article I recently published as a single, independent author.

To be given this kind of independence in pursuing one's interests is, to me, one of the most rewarding aspects of trying to transition from college coursework to professional academic writing as a fully independent, creative professional scholar. Faculty mentors should impress on undergraduates this greater value of (responsible) self-discovery over the automatic completion of one's initial goals.

The String of Rejection Letters

In the spring semester of my sophomore year, two further papers I wrote were pronounced by my professors to be potentially publishable. One of these was a study of the narrative strategies of Emily Brontë's *Wuthering Heights*, originally written for a seminar on the Brontë sisters. Although I have not yet published this manuscript, I consider it a crucial step in my development as an undergraduate researcher. As the first serious research project I brought to completion and worked on independently, it allowed me to experience a productive pattern of working with a single faculty mentor—and, for the first time, forced me to face the full difficulty of transitioning from a student project to a professional publication.

The paper I had written for my seminar did not require extensive revisions, so I was able to redraft it in the course of the same summer during which I was working on my French literature project mentioned earlier. I did not apply for an additional research grant. My faculty mentor (who had taught the course for which I wrote my paper) was on campus throughout the summer and agreed to meet with me to discuss successive drafts. She read and commented on several versions of my paper, but she made no changes to my argument or to my presentation to the extent that the paper would become a collaborative effort. Understanding our mutual roles as mentor-advisor and student-author, we brought the paper to its final form within two months. I then sent the paper to a professional academic journal and waited for a response.

Throughout these editing stages, and as I was waiting to hear from the journal, my faculty mentor continued to advise me not only on the paper itself, but also on the kinds of responses it might elicit and on ways to cope with rejection letters. She underlined how frequently professional academics' works is rejected, and she encouraged me to persist in my efforts even if I was not immediately successful. She also helped me find periodicals that might be most favorable toward the subject I was pursuing.

Two months later, I received a somewhat dismissive rejection letter. Naturally, I was disappointed. My mentor commiserated with me and encouraged me to resend the paper. As of this writing, I have repeated the process of resubmission four times and the manuscript is under review by a fourth journal.

Despite the rejections, the process has been educational. Each rejection letter I receive is usually accompanied by a review suggesting further ways to improve it. Having followed successive reviewers' advice, I have progressively received more appreciative reviews from subsequent periodicals—and less biting explanations of their reasons for not printing my paper.

Undergraduates—myself included—frequently do not realize how difficult it can be even for a university faculty member to publish work. To properly interpret the transition to professional publication, and to benefit from its successive stages, an undergraduate must learn a vital skill: how to cope with the rejection letters she is bound to receive. Thanks to my faculty mentor's frank assessment of what to expect, I learned relatively quickly how best to profit from my reviewers' comments and how to prevent myself from being easily discouraged. Moreover, when I received varied and contradictory opinions from different reviewers commenting on the same paper, I realized that I needed to develop a more independent judgment of my work. I could not base my self-respect as a writer solely on the opinions of the journals to which I sent my pieces.

Another crucial, positive aspect of this project was my communicative and enriching relationship with my faculty mentor. My mentor gave me help and advice that supported, rather than interfered with, the course of my research. She allowed me to feel safe in taking the risk of submitting the paper to external scrutiny, and she worked within the typically accepted parameters of scholars helping each other improve their work, without asserting a need to share authorship credit.

The First Success

My most recent research project has been published in a professional academic journal, *New Literary History*. I attribute its success to the cumulative effect of my prior research experience, an excellent faculty mentor, and, frankly, a stroke of luck. This project showed me how much I had learned from all of my previous research opportunities, but it also reminded me that students need a friendly and supportive external environment to help an undergraduate research project come to fruition.

Like all of my prior projects, this one began as a paper written for a Harvard University course. This time, the paper I had written (also in my sophomore spring semester) concerned the relationship of the early British novel to theater. My instructor for the course encouraged me to develop the paper into an article and offered to help me revise it. He and I exchanged two successive revised drafts of the paper, and he advised me on where to send it.

Four months later, I received my first single-author acceptance letter. The reviewers who read my paper only required that I slightly expand the theoretical parts of my piece. With the help of my faculty mentor, I was able to complete these revisions within two weeks. After another month, the editors officially accepted my article for publication. It was published in the August 2008 issue of *New Literary History*.

In pursuing this project, I was struck by the seeming facility with which it proceeded. Examining the process more closely, I found that some of the ease I experienced stemmed from the skills I had acquired in my prior research. Working previously in a tense relationship with a professor had made it clear to me the kinds of boundaries I should expect to be set by my faculty mentor, and the degree of independence I should insist upon to feel that the paper was fully my own. As a result, negotiating my relationship with my mentor in this case was both nonstressful and highly productive. The practice in writing about philosophy I had gained in the course of my second research project gave me the tools I needed to clearly formulate my arguments. Moreover, having been taught to expect to be sharply criticized—and to stick to my ideas no matter how harshly they were dismissed—I had developed greater confidence and boldness as a writer. This made it easier for me to write a paper that focused on what I knew to be potentially controversial arguments, and to take the risk of sending it to a journal that I considered likely to reject my article. I see this final project as the result not so much of a single idea, but of the entire path on which I had embarked—and the most effective demonstration of how much I had learned even through my initial lack of success.

At the same time, the academics who were part of this process assumed their roles working with an undergraduate student in what should be a model for others. Without the initial suggestion of my faculty mentor, I would not have realized that the paper I had written was potentially publishable. He was able to guide me toward the most productive ways of improving my paper, and he suggested what turned out to be the ideal journal to approach. The editors of *New Literary History* gave my paper serious consideration and accepted it even though they clearly realized that I was a student. Without the goodwill of the more experienced academics I encountered, as well as the lessons and skills I learned along the way, my hopes of publishing this paper would never have been fulfilled.

Conclusions

My experience of publication-oriented undergraduate research has led me to two main conclusions. First, it is possible, and beneficial, for students to attempt to bridge the gap between undergraduate essays and professionally publishable papers. A combination of supportive faculty and university-funded programs is sufficient to give a motivated student the chance to work on an independent research project (see also González 2001; Jacobi 1991).

What my research opportunities have also taught me, however, is that the beneficial effects of undergraduate research depend not only on the undergraduate herself, but also on the attitudes of the individuals she meets on her way. The outcome of most challenges I encountered on my path toward publication greatly depended on my own motivation and on the kind of advice and support I received from my mentors. It is fair to say that an undergraduate is sometimes capable of preparing an innovative academic paper that is entirely her own in terms of authorship. It is also true that, to be able to learn from the frequently difficult stages of transitioning toward professional publication, a student has to show a lot of self-driven motivation and persistence. However, the additional help a student requires to publish even a laboriously researched course essay cannot be underestimated, nor can the value of a faculty member's assistance.

This suggests that, on the one hand, undergraduates should not be discouraged from attempting to publish their work, as the possibility may lie within their grasp. Even if their projects do not immediately culminate in publication, the process of pursuing them is an enriching occasion for personal and academic development. On the other hand, much appreciation should be given to faculty who help students pursue these kinds of projects. We should see behind each such success an equal amount of the individual student's motivation and the faculty mentor's spontaneous support: an achievement of the undergraduate, but also of the department that provided a nurturing environment.

References

Bauer, Karen W., and Joan S. Bennett. 2003. Alumni Perceptions Used to Assess Undergraduate Research Experience. *The Journal of Higher Education* 74 (2): 210–30.

González, Cristina. 2001. Undergraduate Research, Graduate Mentoring, and the University's Mission. *Science* 293 (5535): 1624–26.

Harvard Student Employment Office. *Faculty Aide Program.* http://www.seo.harvard.edu/icb/icb.do?keyword=k59221&tabgroupid=icb.

———. *Harvard College Research Program.* http://www.seo.harvard.edu/icb/icb.do?keyword=k59221&tabgroupid=icb.

———. *Harvard College Undergraduate Research Facts.* 2008.

Jacobi, Maryann. 1991. Mentoring and Undergraduate Academic Success: A Literature Review. *Review of Educational Research* 61 (4): 505–32.

Read, Barbara, Becky Francis, and Jocelyn Robinson. 2001. "Playing Safe": Undergraduate Essay Writing and the Presentation of the Student "Voice." *British Journal of Sociology of Education* 22 (3): 387–99.

Wilson, Reed. 2003. Researching "Undergraduate Research" in the Humanities. *Modern Language Studies* 33 (1/2): 74–79.

IV

Case Studies across the Discipline of English

Research is formalized curiosity. It is poking and prying with a purpose.

—Zora Neale Hurston

Chapter Eight

New Frontiers in Faculty-Student Research Projects in Literature and Journalism

D. Heyward Brock, James M. Dean, McKay Jenkins,
Kevin Kerrane, Matthew Kinservik, and Christopher Penna
University of Delaware

Those involved in English studies are not usually receptive to group endeavors, whether faculty-with-faculty or faculty-with-student collaborations. By *collaboration* we intend the original Latin meaning of the term: *laboring* or *toiling* with others (*con* + *laborare*)—working in groups to solve problems and answer questions, in this case, research questions in English subdisciplines. Although humanities disciplines may not currently embrace collaboration in great numbers, we would do well to study and in some cases to emulate laboratory scientists, who regularly distribute research tasks to cohorts of students, both graduate and undergraduate, and who publish with them. Team efforts can reinvigorate humanities scholarship, bringing faculty and students together around shared interests.

In the English department at the University of Delaware, we have committed energy and some limited funding to support new undergraduate research teams. The first three years of our project (2006–2009) have been supported by the dean's office of the College of Arts and Sciences with an initial grant of $25,000. The dean's announced goal was to trigger "transformational learning"—to create stimulating forms of engagement for undergrads that would give them a sense of purpose and place in the world. A secondary goal of ours was to open new opportunities to undergrads beyond the university's undergraduate research program, which sponsors undergraduate projects on a senior thesis model. We have engaged relatively few of our 800 or so English majors—perhaps twenty-five to thirty—but we see much promise for expanding our efforts, and we believe our model is worth sharing here.

Six faculty members are leading active teams. Following are the participants and their projects, which we describe in this chapter as case studies with student voices:

- D. Heyward Brock: "The Doctor/Healer in Drama and Film"
- James M. Dean: "Chaucer and the Law"
- McKay Jenkins: "Narrative Nonfiction"
- Kevin Kerrane: "Billy Roche and Contemporary Irish Drama"
- Matthew Kinservik: "Treason in the Age of Reason"
- Christopher Penna: "British Literature Wiki"

The projects obviously are unconnected with one another in subject matter, but that is partly because the department is diverse, featuring concentrations in drama, ethnic and cultural studies, film, and professional writing. English education (preparation for teaching grades 7–12) is housed within our department, and many journalism minors are also English studies majors.

Collaboration in English Studies: A Model

For many years the University of Delaware has had a nationally recognized undergraduate research unit, originally established by Joan Bennett in 1980 with the support of a Fund for the Improvement of Postsecondary Education (FIPSE) grant.[1] Our departmental undergraduate research initiative, which we describe in this chapter, derives from the structure and philosophy of the all-university unit. For our projects, which we envisioned as closely knit and coordinated, we wanted to bring students into our workplaces more thoroughly than is normally possible for classroom work in humanities courses. We decided to try to emulate the model in the sciences, especially the laboratory setting, where students engage in meaningful research in collaboration with faculty and graduate students. The result of that collaboration is often publication, with a long string of contributors.

The primary investigator (PI) of the collaborative team, usually the faculty member in charge of the research, assigns research tasks to everyone on the team according to their ability to perform tasks. In this way, the PI can bring even less experienced students into the "community of practice," that is, the research community members who have the expertise to guide others (Lave and Wenger 1991). The "mastery of knowledge and skill," Jean Lave and Etienne Wenger argue, "requires newcomers to move toward full participation in the sociocultural practices of a community." They characterize the movement toward knowledge acquisition—participation in the apprenticeship process—as "legitimate peripheral participation," and they maintain that all knowledge mastery occurs in circumstances of "situated learning." The community of practice that the authors outline achieves coherence through "mutual engagement" (everyone is involved in the enterprise), "a joint enterprise," and "a shared repertoire" (everyone works on the same or similar material) (32–34, 36).

Faculty and students in humanities disciplines do not have laboratories, but they have their own research venues, including library stacks. They consult with colleagues and share their work with others, but often in a limited way. Students usually don't get the benefit of observing the research process as it unfolds. Instead, in classrooms, they witness the end result of the research process without the instructive, but sometimes messy, mechanisms that result in the classroom teaching. In our model, students are personally and thoroughly involved in all phases of the research process. For the projects described in this chapter, we chose research teams for the most part through competitive processes, although sometimes we invited students known to have a flair for a particular subject matter. Part of the selection process involved interviewing candidates. We discovered that students self-selected as they came to understand the demands of a particular research enterprise. Some candidates wanted to participate, and they usually were a good fit for the activity; others, less appropriate for the group, opted out without our having to refuse them. All of the faculty projects required that students have a minimum overall GPA of 3.0.

A significant component of our research activities involved our stipulation of what might count as *success* in our research enterprises. We came up with several measures. If students and faculty gave a talk to colleagues, other students, and faculty, that was one index of success. If they traveled to a national or international conference to deliver a talk, that was also regarded as success. Another kind of success is publication of a website, blog, or wiki. Penna and Dean have both mounted wikis, "British Literature Wiki" and "Chaucer and the Law," respectively. Kinservik's team has created Wikipedia entries on two eighteenth-century Irish revolutionaries, done at the request of an Irish historian they met during the course of their archival research in Dublin. Another index of success is the attempt to publish a collaborative article in a scholarly forum. Even if the journal decides not to publish the article, the endeavor itself is accounted a success. Another kind of success is publishing a scholarly article in an unrefereed journal.[2] A final level of accomplishment is publishing a collaborative article in a refereed journal.[3] (For that matter, this chapter counts as success for our collaborative endeavors.)

The research groups elicited a variety of collaborative experiences. Dean, Kerrane, Kinservik, and Penna engaged in the research with the goal of publishing new findings with students. Brock and Jenkins preferred to allow student interest and abilities to shape the directions of the research. Some of the projects changed as they progressed. Dean initially wanted to produce, with the students, a wiki or website called "A Glossary of Legal Diction in Chaucer's Works." The students, however, voted to change the focus of their research to individual Chaucerian stories and legal issues that appear in them. Some faculty required or encouraged special travel for their students. Jenkins particularly supports his students in travel all over the world to news "hot spots." He has been successful in finding publishing outlets for those students and ushering them into the world of journalistic narrative nonfiction. The following case studies highlight our particular endeavors and give special emphasis to the voices of our student collaborators.

D. Heyward Brock: The Doctor/Healer in Drama and Film

"The Doctor/Healer in Drama and Film" is a large project that involves more than five hundred world dramas and films in which a doctor/healer character plays a significant role. The study considers the evolution of this character over time, and the ways in which the character's portrayal reflects the history and philosophy of medicine and the role of the doctor/healer in society and culture. The goals of the study are to generate two products: (1) a searchable database that will be made available to other scholars and (2) a book on the subject. Nearly twenty years ago, I published a pilot study on the topic that discusses about thirty plays, and that became the model for the student researchers who elected to join the research team with myself as PI. As a broad-ranging study, this project provides an ideal opportunity for collaborative research: it would be nearly impossible, in a reasonable time, for a single researcher working alone to identify, study, analyze, and write about so many works, many of which are not readily available in English. At the time of this writing, about half a dozen students have worked on the project. One former student researcher on the project, Christina Campbell, wrote a degree with distinction undergraduate thesis on the psychiatrist in drama that one member of her thesis defense committee described as "near PhD level quality." Reflecting on her experience in writing the thesis, Christina said that if she had not worked on the doctor/healer research project, she would never have been inspired to write an undergraduate thesis or to pursue a graduate research degree.

All students who wanted to do research on the project enrolled in English 468, Undergraduate Research. Each researcher met weekly with me at scheduled times, and all members of the team stayed in touch via email. Twice during the semester—at the beginning and at the end—the entire team was able to come together.

At the first meeting, we organized ourselves into subteams based on areas of interest and curiosity. Amanda Strickland, for instance, wondered whether there were many plays available with black female doctor/healers in significant roles. This became her research territory. Tammie Sylvia had a general interest in eighteenth- and early nineteenth-century drama, but couldn't remember any plays from the period involving doctors/healers. Tammie became our resident expert in this period and discovered that there were more relevant plays than she had suspected. We used the meeting at the end of the semester to assess what we had all learned, not only about the subject matter but also about the research process, and to plan for the future of the project.

We organized ourselves as a research team into subspecialties. Once each team member had either chosen or been assigned an area of responsibility (medieval/Renaissance plays, American films, foreign films with English subtitles, twentieth-century British plays, and so on), each member was expected to (1) identify the relevant works in the field, using any appropriate special databases or search engines; (2) record the bibliographic information on a master bibliography for the subspecialty; (3) obtain and study the works, making use of interlibrary loan if required; (4) prepare a brief (one- to two-page) plot summary of each work; and (5) write a succinct (one- to two-page) analysis of the role of the doctor/healer in the work. At any point in this process, the student researcher was asked to consult me for help as needed. A searchable database is still in the future. This project is ongoing and will culminate in a book manuscript.

Although to date, none of the students who have worked on the research team has published an article, Joo Young Lee presented her paper at the Hollywood's Physicians panel at the International Film and History Conference in fall 2008. Additionally, all the students have signed a release allowing me to make appropriate use (with acknowledgment) of the information and materials they produced. Along with the beneficial experience of the research process itself, all of the student researchers will have made a contribution to scholarship in the field of literature and medicine—an accomplishment few undergraduates have achieved.

James M. Dean: Chaucer and the Law

Our research team concerned with Geoffrey Chaucer and the law changed its personnel and character from its inception in 2006 until the spring semester of 2008. We began with two handpicked students, meeting every week for at least an hour, with everyone, the instructor included, having a responsibility to report. The students soon developed special interests and expertise. Rachel Garcia concerned herself especially with the legal implications of the late medieval concept of *good fame*, because a good reputation could overcome evidence in a medieval courtroom setting. David Morton became interested in the concept of *covenant*, focusing on the religious implications of late medieval English law in a narrative such as Chaucer's "Physician's Tale," which includes legal proceedings and the concept of justice. David and Rachel helped pioneer the "Chaucer and the Law" wiki.

Depending on the semester, the group had as many as four students or as few as two. Christine Schuck and Rachel Lapp worked on the project during spring 2008. Because Christine had in previous semesters worked on a close, detailed reading of the "Man of Law's Tale," we decided to coauthor an essay on that subject tentatively titled "The *Man of Law's Tale* as Courtroom Drama." I met for at least one hour each week with both Christine and Rachel L., but at different times. Christine wrote sections of our joint essay; Rachel read and prepared notes on her subject. At the time of this writing, the essay is under review.

Rachel L. helped me complete a different project, a commissioned essay on John Gower's tale of a knight and a loathly lady. Under my guidance, Rachel read Chaucer's "Wife of Bath's Tale," Gower's "Tale of Florent" from *Confessio Amantis*, and the "Wedding of Sir Gawain and Dame Ragnell." Those three stories are, in fact, the same story told by three accomplished but different poets of the fourteenth and fifteenth centuries. Rachel researched questions of late medieval nominalism (a philosophical approach to knowledge and truth current in Gower's era); the literary motif of the hunter hunted; and some other issues helpful to my commissioned essay. She constructed an especially helpful table of plot elements in the three works, a chart showing the story components and their differences at a glance.

Both Christine and Rachel L. came to understand the research process and the questions one typically asks of texts. Christine voiced her surprise at the rigor involved in the research process: "I had not considered the amount of work involved in writing an article for scholarly publication. My writing needed to be more concise, I had to cite everything, I had to edit, re-edit, and then edit again." In her collaborative writing, Christine discovered a voice of authority: "By the end of the spring semester of 2008, I was asking Dean the same questions he used to ask of me regarding my research, such as 'So what?' and 'Why is this important?' I tell fellow students that Undergraduate Research is the most rewarding thing I have done at this university." Christine believes that the research methods she learned in her two semesters of undergraduate research helped prepare her for further study. She credits her work with the sources and analogues of Chaucer's "Man of Law's Tale," which include Nicholas Trevet's Anglo-Norman *Chronicle* and John Gower's *Confessio Amantis*, Book 2, as furthering her professional bona fides. She engaged in close reading of all versions, looking especially for legal terms and concepts.

Rachel L. discovered that undergraduate research helped demystify the scholarly and academic process. Like Christine, she engaged first in close readings, studying the organization and structure of the three versions of Chaucer's "Wife of Bath's Tale." Of the research process, Rachel said, "I began to understand why professional researchers know so many things: because the learning process is addictive. The more I read, the more I wanted to know. I uncovered one fact only to be confronted with the need for other facts." A student scholar who wants to know so much more, Rachel is submitting to present her work at the Moravian College Undergraduate Conference in Medieval and Early Modern Studies.

McKay Jenkins: Narrative Nonfiction

I envisioned my "Narrative Nonfiction" collaboration team as a group of globe-trotting journalists modeled on the staff of the *New Yorker* magazine. My role, as "editor," was to handpick a group of gifted students, help them put an idea into a larger context, provide some funding, and then leave them alone to do the work I knew they were capable of doing. The results were extraordinary: each student turned out a remarkable seventy-five-page senior honors thesis, and the experience, for all of them, seems to have been the highlight so far of their respective careers. The students disseminated their work, through readings and slide presentations, in a half dozen public talks on campus, and in one notable forum in the community at large. This last was a joint presentation before seventy-five senior members of the Wilmington, Delaware, community, who filled a room as part of an Academy of Lifelong Learning lecture series.

Over the course of a year, I oversaw four projects. Katie Bennett spent a year following a young girl through her treatment on a pediatric oncology unit at The Children's Hospital of Philadelphia. Dan Jordan traveled to the Peruvian Amazon and charted the lives of people living in a series of villages along a tributary to the Amazon River. Kristin Lindell traveled to St. Paul, Minnesota, and then to a refugee camp in Thailand to interview Burmese refugees. That her project coincided with a catastrophic hurricane in the region only made her work more urgent. Ian Palkovitz spent a month living in a Christian orphanage in (majority Hindu) Kathmandu, Nepal, and then wrote about the complexities facing children living in a war-torn country. The three international projects were funded with roughly $1,500 each in undergraduate research funds. Katie's Philadelphia project cost perhaps a fifth of that.

We met as a group at least every other week for a year. At each meeting, students were required to show tangible work: transcribed interviews, annotated bibliographies, rough pages, or final manuscript copy. We all read and critiqued each student's work, from first week to last. The mood in my office was kept supportive and collaborative; the students were helping each piece to be the best it could be. None of the four was a typical journalism student; indeed, none had ever served on the staff of the campus student newspaper. I considered this a plus: they were all bright and ambitious students, but none had been indoctrinated into the typical newsroom culture. This meant that they approached nonfiction writing with a freshness that can be lost even among undergraduate journalism students, who can exhibit remarkably conservative stylistic traits even at a young age. From the beginning, these projects were deeply researched and vividly composed. It seems clear that the quality of the writing, more than a sense of competition, pushed each student to greater heights.

Dan wrote that both the research funds and the regular team meetings helped his project along:

> I used grants I received from both the English department and from the school's Summer Scholars program to return to Peru the summer after my Junior year. This was another key to my work. I could not have afforded that trip on my own, and without going back to Peru and collecting more information and stories, I would never have been able to write my thesis. Over the summer I continued to work with Professor Jenkins and the other researchers working with him. Being exposed to such a high level of work on a consistent basis was wonderful. The group fostered an excellent working relationship that was centered on collaboration, as opposed to competition (which I believe is too rare in research, especially at the university level). Our bi-weekly meetings kept me focused and improved my writing tremendously.

These collaborative projects inspired students to reach new levels of intellectual achievement and emotional maturity. By requiring both library research and extensive (even exotic) journalistic fieldwork, the projects encouraged work that went deep into and far beyond the culture of the university.

Kevin Kerrane: Billy Roche and Contemporary Irish Drama

A student project on Irish writer Billy Roche originated when I coordinated my own research (a book in progress) with the work of two undergraduates, Hilary Sophrin and Keith Pluymers. These students were pursuing different majors—English and history, respectively—but both had chosen to minor in Irish studies, and both had previously undertaken serious research in courses overseas and in the university's honors program.

In fall 2007, Hilary and Keith were enrolled in one of my advanced undergraduate courses, Contemporary Ireland in Literature. The syllabus included writing by Billy Roche—the author of seven plays, two film scripts, a novel, and a collection of short stories. All of Roche's works are set in his home town of Wexford, on Ireland's southeast coast, but in a classroom interview via speakerphone in November 2007, Roche discussed his literary alterations of this setting: "James Joyce once said that if Dublin disappeared, the city could be reconstructed from his pages. My work is different. It's firmly grounded in Wexford, but it's not a transcription of the town. It's a transformation."

Hilary and Keith developed this insight into a full-scale research project. They wrote a grant proposal requesting funds for a weeklong trip to Wexford; they established email contact with Billy Roche and such Wexford historians as Tom Mooney, editor of the newspaper *The Wexford Echo*; and they enrolled in a special research course with me in spring 2008. The grant proposal was approved, and by the time of their research trip—March 28 to April 5—Hilary and Keith had read all of Roche's published work. In our weekly meetings, and in short writing exercises, they discussed Roche's uses of setting, and they formulated a list of priorities for their research in Ireland.

I focused on Roche's plays, while the students put greater emphasis on his fiction. Hilary isolated several key stories in Roche's 2007 collection, *Tales from Rainwater Pond*, while Keith examined an early apprenticeship novel, *Tumbling Down* (1986), which Roche was in the midst of revising for a new edition. When the students met the author in Wexford, he took them on an extensive walking tour and pointed out specific sites of events depicted in his writing. Hilary and Keith also explored the area on their own, conducting other interviews and taking more than a thousand photographs. They later offered this perspective:

> In many ways, the blending of the town with Roche's work made our project challenging, because his stories are neither purely autobiographical nor purely fictional. We began to recognize the subtleties of his technique. His transformations of places are small but significant—even in the slight shifting of a pond from one side of the railroad tracks to the other. In *Tumbling Down,* Roche centralized the characters and action around an area known as the Bull Ring. In real life, the Bull Ring is a small market square, but in Roche's work it becomes an epicenter for romantic encounters, dramatic or comedic scenes, or moments of quiet reflection.

Back at the University of Delaware, the students' research meetings with me led to a critical vocabulary for mapping Roche's transformations of landscape. Hilary and Keith juxtaposed photographic images with quotes from Roche's fiction to exemplify such concepts as *condensation*, *magnification*, *relocation*, *centralization*, and *isolation*. To illustrate *condensation*, for example, Hilary noted that the place called Rainwater Pond is a composite of two large tidal pools, Blue Pond and Otter Pond, which lie just outside of Wexford. In combining them, Roche has created a mirror of the town's consciousness: a trysting spot for lovers, a training site for athletes, or a refuge for the lonely. Hilary found "a seamless quality" in Roche's comments about fictional characters or places and his real town: "They blend together in a way that makes all of his work distinctly local and yet part of a bigger picture. Rainwater Pond is not merely a swimming hole, but a sanctuary and sacred place."

Similarly, Keith observed that The Rock—a pub that serves as the central setting of the novel *Tumbling Down*—is based on The Shamrock Bar, which Roche's father leased and managed during Billy's formative years. The real pub was located in Roman Lane, a small alley on the edge of town; the fictional pub has been relocated to Circular Quay, at the heart of Wexford, offering a stunning view of the harbor and the sea beyond. Keith contended that "Roche translates the emotional importance of The Rock to the characters in *Tumbling Down* by moving the bar to a physical setting that matches its emotional setting in the center of the town."

In May 2008 Hilary and Keith gave an illustrated research presentation, open to the campus community. Based on their success, I proposed a panel titled "Billy Roche's Wexford" for the northeastern regional meeting of the American Conference for Irish Studies. The proposal was accepted. To continue this research initiative on Billy Roche, both Hilary and Keith want to take their work beyond the conference stage and into the realm of scholarly publication, ideally in a journal like *Irish Studies Review*. My projected book on Roche will credit the significant findings of these students—and may even include a chapter by them, possibly with illustrative photos.

As I continue to teach courses in Irish literature, I intend to match students with worthy research projects, focusing on additional Irish writers. The special collections holdings at the University of Delaware library include a wealth of materials related to Irish drama—for example, original manuscripts by Patricia Burke Brogan, an unjustly neglected playwright. I have begun to schedule some seminar classes at the library, aiming to use specific documents as starting points for undergraduate research.

Matt Kinservik: Treason in the Age of Reason

I directed three different teams over the past three years, all relating to research on my new book project on the 1794 treason case of Reverend William Jackson, an Irish-born spy for the French government during the Reign of Terror. This wide-ranging project includes political history, religious controversy, print culture, drama, novel writing, and so on. After giving the first two teams great latitude in their choice of research, I chose to provide much stronger direction for the third team. I was interested to learn of the impact of the Jackson treason case in America. The 1790s saw a flood of Irish immigrants to the United States, many of them political refugees, including some important figures connected to the Jackson affair. So I drew up a list of the eight most significant exiles, and divided them among the three members of his third research team. The students' task was to research the biographical tradition on each subject as best they could using local library resources. Then they would identify archival material in other places, and travel to those archives to do original primary research.

After about six weeks of preliminary work, I took the students to the library of the Delaware Historical Society, in nearby Wilmington, to look at the papers of Archibald Hamilton Rowan, an exile who spent four years in Delaware. The idea was to use this local collection as an opportunity to introduce the students to a rare books and manuscript collection, and to show them how to handle, read, and transcribe eighteenth-century manuscripts. The students found so much rich and surprising material on Rowan in that collection that they scrapped the other exiles entirely and focused all of their efforts on Rowan alone. A dozen unpublished letters challenged the biographical tradition on Rowan's time in America, and the students also found several early versions of Rowan's memoirs, produced on his own lithographic press.

Two of the three students, Alice Lippincott and Brion Abel, continued on with this research the following semester. Between semesters, these two students and I traveled to Dublin, where we consulted Rowan manuscripts in the Royal Irish Academy. The letters all date from after Rowan's return to Ireland, and they are significant because they reveal a long-term correspondence with his Delaware friends that indicates (sometimes quite explicitly) that he remembered his time in exile with fondness, and sometimes regretted having left Delaware. The biographical tradition tells quite a different story, representing his time in America as an unhappy and disillusioning experience. The letters also reveal Rowan's continuing political radicalism, something the biographies suggest he left behind him in America.

The students then went to Belfast to work in the Public Record Office of Northern Ireland, but were prevented from using the collection because on the morning of their visit, the ceiling fell in on the documents storage room! The research trip ended with a visit to Rowan's ancestral home, Killyleagh Castle, County Down. There, we all met with and spoke to Rowan's descendants, who still own the castle, and were allowed access to the library and portraits of Rowan.

The students met with Irish historians during their travels, and were encouraged by one of these historians to produce Wikipedia pages on Jackson and Rowan in order to share their findings quickly. The students and I are currently drafting a piece on the Rowan letters in Delaware for the journal *History Ireland*. All have also shared transcriptions of those letters with the historian who is producing the new *Dictionary of Irish National Biography* for the Royal Irish Academy. Alice and Brion both believe their undergraduate research experience has been vital to their education. Alice wrote,

> Undergraduate research has been an extraordinary experience. I learned everything from basic document handling to the publication process. We were able to follow our research all the way

> to Ireland where we were allowed access to several scholarly libraries and archives. This was perhaps the most important part for me because it confirmed my passion for library science. While sitting in the library at the Royal Irish Academy looking through a book of Archibald Hamilton Rowan's newspaper clippings, I realized how important the preservation of such artifacts is to me. And the transformational experience continued when we returned home to give a presentation at the University of Delaware's Academy of Lifelong Learning about all that we had found over the course of our research.

The students' remarks affirm the tremendous value and opportunities of faculty and undergraduate research collaborations in literary studies.

Christopher Penna: British Literature Wiki

Our collaborative research project, "British Literature Wiki," grew out of a modest course project for students in a British literature survey course. The goal in that setting was to have teams of students work on research projects created on a class wiki site. While the resulting wiki of well over a hundred pages served its purpose within the limitations of the course, the undergraduate research team's goal was to take it a step further by adding new material, editing existing pages, and producing a reliable source of readily available information for students of British literature. Early on, the idea emerged that the wiki's audience would be students talking to and teaching other students.

The choice of a wiki was appealing for several reasons beyond its being simply a convenient collaborative tool. The public nature of wiki writing was a useful means of reinforcing for the students the important role that audience plays in shaping one's writing—something students quickly recognized. They were further reminded of the presence of a real audience when they began to see their work turning up near the top of Google searches. Closely related to this notion of audience was an awareness that the wiki was a publication of their research. They were, in effect, creating and disseminating new knowledge, or in the words of one of the students, Stephanie Polukis, "[T]his project gave us a sense of pride in leaving behind a legacy." Their goal was to do more than simply replicate what was already available. Thus entries would go beyond Wikipedia-type articles, to include the students' research-based, interpretative analyses. Another benefit of the wiki was that its multimedia capabilities allowed students to rethink ways in which typical English research projects could be presented, to "give a voice to the information," as another student, Julie Wigley, put it. Finally, the paradox of a wiki as an ostensibly fixed artifact that is constantly being revised seemed an appropriate metaphor for the tentative, speculative nature of academic research.

Project Goals and the Research Team

Students who had done well in the original survey course, and who seemed to have an interest in the potential of creating material for the wiki site, were invited to join the project. During the spring 2008 semester, six students participated (Diane Aiken, Kathryn Kummer, Lindsay Milbourne, Allie Myers, Stephanie Polukis, and Julie Wigley). All were English majors with varied interests. The variety of talents and interests allowed the project to move in many complementary directions.

At the beginning of our sessions, we collectively generated a list of specific goals:

- Create more content through continuing research on topics in British literature.
- Learn about how technology influences collaborative work.
- Develop editorial uniformity throughout the wiki.
- Understand issues of online publication (copyright, intellectual property).
- Mentor students enrolled in the survey course who would be first-time contributors to the wiki.
- Treat each student's work as a publication.

We met as a group once a week in person (in addition to meeting online) to report on progress and provide feedback to each other. Early in the semester, our meetings focused on these larger goals and on editorial decisions to assure the overall unity of the site. As the semester progressed, the students identified additional projects they wanted to research and publish on the wiki. Diane investigated the historical realities of daily life in Victorian England and compared them to George Eliot's rendering of them in *Middlemarch*. Kathryn explored the relationship between Samuel Taylor Coleridge and William Wordsworth in composing *Lyrical Ballads*, specifically trying to identify how and where Coleridge diverged from Wordsworth. Lindsay researched the history and emergence of newspapers and periodical literature in early eighteenth-century England. Allie wanted to tease out image clusters in T. S. Eliot's "The Love Song of J. Alfred Prufrock" and explore the influence of imagism on the poem. Stephanie investigated what she saw as Romantic and Augustan conflicts in Jane Austen's novels, concluding that Austen was a "mock-Romantic." Julie created documentary-style videos by interviewing professors about the historical contexts of the Romantic and Victorian periods—videos that were then mounted on the wiki to enhance the appropriate pages.

Reflections

During the course of our work, I asked the students to reflect on what they were doing and to post their observations to a "Reflection Journal" page on the wiki. Their reflections speak to their engagement in the research process. In tightening and revamping the extant pages, the students realized some of the difficulties of collaborative writing. Stephanie, for example, ran into a problem while working on the Romantics page: "I'm not sure about the French Revolution just yet since I don't know what the original authors of the page were implying or what sources they read." Kathryn noted, "I have learned when it comes to editing that clarity is most important. It is much easier to see those problems when editing rather than writing on my own."

When considering the overall research experience, the students expressed interesting insights on its challenges and rewards. Lindsay commented on the process of discovery and revision: "It was fun going back through the books from class and relearning information to add. [. . .] And it has been a challenge, just researching and attempting to find anything that could be useful. I'm still not exactly sure how everything is going to work out." She added that her goal was "to bring the thoughts that I have together and create new ideas." Stephanie discussed the recursive nature of research, the vision and revision of testing of hypotheses: "I can't decide whether Jane Austen is a Romantic writer or not. The dates of her novels' publications fall into the Romantic Period, but I suspect she dislikes Romanticism." Reading Austen's letters led Stephanie to Ann Radcliffe's stereotypically Romantic novel *The Mysteries of Udolofo*, and to the observation that "it didn't take long to note the heavy contrast between the styles of Radcliffe and Austen." Diane recognized the scope and unexpected byways of research. In her investigation of everyday Victorian life and its representation in George Eliot's *Middlemarch*, she appreciated "learning about the small, inconsequential aspects of Victorian life" and noted that she was "learning about aspects of life that [she] wouldn't [ordinarily] think to research."

At the end of the semester, I asked the students for some final thoughts—to sum up, if they could, some of what they took away from the project. If we take these students at their word, they seem not only to have benefitted from the project, but to feel that they've made a contribution similar to a publication. Stephanie confirmed this when she wrote, "[T]hese projects [. . . gave us] a better understanding of the literature and the contextual significance of the text. This wiki will also serve as a handbook for future students." Julie expressed satisfaction at being able "to experiment with different ways to share information with my peers, something I would not have normally gotten to do in a classroom setting." Also typical of the students' reactions is Diane's comment: "Working on the wiki pages has really helped me better understand all of the different literary movements since the 18th century, and the information provided on the pages complements all of the knowledge I gained in my English 206 class. I think if I had had access to this information during the course, I would have benefited greatly." Of course, the very nature of wikis undermines the notion of a "last word." Nevertheless, these optimistic assertions do suggest a continuing conversation and fruitful collaboration between student and faculty researchers.

Although we believe that the previous case studies make a strong case for collaborative endeavors among students and faculty, we would be remiss if we failed to acknowledge special problems that arise in engaged, intensive research—research that involves faculty development as well as student advancement. The undergraduate research projects we have outlined in this chapter go beyond typical independent studies for undergraduates, so they make special demands on faculty time and energy. They are not for everyone. Even if the chosen students are quick learners and self-starters, they may need considerable guidance and support. Groups may be obliged to meet for at least an hour each week, with reports on the status of everyone's research. Projects like ours inevitably turn out to be labor intensive; hence, they are most likely inappropriate for untenured faculty unless such instructors are exceptionally well organized.

All of this acknowledged, there are rewards to collaborative research in humanities disciplines. One compensation that experienced faculty will doubtless immediately grasp is that we can bring undergraduate students into our professional lives more intimately than we ordinarily find time to do. We can help renew our disciplines and subdisciplines in important ways. Conducting research with undergraduates helps faculty explore the grounds and assumptions of their disciplines. Undergraduates often raise the questions "So what?" and "Who cares?" for us and for our colleagues—questions we need to hear and address as often as we can.

Notes

1. See the Reinvention Center "Spotlight" on the undergraduate research program at http://www.reinventioncenter.miami.edu.

2. See, for example, Kaiser and Dean (2006).

3. See, for example, Dean and Kaiser (forthcoming).

References

Dean, James M., and Melanie L. Kaiser. Forthcoming. Faculty-Student Collaborative Research in the Humanities. *CUR Quarterly*.

Kaiser, Melanie L., and James M. Dean. 2006. Chaucer and the Early Church. *Medieval Forum* 5 (January). http://www.sfsu.edu/~medieval/Volume5/Kaiser.html.

Lave, Jean, and Etienne Wenger. 1991. *Situated Learning: Legitimate Peripheral Participation*. Cambridge: Cambridge University Press.

CHAPTER NINE

Undergraduate Research Fellows and Faculty Mentors in Literary Studies

CHRISTINE F. COOPER-ROMPATO, EVELYN FUNDA, JOYCE KINKEAD, AMANDA MARINELLO, AND SCARLET FRONK
Utah State University

Utah State University (USU), a research and land-grant university of 23,000 students, offers the Undergraduate Research Fellows Program to support incoming students who are interested in graduate or professional study following the undergraduate degree, and who may be interested in preparing for major fellowships such as the Rhodes. A goal is to give students—particularly the first-generation students who are the traditional target of a land-grant mission—opportunities that exist at more elite institutions. The fellows program offers students the opportunity to engage in scholarship and research from the outset of their undergraduate career. Students interview with faculty teams in a spring competition before arriving on campus for the fall term. Working with the associate vice president for research, who oversees the program centrally, the new fellows find a match for mentors among the faculty, based on their own stated interests and educational trajectory. (A complete description of the fellows program can be found in Kinkead [2008].) This chapter focuses on fellows who major in English.

What does a research fellow do? Each field defines what it means to engage in *hands-on learning*. In some departments, a fellow might have immediate immersion in a lab or studio, whereas in other departments, fellows might be asked to attend seminars, visit labs, or meet with potential faculty mentors. For students who major in degree programs within English, the choice of program determines the experience, as a technical writer's goals will differ from those, say, of an English education major.

The two case studies of research fellows described here provide models to consider. Through the research fellows program, which excites students about inquiry and discovery from the outset and provides the scaffolding for them to continue and grow as scholars, we have been able to create a foundation for enhanced undergraduate research in English.

The Fellows Program

Scholar's Day, held annually in March, provides a venue where students compete for research fellowships. The students submit an application in advance, and then have an interview with faculty from their field of interest. Our humanities faculty members who participate start setting the tone during the interview. They query the applicants about their career goals, and they also begin to reveal what it means to undertake academic scholarship. Their task is to tease out the interviewees who not only have the academic track record, but also have the ambition, confidence, and tenacity to undertake research at an early stage. Faculty members on the selection panels often get first choice of students with whom they would like to work, or they alert colleagues about fellows who may have an interest in their area.

Once fellows are selected, the process of matching students to mentors begins. Whereas the sciences have a tradition of mentorship and apprenticeship, humanistic fields such as English typically do not. Faculty members traditionally perform every phase of the research process, rarely having a student assistant to help with the review of literature. Certainly this is the result of long-established practice and custom; however, it is also due to a lack of funding to hire assistants. As the 1937 Nobel Prize winner Albert Szent-Gyorgyi explained, scientific research is composed of four things: "brains with which to think, eyes with which to see, machines with which to measure and, fourth, money" (qtd. in Sullivan). Humanists rarely have any money. Consequently, there are good reasons why a culture of undergraduate research does not exist in the humanities. The fellows program is designed so that students initially work on faculty mentors' projects, and then branch out into more independent projects as they assimilate the inquiry process. As a result, both partners benefit.

This chapter illuminates two faculty-fellow relationships, one following the completion of the student's initial year of fellowship work, and a second spanning several years of the student's research experience. The two research fellows and their faculty mentors, all in literary studies, take up the thread of the narrative from here. Christine F. Cooper-Rompato begins with a description of year one of Scarlet Fronk's research fellowship. Evelyn Funda continues with an account of her work with Amanda Marinello over a period of three years. One begins the relationship by focusing on a large topic—the Middle Ages—while the other chooses a more discrete topic, the friendship album. Their stories illuminate the challenges and opportunities that lie in collaborations between faculty and undergraduate researchers. They also incorporate information about assistance undergraduate researchers received from the Office of the Vice President for Research.

An Undergraduate Research Fellow in Medieval Studies: The First Year from a Faculty Mentor's Perspective

Christine Cooper-Rompato

Scarlet, a first-year undergraduate research fellow in the English department, works five to ten hours a week during the school year with me on various projects. Although Scarlet declared creative writing to be her main area of interest during her initial interview—at which I was present—after being accepted to the program, she requested to work with a medievalist because she was interested in that time period. I also hold an MFA in creative writing, so our match was a good fit. Before I met with Scarlet, I was unsure about the kind of project we could work on together. My department head suggested combining medieval studies with something "modern" and technological (a medieval podcast, for example) and offered to promote our results on the departmental website. So I went to our first meeting wondering what a medieval studies project that could be easily showcased might look like.

Fellows in science work in their mentors' labs, and my equivalent of the lab is the library. How could I get a first-year student up to speed on something as vast as the Middle Ages to help with my research? I decided that my goals for the first semester would be to allow Scarlet to explore her own interests and to encourage her to read deeply about the Middle Ages. Initially, I imagined that I would design a directed reading project on medieval history and literature, or perhaps (because I knew she wanted to write fiction) on modern writers influenced by the medieval. I arrived at that initial meeting expecting to do all the talking but quickly realized that Scarlet had creative ideas of her own. We discussed possible projects; and at our second meeting, we ranked the list of projects and agreed on our top choice: a musical set in the Middle Ages. I thought this had great potential for showcasing. I imagined a fantastic musical based on Geoffrey Chaucer's *Canterbury Tales*, with witty (and slightly naughty) musical numbers of the "Miller's Tale" and "Nun's Priest's Tale." Scarlet had other ideas, however, for while in high school, she had already started thinking about and writing some lyrics for a musical featuring star-crossed lovers.

I had to trust Scarlet to follow her own interests and instincts, while encouraging her to expand her horizons. I insisted that she decide on a particular medieval setting for her musical, and after reading some English history, she chose Anglo–Saxon England during the Danish invasions, creating a fictional kingdom of "Southumberland." Scarlet read a good deal of background material, including *Beowulf* and information on *scops* (Old English bards) and *skalds* (Old Norse bards). Although the basic romantic plot of the musical did not change, she added scenes and songs based on her research: an Anglo–Saxon feasting song and a rivalry between a scop and a skald. Next is a stanza from Scarlet's "Feasting Song." The lute is being passed around, and all are expected to sing. This is Caedmon's stanza, inspired by Bede's account of Caedmon from his *Ecclesiastical History of the English People* (248–49).

> I was despairing for my soul could not sing
> Until I was visited by God the great king
> He taught me to play and he taught me to sing
> So I praise the creation and God as I sing.

Scarlet's enthusiasm was delightful, and every week I looked forward to hearing of her progress and the questions that arose during her research. Several times, though, I had to temper my enthusiasm and not push too much on her—when Scarlet expressed an interest in lute making, for example, I waxed on about the grants we could write so that she could attend a summer lute-making camp. I had to learn to strike a good balance between trying to show Scarlet the many opportunities out there (Study Abroad programs, for example) and *not* trying to plan the next four years of her life to create the "perfect medievalist."

By the end of the first semester, we realized that the musical would be a long-term project and might take several years to finish; we had been too optimistic in our original goal of finishing it the first year. In one semester, Scarlet had written out much of the plot, started filling in dialogue, composed music to several songs, and added several more "period" songs. We then had to choose whether to continue with the musical during the spring semester, or to work on something else in tandem. Scarlet said she would like to help me with one of my own projects, too, so over the winter break I decided a multipronged attack on the Middle Ages would be best: in addition to approaching the Middle Ages through creative writing, we would also focus on scholarly research and manuscript studies.

Scarlet and I agreed that during the spring semester, she would help me with a research question for my book project on medieval miracles of *xenoglossia* (the miraculous ability to speak, read, write, or understand a foreign language). I had found a reference to xenoglossia in a thirteenth-century legend of St. Francis of Assisi, but other popular medieval versions of his vita do not contain any reference to this miracle. I initially gave Scarlet a list of more than twenty medieval legends of St. Francis, and asked her to find translations to see if xenoglossia made an appearance. This would give her experience with electronic databases. Scarlet began this project, but I soon realized that what was an exciting research avenue for me might not be a particularly interesting introduction to primary research. So we chose to work for most of the semester on prong three of our plan, a hands-on manuscript experience. In January, I arranged to meet Scarlet in our library's special collections to examine a fifteenth-century Latin prayer book, the Merrill-Cazier Library MS *De Villers Book of Hours*, which contains a seventeenth-century French genealogy of the De Villers family on the flyleaf. In the 1970s, a USU history master's student had transcribed the French in his thesis, but he had not translated it. This seemed like the perfect project for Scarlet: she would have to check the transcription against the original manuscript, translate the French passages, and then design a poster for the university's undergraduate research day in April.

As fascinating as it was, this project presented a number of challenges for both of us. Scarlet was enrolled in first-year French to build on her high school coursework, so in order to translate the seventeenth-century French, she had to find early French dictionaries in the library and meet with a professor of medieval French to go over her translation. To check the transcription against the manuscript, she had to have a crash course in paleography. To design the poster, she had to learn how to put together a professional poster that would be attractive, argumentative, and informative. She then had to feel confident enough to stand by her poster for three hours and answer questions from both students and faculty. All of these steps required a great deal of personal direction and guidance.

This project was also challenging for me as the mentor. As the deadline for the on-campus undergraduate research day, Student Showcase, approached, I was concerned that I was asking too much of Scarlet. After all, she was only in first-year French, and the translation proved quite difficult in places. I had never designed a poster before and was unaware of how much time it required. Once again, the biggest challenge for me was to step back and let Scarlet be in charge of the poster—because the choices that go into designing and formatting a poster are all part of learning how to build an argument, an essential skill for scholars.

Despite my concerns, Scarlet's poster was a success, earning second place in the humanities division. After the research day, the poster was moved to the English department's office for showcasing, where many faculty and students commented on it. We have discussed further venues, including submitting a paper to the International Medieval Congress in Kalamazoo, Michigan, which offers several panels on undergraduate research. Undergraduate research expenses are funded via the research office or the student government–sponsored travel fund.

At our last meeting of the spring semester, we discussed our plans for next year, focusing on several possible projects, including taking the genealogy that Scarlet translated from the *De Villers Book of Hours* and researching the particular family members mentioned. Because Scarlet is familiar with the library databases and interlibrary loan, I won't hesitate to ask her to help me with further research projects. We expect to continue working together through Scarlet's undergraduate career. I look forward to watching her develop as a scholar, much as Evelyn Funda describes her delight at seeing Amanda develop into an independent researcher.

An Undergraduate Research Fellow in Medieval Studies: The First Year from a Student's Perspective

Scarlet Fronk

I began my undergraduate research experience by enrolling in the Research Fellow Connections class, a weeklong orientation before fall term, taught by Dr. Kinkead. The class included research fellows from many fields. The other new fellows and I received important information about what a research fellowship entails, what to look for in a mentor, how to find our way around campus and town, how to sign up for classes, and where to get help.

As part of the class, I met with the department head, who gave me several names to consider. I decided to visit Dr. Cooper-Rompato because she had been one of my interviewers, and I knew that she was interested in the Middle Ages, a subject that has always intrigued me. I was fortunate to find such a good mentor on my first attempt. Dr. Cooper-Rompato was enthusiastic and eager to produce a project that we could both enjoy and learn from. I had long considered writing a musical with a medieval setting, and she liked the idea immediately. Although I had always been interested in the time period, I knew little, so I spent most of my first semester reading appropriate texts, such as "Caedmon's Hymn" and *Beowulf*. I also began taking music composition lessons to help me write the music.

Starting in spring semester, we put the musical on hold and began a new project. Dr. Cooper-Rompato had discovered a fifteenth-century prayer book in the special collections of the library. The text itself was in Latin, but on the flyleaf the De Villers family had written their history in French. During the course of three months, I read over the transcription rendered by a former graduate student, and translated it, drawing on advice from a French professor when needed. It was a little frightening to translate something that no one else had translated, but at the same time it was fascinating to be able to translate writing penned by people who lived nearly four hundred years before I was born. Presenting my poster at the Student Showcase was amazing; it was a new, enjoyable feeling to realize that I knew more than anyone else about this subject.

In my second year, I hope to finish writing my musical. I also intend to research more on the De Villers family. If I can find out enough about their background, I may be able to visit the area where they lived when I study abroad in France next summer, and present any new information at another poster presentation. Looking back at my first year, my only regret was that I didn't do more to help Dr. Cooper-Rompato with her research, something I intend to make up for this year. I felt that I could have served in an apprentice role in her scholarly work, learning from her as a model, and seeing a mature scholar in action.

An Undergraduate Research Fellow in Literary Studies: A Faculty Perspective on Three Years of Mentoring a Fellow

Evelyn Funda

A large portion of the success of my three-year mentorship of Amanda Marinello undoubtedly goes to Amanda ("Mannie") herself, who was an uncommon student with a clear sense of what she wanted and how she would achieve her goals. Yet I believe that an examination of the way Mannie approached me, and the methods we used to work together, offers a model for mentoring that can be replicated by others.

Several years ago, a junior colleague, Susan Andersen, and I coauthored an essay on teaching the early writings of Willa Cather to undergraduate students. That essay, published in *Teaching Cather*, focused in part on Cather's written responses from 1888, when she was only sixteen, to a questionnaire about her opinions on everything from favorite authors to dressing habits. A revised and expanded version of the essay was slated to be published in a book-length collection on Cather and classroom pedagogy (Funda and Andersen 2009). The questionnaire that Andersen and I were analyzing had appeared in Cather's friend's confession album, a Victorian version of an autograph album that includes various prompts for friends to fill out. The document had never been seriously considered in Cather scholarship, in part because most scholars thought Cather's answers quaint and the album a minor piece of Victorian ephemera. However, Andersen and I argued that Cather's responses were revealing when considered in the context of the development of Cather's career and her engagement with the cultural issues evoked by the questions in what we had been calling a *survey* or *ephemera*. Although we had discussed the cultural and historical significance of some of Cather's responses, we hadn't discussed the historical significance of the form itself, its development, or its cultural aims. Revising the essay for the book allowed us to do further research, which is where Mannie came in.

Mannie had previously taken a class from me, in which we studied women in the nineteenth century, and a course from Andersen, in which they had discussed a Cather short story. Mannie was interested in Cather, modern writers more generally, and women's culture. Her interest in women's studies meant that looking at this document from a feminist perspective, as Andersen and I had done, intrigued her.

I set Mannie on the task of finding out more about the form. This was a focused, manageable task, and very different from the beginning described by Cooper-Rompato and Scarlet in their narrative. We sought a more accurate term than survey or ephemera, and we wanted to know as much as we could about these kinds of albums, in particular if anyone had begun to look at them as cultural documents. Our own best efforts hadn't turned up much on this kind of document, but we were hoping that under my direction, Mannie would have greater success. We needed someone who had the time and ability to methodically sort through the variety of databases and indices available in sociology, history, women's studies, and cultural studies. Mannie had a good sense of the research process, and she felt no discomfort in seeking help from our library staff if and when she came to a dead end in research. Therefore, I didn't need to take time to teach her about research methods, and Mannie set off on the task. The plan was that she would find and read scholarly essays that promised to be relevant, and then submit an annotated bibliography (complete with key quotes and summary of the thesis) and copies of what she considered the five most useful works. Along the way, Mannie and I met to discuss her progress and findings. We agreed to be watchful during this process for some related topic that she might work on as her own project. Because Mannie was in year two in her fellowship, and on track to graduate within three years rather than four, we wanted to make sure that she was on a trajectory to conduct her own research and develop a thesis for her honors degree.

Because Mannie had a talent for conducting independent work, she came up with more than I had expected. She provided accurate names—*friendship album*, *confession album*, or *autograph album*—and a groundbreaking essay from a rather obscure publication about the cultural significance of this form and its function as a Victorian tool of courtship. She also found other authors who had completed these albums, in particular, a series of surveys completed at different times by J. M. Barrie, author of the *Peter Pan* plays. Mannie showed me the Barrie responses and asked if I knew whether the two authors had known each other. I had directed a master's thesis nearly ten years earlier that established that the two writers had corresponded briefly, but I was not aware of any Barrie friendship albums. The Barrie connection was interesting but outside my research plans; however, laying Cather's responses alongside those of Barrie, something no other scholar had done, offered evocative possibilities that excited Mannie. This, clearly, was going to be her research project—the outgrowth of my research that we had been seeking—and it was a joy to see her arrive at such a significant moment in her intellectual life.

Mannie's subsequent research into the history of these albums led her to opportunities we had never initially imagined. After some preliminary reading that included biographies of both authors, as well as several primary works by Barrie and Cather, Mannie proposed an honors senior thesis on the social use of those albums within the Victorian era, and how the two authors had resisted their courtship function. That, in turn, created an ever-widening series of possibilities: the proposal for the thesis helped Mannie succeed in her application during her junior year for a Study Abroad program in Scotland (where Samantha Matthews, the friendship album scholar Mannie had discovered, resides, and where Barrie papers are archived). That opportunity helped her secure an Undergraduate Research and Creative Opportunities institutional grant) that funded travel and archival research. In Scotland, Mannie conducted research and extensive interviews with both Matthews and R. D. S. Jack, a top Barrie scholar in Scotland. That an undergraduate student should carry out such primary research so well is testament to her initiative. Professor Matthews, who was still researching friendship albums for a forthcoming book, was not only impressed with Mannie but surprised to learn she had discovered the Barrie album, a document that Matthews herself did not even know existed.

When Mannie returned to the United States, her writing was informed by research conducted in Scotland, and her senior year was spent completing the thesis. Also during that time, Mannie was accepted to present a paper at the 2007 National Conference on Undergraduate Research (NCUR). In her final honors thesis, she deftly considered the albums of J. M. Barrie and Willa Cather as autobiographical texts written in the midst of Victorian culture, and also considered how they had addressed the concerns and duties of Victorian adolescence—a far cry from what Andersen and I had been researching when Mannie first joined the project. Equipped to respectfully join in the scholarly conversations about both writers, Mannie made a new and significant contribution to the field.

Now graduated and living permanently in Scotland, Mannie finds that the ripple effects of that project continue. At the invitation of the editor of *Teaching Cather*, the journal in which Andersen and I had first published our essay, Mannie is preparing a portion of her honors thesis for submission. Because the thesis also considered the friendship album in terms of autobiographical writing, Mannie and I have discussed the possibility of submitting a different part of her essay to a journal focused on autobiography theory.

Although Mannie's research path during her undergraduate career was a professional and personal growth experience for her, she was not the only one to benefit from the mentor-fellow association. The close working relationship that she and I developed was the kind I had only previously known with graduate students. As I came to an enhanced understanding of the possibilities of a scholarly relationship between a faculty mentor and an undergraduate researcher, I also began considering what about the experience made our collaboration so successful.

An Undergraduate Research Fellow in Literary Studies: The Student's Perspective Post-Graduation

Amanda Marinello

Although Dr. Funda's narrative may give the impression that I exuded confidence from the very first meeting, I'll admit that coming to a level of self-assurance in my work with other scholars and with my honors thesis project came much more slowly, and only through a series of unexpected events. I was originally planning to attend USU's flight school and conduct research in aircraft design, but a few weeks after I received the undergraduate research fellowship, I was diagnosed with an eye disease that prevented me from passing the required medical for the flight program. I needed a new major, and because I had enjoyed English in high school, I switched and spent my first year as a fellow working with the department's outreach and publicity staff person on projects that included research and writing for a literature-based radio program that aired on Utah Public Radio. However, I knew that this kind of work wasn't the research path that I wanted to pursue. After finishing a class taught by Dr. Funda, I spoke with both her and Susan Andersen about the research they were conducting. As Dr. Funda brought me up to speed about the current status of their project and talked about where I could start, I was relieved that she didn't just say, "So, what do you want to do?" because I still didn't have the vaguest notion about my own project. I was happy to spend the next few months just trying to find answers to Dr. Funda's research questions.

My own research project began to take shape when I came across a confession album survey that had been completed by author J. M. Barrie. I knew very little about Sir Barrie or his work, but had recently seen the film *Finding Neverland*. The film depicts Barrie's relationship with the Llewelyn Davies family, including the effects on the family and Barrie caused by the death of Sylvia Llewelyn Davies from cancer. Having recently lost a close friend to cancer, I became interested in finding more information about Barrie's relationship to the Llewelyn Davies family. I never intended to even mention the album in my report to Dr. Funda, thinking that my interest in Barrie was separate from the research I was performing with her, but as we were discussing what I had found generally on confession albums, I showed her Barrie's album. She was intrigued and encouraged me to do some more research on connections between Barrie and Cather.

Gradually, as I started making connections between Barrie and Cather and the confession album genre, I was able to see how both authors had personal and profound experiences with death that affected their characters and their writing. The result was that I was really working on two different levels: the academic level, searching for angles to make a scholarly contribution; and a personal level, searching for perspectives on loss. I had signed on for literary criticism research, and I had never intended my work to be memoir. At one point, I wrote two copies of my thesis: the one I gave to the committee, focused on confession albums in Victorian culture; and another one following the influence of death on Cather and Barrie. My extensive notes from the Barrie archives include topics that could fill a second thesis, but I used only a smattering of the information in my final thesis. I'm happy that I decided to take that route, because ultimately, my honors thesis was not the place for catharsis. But my personal loss was certainly a significant driving force behind the research. Dr. Funda taught me how to use personal interests as a catalyst to stimulate academic questions, and eventually publication and presentations.

Lessons Learned: The Faculty Perspective

1. Be sure the student takes an active role and is a decision-maker in the faculty-student relationship. Mannie interviewed potential mentors before choosing Funda. A good match between student and mentor is essential; after all, the undergraduate researcher is a potential partner in scholarship. This means that the partners must commit to regular meetings and good communication. The faculty mentor also needs to consider how he or she can contribute to the student's overall educational experience, and this might include introducing the student to other faculty at departmental functions or accompanying the student to a research presentation.

2. Be aware of the ethics of student-centered versus faculty-centered projects. Our goal for undergraduate researchers is to give students practical experience in research, to allow them to witness and *participate in*, firsthand, the world of academic publishing. We are modeling the process of scholarship for students who may have read literary criticism but have little or no experience doing it. The goal for undergraduate research fellows, then, is to correct the disconnect between the kind of scholarship regularly published by their professors and the skills students learn in their coursework.

3. Be reflective and ask students to be reflective as well. In order to make this experience effective, students need to be self-conscious about their research process. A mentor can help them do this by asking them to articulate in meta-narratives what they are doing and learning. Funda wanted Mannie to be aware of how and why she was making the choices for the essay; what it means to do primary, theoretical, and cultural research; and what a scholar does to strike a balance between stimulating further consideration from other scholars and aiming to be exhaustive or to have the last word on a subject. Conversations between mentor and students are as much about the *process* of applying research as they are about the specific research.

4. Be watchful for the transition. Mentors should be hyperaware of when they need to initiate the transition, or evolution, from research assistant working on our research projects to a new phase, where the student is working on her own project. McDorman (2004) defines different models of undergraduate research with faculty mentors. Funda and Mannie began with a faculty-driven collaboration in which the student supplied meaningful contributions to the Cather research. From there, they advanced to a student-driven collaboration, where Mannie was the lead author and final decision-maker on her own project. At that point, the relationship became more reciprocal, and they were able to provide meaningful feedback on each other's projects.

5. Be watchful for interrelated possibilities. One of the best lessons learned during this process is that knowledge is an evolving thing. One project may have many different lives, be made of different component parts, and be applicable in different venues. For instance, Mannie's project moved from tracking down cultural information to adding to the scholarly conversation through her own honors thesis—a document with significance for an audience of Cather scholars, Barrie scholars, and those interested in how to read the form of confession albums as a text that illuminates the motives of a culture. Both Mannie and Scarlet enjoyed a support system including a faculty mentor, the honors program, and the undergraduate research program. This system initiated them into the entire web of academic life, from primary archival research to grant writing.

6. The payoff for faculty in mentoring an exceptional undergraduate can be substantial. Cooper-Rompato, named Teacher of the Year for the English department, enjoyed working with a student who was fascinated by the Middle Ages. Faculty also received credit in tenure and promotion documents for mentoring undergraduates. As this volume's introduction points out, a faculty reward system for mentoring undergraduates must be in place if a culture of undergraduate research is to emerge.

Lessons Learned: The Student Perspective

1. Open communication is a must. Even if there isn't time to meet every week (although that is advisable), it's important that the student and mentor communicate often to ensure that they are still on the right track with their research, and to resolve any confusion. Faculty and program directors can offer suggestions and help even if the questions do not relate directly to research but relate to college life in general.

2. The student should not be afraid to do things herself. Although both Mannie and Scarlet had some initial anxieties, each learned so much more than might have been possible otherwise. Taking risks, they agree, can be a good thing.

3. Help students find the personal stake in a research project. All scholars need a driving force behind their research. Mentors can share why they are interested in their specific field of research, and can assure undergraduate researchers that projects can have personal connections as well as academic ones.

4. Remember that the student is a novice. A faculty mentor should keep in mind that the student is new to conducting genuine research. The mentor should help the student take the research process one step at a time. Mentors can help students keep an even pace and enjoy all aspects of the undergraduate experience.

5. Recognize the payoff for research fellows. For Mannie and Scarlet, not only did the research teach them much about specific areas, but they learned about the research process, time management, and teamwork—skills useful in classes and daily life. Both undergraduate scholars became proficient in using interlibrary loan and databases, even in the special handling of medieval manuscripts. Further, the experience as an undergraduate research fellow opened many doors for Mannie that she had never anticipated. When it became apparent that the fees required to study in Scotland for a semester were beyond her financial abilities, the University of

Strathclyde made an exception because of her project. The title Research Fellow allowed her access to the National Library of Scotland, typically closed to undergraduates, to read J. M. Barrie's personal journals. The Barrie scholars she met with in Scotland were impressed that a university supported such advanced research at an undergraduate level.

Lessons Learned: A Central Administration Perspective by Joyce Kinkead

As associate vice president for research, I am responsible for overseeing undergraduate research on campus, particularly our signature effort, the Undergraduate Research Fellows Program. Although English is my tenure home, I found that integrating fellows into the department was more difficult than I had anticipated. There was, in essence, not a vibrant culture of undergraduate research. Activity that might be viewed as *research* included the regular classroom papers, independent study, directed reading, and thesis writing for honors. Because faculty colleagues were not accustomed to faculty-student scholarly collaborations, they asked questions typical for humanists: What credit do I get for mentoring an undergraduate researcher? Will I be paid for mentoring? What might I have an undergraduate do?

What happened as a result of the partnerships described in these case studies? It became apparent that a student could provide valuable assistance to a faculty member on a research project and lessen the workload, even bringing in information not anticipated by the scholar. The synergy between the student-faculty partners was a factor in enriching both of their projects. Mannie became a gold standard for what an undergraduate could accomplish. Cooper-Rompato and Scarlet took a different tack in pursuing scholarship. Their relationship is still developing as they explore their mutual scholarly interests and also how they work together. They demonstrated that scholarship could be disseminated in a poster format rather than the traditional oral presentation. A more recent fellow, Natalie Marie Hatch, working with Dr. Paul Crumbley, began the year creating didactics for the exhibits in the May Swenson Room in the English department at USU, helped with the bibliography of this volume, and ended the year with a grant that saw her working with several state and federal agencies to memorialize poet Swenson in public arenas.

With the help of my colleagues, we have developed a set of guidelines for humanities faculty that suggests ways in which an undergraduate researcher can be of assistance. We piloted a new undergraduate research assistant program in humanities to enhance the pipeline of student scholars; in this program, faculty members apply for a grant and then choose the student with whom they would like to work. In addition, I have learned that I need to be more proactive about communicating opportunities for student financial support to my colleagues in English. The culture that exists currently operates on a shoestring. The members of the English faculty are pleased to find that we fund students to do grant work, travel to conferences to present, and study abroad. The fact that an English undergraduate (not in the fellows program) won the University Undergraduate Researcher of the Year prize, and was awarded the inaugural Undergraduate Research Fellowship from the state's humanities council, seems to suggest that the culture of undergraduate research is becoming more pervasive in the department.

One of the most heartening aspects of this collaboration was learning that the head of our English department valued highly the mentoring of students by faculty members. "It would look good in your tenure portfolio." This endorsement, not only by the head of a department, but within the tenure/promotion documentation in the faculty code, bodes well for enhancing the culture of undergraduate research. The university undergraduate research fellows provide the lead examples to help us rethink student scholarship in literary studies and to strive for an exciting culture of undergraduate research. These students illuminate the possibilities.

References

Bede. 1955; rev. ed. 1990. *Ecclesiastical History of the English People.* Trans. Leo Sherley-Price. London: Penguin Classics.

Funda, Evelyn and Susan Andersen. 2004. Predicting Cather: Using "Peter" and "The Opinions, Tastes, and Fancies of Wm Cather, M.D." as Introduction. *Teaching Cather* 4.2 (Spring): 4–12.

Kinkead, Joyce. 2008. A Successful University-Wide Model of Undergraduate Research: Utah State University. In *Developing, Promoting, and Sustaining the Undergraduate Research Experience in Psychology*, ed. Richard L. Miller, Robert F. Rycek, Emily Balcetis, Steve T. Barney, Bernard C. Beins, Susan R. Burns, Roy Smith, and Mark E. Ware, 65–68. Washington, DC: Society for the Teaching of Psychology.

McDorman, Todd. 2004. Promoting Undergraduate Research in the Humanities: Three Collaborative Approaches. *CUR Quarterly* 25 (1): 39–42.

Sullivan, Walter. Albert Szent-Gyorgyi Dead; Research Isolated Vitamin C. Obituary. *New York Times*. 25 Oct. 1986.

Chapter Ten

Advancing Research in English through Honors

Christie Fox
Utah State University

The marriage of undergraduate research and honors seems obvious. Honors programs provide opportunities for students to test themselves, to go beyond the classroom experience to engage firsthand in the grasp and creation of knowledge. We actively seek students who are interested in inquiry, in exploration, and in making an original contribution, and we match them with professors who share their passions. We also seek new ways to help students and professors collaborate in the creation of this knowledge. In this chapter I provide an honors director's perspective on undergraduate research in English studies. I describe examples of two forms of undergraduate research in English: the first, a poster presentation that arose from an honors contract in a literary studies class; the second, exemplary undergraduate research conducted by English education students. Both of these cases demonstrate how an honors program can serve as a site for innovation and experimentation to open up greater opportunities for undergraduate research in English.

"Why wouldn't you do honors?" This is the kind of student comment that makes an honors director's heart sing. The two *best* things about honors are, arguably, the more intimate, focused teaching that happens in honors classes that are generally smaller than the university average, and the chance to build a mentor relationship with a professor. Honors programs also contribute to the health and success of the university through recruitment and retention of high-ability students.

In the case of Utah State University (USU), undergraduate research is the key to attracting and keeping the most motivated students. High-ability students are more likely to graduate and, as Bridget Terry Long (2002) notes, provide positive outcomes to their peers in the form of increased intellectual interaction in the classroom. They are also one way to increase faculty satisfaction and retention (2). USU enrolls more than 18,000 undergraduates. We are a land- and space-grant institution in rural Utah, and the majority of our students come from inside Utah. The honors program attracts about 4 percent of the undergraduate population, within the national norm of 3 to 4 percent. We actively recruit students to USU through recruitment nights, special on-campus events, direct mail, and email. As a recruitment tool, an honors emphasis on undergraduate research helps us attract high-ability students who might otherwise leave the state.

High-ability students tend to be interested in hands-on learning and in finding answers for themselves. Tricia Seifert and her coauthors (2007) found that honors programs positively affect students' cognitive development throughout college, particularly in the first year (11). Thus, the honors mission contributes to the overall goals of a university by drawing talented and motivated students; providing them with stimulating, meaningful challenges; and introducing them to the world of (academic) research. Students who engage successfully in undergraduate research learn how to manage time more effectively, how to synthesize and present material to specialized and general audiences (in the important step of dissemination), and how to talk to people about their work. Not all of them will continue on to graduate school. Some will go into industry or participate in a service corps, such as City Year or Teach for America, while others will head to medical or law school. All, however, will find that the tools they've learned as undergraduate researchers help them attain their post-baccalaureate goals.

Creating a Scaffolding of Habits of Mind

It generally has been easier for students in the sciences and the social sciences to create a workable model for turning the traditional honors thesis into an undergraduate research experience, resulting in a paradox. Honors tends to be most popular in the humanities, but these students often have trouble accessing meaningful undergraduate research experiences. At USU, however, we have created a process through which students in all fields work with professors in stages, and both the students and professors have a chance to "try out" the mentor relationship. Most honors programs emphasize undergraduate research through the thesis; we have intentionally created a process that exposes students to undergraduate research in their first year. Then, ideally, they become more involved in undergraduate research as they progress through their majors. Once our goals are made clear to the students and professors, we find that the quality of honors theses and the number of those engaged in undergraduate research increase.

In their first year, honors students enroll in a discipline-based class called Honors Inquiry, in which they hear presentations from professors about the nature of academic inquiry in their discipline.[1] Advanced undergraduate researchers, often from the ranks of our university research fellows, also present their work to the novice researchers. Students in Inquiry try their hand at research. During one semester, the students enrolled in Honors Inquiry for Humanities conducted undergraduate research for the university's anthropology museum, collecting information on objects for which not much data exist. The museum published the students' results on its website: the advanced research skills and real-world application—the museum needs this information—emerged as the strengths of this project.[2] Asking students to dive into research in the first year rather than wait for the honors thesis helps them to define what "research" means in the humanities, and to get involved in the shaping of knowledge.

Once students begin upper-division coursework in their major, they start honors "contracts," in which they work one-on-one with professors on independent, ungraded, extra work (a common feature of honors programs). The outcomes of these contracts range from annotated bibliographies to conference presentations. The goals include strengthening professor-student mentor relationships, leading to stronger letters of recommendation, and building students' research skills.

Honors contracts further the scaffolding of habits of mind onto which the writing of a thesis can easily be drafted. Students are required to complete twelve credit hours of such contracts to graduate with honors. These are not undergraduate research per se, but can be, and they provide an opportunity for a student and professor to work together for a semester on a class-based project. The twelve credits allow students to get to know a variety of professors better and to begin to delve into a topic that they might choose for the senior thesis. At USU, all honors students are required to complete a thesis for graduation; we encourage students to turn this project into undergraduate research, and we equip them with the tools to do so. Honors students routinely cite their honors thesis as the best experience of their education, as it gives them the confidence and skills to work independently, with the benefit of a research mentor. As Richard Light (2001) notes, "The key point is designing a project from scratch, rather than simply carrying out professors' instructions. This is hard work, yet students praise it as an especially powerful kind of learning experience." Light identifies the clue to encourage undergraduate research in honors theses: students should be guided to take on the work of undergraduate research rather than do an extended research paper (97–98).

Contracts help students determine the best way to design an independent project, but students still need assistance in carrying out these projects. In 2006, we introduced an Honors Thesis Guidebook[3] and a preliminary thesis proposal—due a full year before graduation—that asks students to frame their theses in terms of research questions, such as "What creative activities, research questions, and/or design features are foundational to your thesis?" and "How will you discover answers to research questions, create artistry, and/or develop design projects?" We inaugurated a course titled Thesis Research and Writing, team-taught by librarians and open to students in any college, designed to give students the research skills necessary for an honors thesis based in undergraduate research. The class, taken in the student's penultimate year, provides a supportive community of the kind more commonly seen in master's or PhD dissertation groups. Students are required to present their honors thesis work in the interest of dissemination as well as for the experience of public presentations, as noted by Joan Digby (1985). Students then archive a copy of their thesis or project in the thesis library in the honors office and online, in our digital commons.

The Honors English Program: Centers of Inquiry and Experimentation

English honors students initially approach honors contracts as opportunities to write additional papers. Once we can expose students to the types of research their professors are doing and provide them avenues into that research, they can reimagine contracts as sites to experiment with their own research questions, and as places to bring in their own interdisciplinary drives and experiences. Recent English honors contracts have propelled students to seek funding for research in Brazil, and to expand a case study in social justice learning into an undergraduate research-focused honors thesis. In this chapter I describe three other examples of English students reaching beyond the additional paper and into undergraduate research. These cases are atypical, but with solid models, we hope to encourage more English students to incorporate undergraduate research into their theses.

The Honors English Poster Presentation

Students easily create projects or devise research questions, but they sometimes struggle when it comes to presentation. We needed to reinvent the senior honors project in English for students in all tracks of English, including literary studies and English education. We found a novel way for the students to present their findings—the poster, a medium traditional to the sciences. In one case, Amber Bowden worked with Professor Phebe Jensen to research the laws regarding attire (known as sumptuary laws) in Elizabethan England, and how actors and theaters actively subverted these laws, perhaps leading eventually to their repeal. Amber has a background in high school theater and an interest in textiles, so for her the project was mapping a rigorous academic dimension onto something that already interested her. Her project involved researching and creating a period costume design for Shakespeare's *King Lear*.

Amber's poster and our chance to experiment grew out of an opportunity to take her and another undergraduate researcher to the 2007 National Collegiate Honors Conference (NCHC).

Although there are student research panels at this conference, most of the presentations focus on honors best practices. A student-research poster session runs parallel to the institutional presentations. Though the majority of the posters represent the STEM areas (science, technology, engineering, and math) and social sciences, a few humanities disciplines, such as folklore and theater, participate in the poster sessions. English is rarely represented.

The process of creating Amber's poster was an adventure, a first for all of us. We were all fairly familiar with posters as they are displayed in science and engineering buildings on campus and at the undergraduate research day on campus. But we had no experience in turning an English paper into a poster, although as other chapters in this collection suggest, poster presentations are becoming increasingly common for undergraduate research presentations in English.

Online guides and suggestions provide clear parameters in terms of font size and organization—but they remain very science oriented in their language. Amber did not at first think she had a research question, a methodology, or results. Once we started talking, however, she realized that she did have a research question and most certainly had results, even if we do not normally call them that: she had reached a conclusion from her research and answered her initial question of the relationship between sumptuary laws and theater. After six drafts, the poster was visually interesting and contributed to our understanding of dress and class in Elizabethan England. The most exciting part, of course, was the actual poster session at NCHC. English majors, theater majors, and professors made a beeline to Amber's poster, and she was engaged throughout the hour.

What strikes me most about this experience is not that we could turn Amber's information into something visually interesting, but that the poster format fostered a scholarly conversation, exactly what we ask students to attempt in papers. People took an interest in, asked questions about, and contributed to her work. English students can get caught up in the beauty of their language; honors students in particular can be too obsessed about the words they choose rather than the merits of their argument. Turning an English project into a poster forces the student (and mentor) to think differently about the work. It further helps students develop their ideas and determine what contribution they are making. They must be prepared to defend their thesis statement and research methods, and to field questions about the larger implications of their work. I found it to be a remarkable method of communicating an academic project.

English Education: Practice-Oriented Undergraduate Research

In English education, we often see students filled with enthusiasm about bringing new techniques into their classrooms. We have learned to match that enthusiasm with an action-based approach to undergraduate research and the honors thesis. English education students are eager to learn how to improve their teaching skills but often are less interested in doing library research. Connecting them to undergraduate research allows them to conduct research that is immediately applicable to their classroom through *action-based research*, a paradigm that involves practitioners in finding ways to improve their practice (Dick and Swepson 1997). Turning teachers—or in this case, English education students—into principal investigators (PI) in the research project ensures that the research question stays focused on applicability while relying on contemporary theory and an exploration of what is already known about the subject. Student teachers may then experiment with a new technique grounded in theory and historical perspective.

Unfortunately, we often lose education majors at the thesis stage. They complete fascinating contracts, but balk at trying to tackle a research-based thesis while student teaching. Action-based research allows students to see the immediate applicability of undergraduate research and can retain English education students in undergraduate research and honors. A 1988 article in *Action in Teacher Education*, the journal of the Association of Teacher Educators, highlighted the potential of honors programs to attract high-ability students to education programs (Reed 1988). The article noted the option for students to participate in faculty research projects, yet the author omitted the possibility that students themselves could design and implement research projects that would enhance their efficacy in the classroom, perhaps because the idea of undergraduate research was still developing.

Since 2002, at least one English education student per year at USU conducted undergraduate research for the senior honors thesis. Two projects with direct ramifications in the K–12 classroom involved collecting information directly from students and teachers through participant observation or interviewing. Research that involves working directly with people requires a different approach from library research, and students working in the schools may have to acquire institutional review board (IRB) approval. The IRB on campus ensures that all research involving human subjects is conducted ethically and with full disclosure. We require students to include IRB approval in their thesis proposal; learning the ethics of working with people often makes a strong honors contract.

One 1999 thesis focused on English as a Second Language (ESL) programs in the state, centering on the most developed ESL program in Salt Lake City. The student combined a substantial amount of library research with data she collected from the school district and the schools. She shadowed four English language learners (ELLs), one at each "level" in one Salt Lake City school. She found that the students who were better integrated with non–language learners and had more formal schooling before coming to the United States were more likely to be successful in learning fluent English and assimilating into the U.S. educational system. Her astute conclusion incorporated her research methods to make recommendations for the state, district, schools, and individual teachers, and can help us better understand the experiences of immigrants from countries with less developed public education.

A second example also focused on ELLs. In 2007, Kimberly Call Gleason combined a strong love of poetry with an interest in teaching English as a foreign language. Gleason reported "despis[ing] the redundant, boring drills" most often used to teach English pronunciation, and asserted that "poetry could serve the same purpose in an interesting way" (ii). She felt strongly that "the same practice that occurs in ten pronunciation drills could also occur in a single poem," so she embarked on a lesson plan with an individual ELL, resulting in her honors thesis. Gleason brought in poems she loved from a variety of periods and authorial backgrounds, including Christina Rossetti, Carl Sandburg, Gwendolyn Brooks, Emily Dickinson, Edgar Allan Poe, and Shel Silverstein. She learned that it worked better to introduce a small amount of poetry into each class rather than spend all day on it. This method piqued student interest and prevented fatigue with the form or the process.

Gleason blended a study of the theoretical research behind the teaching of pronunciation with a field study. She found that short, interesting poems kept the students' interest better than traditional textbooks: "I love Mondays," the student reported, "because I like to see the new poem." Poetry motivated this student to become interested in reading, which was positively correlated with better academic performance.

Gleason's desire to theorize and quantify what she did created a formal academic study out of a semester of student teaching. Traditionally, student teaching involves placement in a classroom with a supervising teacher. The student gains experience in creating and delivering lesson plans, working with diverse students, and learning how schools work. When combined with action-based research, the student-teaching semester can be a powerful tool for innovation that instills the expectation that teaching should be a site of inquiry and excitement.

Honors Programs and Undergraduate Research in English: Happily Pushing the Envelope

Students and parents routinely ask me, "Why should I do honors? What are the benefits?" I tell them that the best benefits are intrinsic: knowing that you did more than we asked of you, and in the case of undergraduate research, knowing that you contributed to the larger body of knowledge in the field. But there are also tangible benefits. In addition to learning time management and study skills, students engaged in undergraduate research in English studies learn very quickly how to synthesize large bodies of information, and to encapsulate that information into easily digestible pieces for a poster or presentation. They learn how to distill what is important about a book, an argument, or a piece of scholarship, and they learn communication skills. A reader could correctly argue that any English student should learn these skills, but students should realize that their work is meaningful, and that realization is most likely to happen during the dissemination of undergraduate research.

Honors and undergraduate research are inextricably linked at USU, where undergraduate research helps our students achieve excellence. Honors programs encourage innovation on campus and can build the scaffolding to support students engaged in undergraduate research. I hope that honors programs can continue to be centers of inquiry and experimentation as we develop undergraduate research in English studies. The number of English education students doing action-based research has increased, along with the number of literary studies students presenting their work at conferences, and creative writers submitting their work for publication. We are generating excitement in English, as we see a jump in English students completing contracts and graduating with honors. Students and professors are taking advantage of the scaffolding offered by honors contracts to find the best avenues into undergraduate research, either through traditional literary studies models or through action-based research; both culminate in poster presentations and other opportunities for dissemination beyond the honors library.

Notes

1. For the most part, the instructors of these classes (in a typical semester, we offer nine sections) are professors who are active in undergraduate research. Last year, three of the contributors to this volume spoke to my class, Honors Inquiry for the Humanities. Find more information on classes at http://honors.usu.edu.

2. See http://www.usu.edu.

3. See http://honors.usu.edu.

References

Dick, Bob, and Pam Swepson. 1997. Resource Papers in Action Research: Action Research FAQ: "Frequently Asked Questions File." Web.

Digby, Joan. 1985. Should NCHC Sponsor a National Honors Thesis Archive? *The National Honors Report* 6 (1): 16.

Light, Richard J. 2001. *Making the Most of College: Students Speak Their Minds*. Cambridge, MA: Harvard University Press.

Long, Bridget Terry. 2002. *Attracting the Best: The Use of Honors Programs to Compete for Students*. Chicago: Spencer Foundation.

Reed, Daisy. 1988. Honors Programs in Teacher Education. *Action in Teacher Education* 10 (3): 35–41.

Seifert, Tricia A., Ernest T. Pascarella, Nicholas Colangelo, and Susan Assouline. 2007. The Effects of Honors Program Participation on Experiences of Good Practices and Learning Outcomes. *Journal of College Student Development* 48 (1): 57–74. http://findarticles.com/p/articles/mi_qa3752/is_200701/ai_n17220520/?tag=content;col1.

CHAPTER ELEVEN

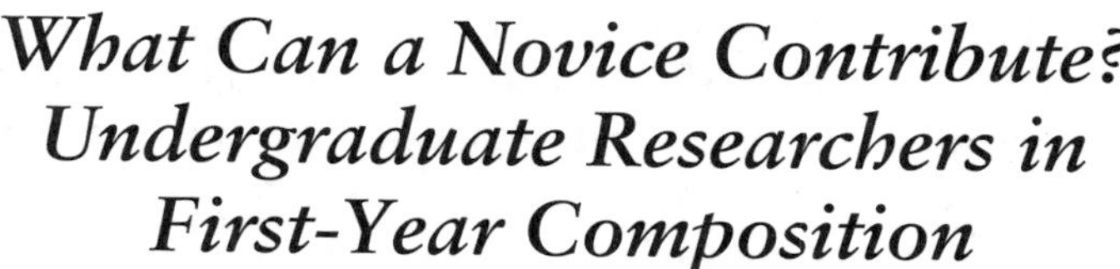

What Can a Novice Contribute? Undergraduate Researchers in First-Year Composition

DOUGLAS DOWNS
Montana State University

ELIZABETH WARDLE
University of Central Florida

Writing teachers are familiar with the many complaints about and characterizations of first-year students' research papers: they are shallow, regurgitative, "grave robbing" (Russell 2002). If we listen to Stanley Fish (2002), this is perhaps all that first-years are capable of producing:

> [Students] have been allowed to believe that their opinions—formed by nothing, supported by even less—are interesting. [. . .] The instructor who hears them coming from the mouths of his or her students should immediately tell them, "Check your opinions, your ideas, your views at the door; they are not fungible currency here." [. . .] Every dean should forthwith insist that all composition courses teach grammar and rhetoric and nothing else. (par. 13, 14, 16)

But the 1998 Boyer Commission report, *Reinventing Undergraduate Education*, rejects such passive absorption for undergraduates in general: "The ideal embodied in this report would turn the prevailing undergraduate culture of receivers into a culture of inquirers, a culture in which faculty, graduate students, and undergraduates share an adventure of discovery" (16). The Council for Undergraduate Research (CUR) has long argued that undergraduates can do much more than regurgitate if they are given the opportunity and appropriate guidance.

The Boyer Commission's recommendation that "undergraduates should have the opportunity to work in primary materials, perhaps linked to their professors' research projects" (1998, 17), implies that such research will take place in the major, at an upper level. Generally, only upper-level undergraduates in a major have had the opportunity to form relationships with professors and read enough in the field to be able to contribute in a meaningful way to a research project. Therefore, we wonder, along with the contributors to the fall 2008 *CUR Quarterly*, which focuses on "Undergraduate Research: An Early Start," whether there is a place for genuine, contributive research in first-year general education courses, particularly in first-year composition. This course is often charged with teaching "the research paper," but such papers are usually written in only a few weeks, outside any disciplinary knowledge, for a nonspecialist reader. Still, as Joyce Kinkead (2007) has demonstrated, composition courses already contain teaching and assignments that offer groundwork for students to become undergraduate researchers later. Is it possible to have students from many majors, with a writing studies or English studies instructor, apply that groundwork directly in the composition course? We believe it is. In this chapter we outline what we believe genuine, contributive research might look like in first-year composition and how that experience can benefit students.

A Picture of Contributive Research in First-Year Composition

While first-year composition courses can be focused in many ways, we will argue specifically for courses whose content is writing itself, including discourse, literacy, rhetoric, composition processes, new media, and the like; we believe that writing as course content increases the likelihood that the research students conduct will be genuinely contributive. We'll cover some reasons for this focus briefly, referring readers to our 2007 *College Composition and Communication* (*CCC*) article "Teaching about Writing, Righting Misconceptions" for fuller explanation.

First, a writing course must primarily teach *writing*. Writing courses with some content other than writing—say, environmental issues—must teach *two* fields of knowledge if students are to write contributively. The likelihood of students gaining sufficient background in a content field while the course remains focused on writing is greatest when the course content is writing *about* writing. Second, undergraduate research demands mentoring by faculty in the field to which students are contributing. Although it is true that many writing instructors are *not* experts in rhetoric and composition, it seems reasonable to believe that the average writing instructor is far the greater authority on writing and literacy than on (continuing our example) environmental issues. A third argument for writing-about-writing research is the relative accessibility of scholarly conversations on writing-related subjects. Composition studies has not only had less time to specialize than have most other academic fields (its major professional organization forming only in 1949), but it has also been a field with an ethic of inclusion and a focus on pedagogy; all of these factors yield accessibility in both the field's questions and its language. Unlike fields such as environmental biology or hydrology, then, composition allows first-year students to garner a reasonably good understanding of much of the work in the field. Another source of that accessibility is our fourth and most important reason for advocating writing about writing: students have firsthand, daily experience with language, discourse, literacy, writing, and rhetoric. If contributive research emerges from genuine questions that puzzle the researcher, all students should be able to identify a research project on writing that emerges from their own experiences.

We also find writing-about-writing courses effective because excellent opportunities for dissemination of students' research on writing and rhetoric already exist. Unlike many other fields, composition studies has an international, peer-reviewed undergraduate journal, *Young Scholars in Writing*, with a feature on first-year composition students' research on writing and rhetoric (coedited by Douglas Downs). The field has also long fostered undergraduate conference presentations, particularly through its work on writing centers. First-year composition programs have pioneered more local dissemination in the form of "celebrations of student writing" at several institutions nationwide. Finally, the past year has seen the emergence of a new venue for first-year students' work on writing and literacy: the National Conversation on Writing, a project of the Council of Writing Program Administrators' Network for Media Action, which offers a Web 2.0 clearinghouse for writers researching and talking with others about writing nationwide. When students research on writing and literacy, they can upload their work to the site for review and posting.

In our own writing-about-writing research classes, we ask that students begin by reading articles that might relate to or contrast with their own experiences with writing. As they review Sondra Perl's (1979) research on "Tony" or Nancy Sommers's (1980) research on students' understanding of revision, we ask them to explore their own experiences with writing or their own understandings of revision. Out of such reading and reflection come questions that serve as the basis for research projects, questions that are meaningful to the student and have generally not been answered in published literature. For example, our students have looked at how sports impact boys' reading habits and attitudes, how various kinds of music affect reading and writing, how students at a particular university understand plagiarism, and so on. These projects tend to take up most of a fifteen-week semester, in close imitation of the way professional scholars conduct research, with at least some opportunity to collect data, reflect, analyze, write, revise, and consult with others. We also have students conduct shorter research projects that, again, begin with their own experiences and questions: students keep logs of the kinds of writing they do over several weeks, or the technologies that mediate their writing, and then compare their processes and purposes for the various texts and technologies. They keep logs of the writing they do in different classrooms, and then compare conventions and purposes across disciplines. They also conduct mini-discourse community ethnographies of groups with which they are familiar (say, church or sorority or workplace); later they conduct mini-discourse community ethnographies of language use in their desired majors. All of this work emerges from genuine questions and requires some grounding in published research and in fieldwork.

Published examples of student papers about writing and rhetoric are available to offer concrete examples of genuine inquiry at the first-year level. The inaugural first-year feature in *Young Scholars in Writing* included a commentary on the content of first-year composition (Strasser 2008), a survey-based study on perceptions of "classic" literature (Augino 2008), an ethnography of the punk scene in mid-1980s Waco (Pleasant 2008), and an interview-based study of the effects of past praise of writing on future literacy experiences (Jackson 2008). The 2009 volume included rhetorical analyses of presidential campaign speeches by first-year students. In the 2010 volume being edited as this chapter goes to press, first-year writers are revising studies on the positive and negative effects of blogging in recovery from eating disorders, on a "rhetoric of magic" in environmental discourse, on the effects of direct grammar instruction in second-language instruction, and on other equally intriguing subjects. In every case, these papers say something that hasn't been said before. They were researched and drafted during a semester in a first-year composition course. They use professional methods. They were never conceived as library research papers, regurgitation of sources to "take a stand." Rather, they respond to assignments that required primary research on an open question of import to the writer and a field, and a written account of that research and its implications. The important point, neither subtle nor intuitive, to understand about this difference in purpose is that a library research paper, for all its hope of having the writer reach a new insight, is not learning based on discovery new to *other* inquirers. Such discovery is simply not expected. In stark contrast, the teachers who made the assignments that resulted in these *Young Scholars in Writing* submissions explicitly *did* expect to read something in their students' papers that they did not already know.

What Undergraduate Research in First-Year Composition Can Offer

Clearly, first-year students cannot conduct the same sort of research that upper-division or graduate students can. They are not yet immersed in the work of a field, have not yet read broadly on any one subject, and do not have relationships with faculty in their chosen fields to serve as apprentice researchers. Yet we believe that teaching contributive research in the first year can have important benefits even if the student does not actually end up making a contribution: it can teach habits of mind and an understanding of scholarship; it can teach students how to read and use difficult scholarly texts; it can teach writing as transactional and genres as content- and purpose-driven; and it should result in better transfer (generalization) of writing-related knowledge to other courses. While we can anticipate concerns that first-year research could lower the standard for what counts as "research," we see these other benefits as lessening that pressure: success might be viewed as a contribution to the immediate class's knowledge rather than to a discipline in the pursuit of these other benefits. These students, engaged in small-scale but meaningful research in the first year, gain an understanding of what research is and how it is done that can be built on in the following years.

Teach Habits of Mind

Conducting primary research in writing courses teaches writerly and scholarly habits of mind. Sarah Wyatt (2005), in an argument for the efficacy of original experimentation in inquiry-based learning, offers examples of what students can learn from contributive research that they *must* learn in college but are unlikely to learn in many other ways:

> Students, and teachers, have been groomed to believe there is a single correct answer and that education is about finding that answer. With original research there is no "right" answer to find; there is only data to be collected. Students must learn to think and to evaluate that data, and trust the process of so doing. They also must be willing to be wrong. (84)

In other words, training in contributive research does teach ways of thinking that benefit not only future graduate students but also the vast majority of college students, those who won't have research careers. Students' research in college is worth their time and ours, even as they pursue other directions afterward.

Therefore, even when students try but don't succeed at conducting contributive research in their first year, there is great value in the *attempt*. Failure to contribute is not synonymous with failure to learn; even failure in contribution does not diminish the value of framing undergraduate education as learning through discovery. It makes more sense to have students try to contribute and not succeed than it does to simply assume first-year students to be incapable of contribution, locking them out of the discovery culture as a whole. In arguing thus, we concur with Alan Jenkins and Mick Healey (2007) that the value of undergraduate research has to be considered more broadly than just in terms of students' actual contributions: "To say that the student learns as a researcher, is to state that the university, particularly through its curricula, supports students in gaining new insights and opportunities to learn about research and the way knowledge is constructed" (210). Institutions that would claim a culture of undergraduate research consequently seem obligated to include first-year students on principle alone.

Teach How to Read and Use Scholarship

As most teachers can attest, undergraduate students do not come to us knowing how to read scholarly research; much less do they know what to do with it, or even that they could do something with it. Students who can successfully integrate a *Time* magazine commentary into their marijuana paper do not necessarily know how to use scholarly articles and books. Reading is no mere act of text recognition (words on a page); it's an act of constructing representations of the writer's meaning by integrating text *and context* with prior knowledge. As Christina Haas and Linda Flower (1988) have demonstrated, younger students tend not to read rhetorically, understanding that the meaning of the text is contingent on the writer's motivation and the circumstances of its writing. Explicit reading instruction that demonstrates how scholars read and has students practice reading is essential to students' abilities to conduct their own research. Teaching students the "moves" (Swales 1990) in research introductions or the types of citation practices used in different disciplines (Hyland 2002), as well as the conventions of various scholarly texts, can help them focus on content and research questions in a way that supports their own research interests. No matter what their intended major, students who can read and use scholarly sources after completing first-year composition are better prepared to conduct research than those who cannot. And the fact that they are receiving this reading instruction in the composition classroom itself increases the likelihood that they can do unexpected contributive work.

Teach Writing as Transactional, Genres as Emerging from Purpose

It is by now axiomatic in rhetoric and composition that writing instruction must be situated—we cannot teach "writing" generally. Condemnation of "general writing skills instruction" is most focused in Joseph Petraglia's (1995) volume *Reconceiving Writing, Rethinking Writing Instruction*, where, for example, David Russell (1995) argues that imagining general writing skills is equivalent to imagining "general ball handling skills" for all sports involving a ball, from table tennis to American football (57–60). Petraglia labels unsituated writing assignments as "pseudotransactional" (92), asserting that first-year composition has specialized in such assignments rather than writing that genuinely participates in specific rhetorical situations. Gerald Graff and Andrew Hoberek (1999) echo this sentiment in their *College English* commentary "Hiding It from the Kids," pointing out that students "who submit writing samples that are studiously pointless would never think to speak that way in real life. It took them years of education to learn to speak with no context to no one" (252).

In marked contrast, scholarly inquiry is some of the most situated writing that teachers can assign, as contributive research grounds writing firmly in tangible audiences and purposes. As Graff and Hoberek assert, students who attempt to answer the questions most basic to scholarly inquiry—"so what?" and "who cares?"—will be situating their writing realistically (1999). The field has concrete evidence that students learn tremendously from seeing actual readers attempt to *use* their writing. Literacy researcher Gert Rijlaarsdam (2008) asked elementary students to write process instructions, watch readers try to use them (but not get direct feedback from those users), and then revise. Another group of writers did not get to watch readers but instead got additional practice writing. The group that ultimately produced the best writing was the group that wrote the least but saw readers attempting to use their document. Writers travel miles farther in the presence of genuine attempts to use their writing than in endless loops of "process" that lack any actual transaction with readers.

The connection between that finding and undergraduate research in first-year composition will be clear to teachers who have tried to publish: the attempt to create contributive writing is so genuinely recursive and interactional that writers truly get a sense of how their writing is *used* by readers, and thus where its shortcomings are. Research conducted by Downs, Heidi Estrem, and Susan Thomas (2009) on submissions to *Young Scholars in Writing* shows exactly this: the most striking aspect of students' publishing process was the interaction between readers and writers making sense of feedback by some of their intended but heretofore imagined readers.

We also want to stress that first-year students need instructors to *show* options for dissemination in order to fully imagine them. Bringing copies of *Young Scholars in Writing* into class, asking others who have presented at conferences to present to the class on those experiences, demo-ing websites that accept student work, showing videos of previous local conferences—all are strategies instructors can use to offer their students tangible goals for dissemination of their work.

Facilitate Transfer

A major consideration for first-year composition is (or should be) transfer, or generalization, from first-year composition to other classes. Much research has demonstrated the lack of transfer from school activities generally; the minimal research on writing-related transfer from first-year composition seems even bleaker. There is little evidence on whether and how students later deploy knowledge gained in first-year composition, in part because transfer seems to depend as much on context and situation at the far end as it does on first-year composition (Wardle 2007, 82). But there are ways to better encourage and facilitate transfer, and some of those methods are natural to research-based writing. For example, teaching researched writing as transactional, and genres as emerging from context and purpose, can encourage the meta-awareness about writing needed for transfer. Teaching ways of reading scholarship, and ways of understanding the conventions employed in that scholarship, teaches flexible principles rather than rigid rules, again encouraging transfer to other contexts. Elizabeth Wardle's (2007) longitudinal study of students post-first-year composition does show that the writing-about-writing version of first-year composition can "help students think about writing in the university, the varied conventions of different disciplines, and their own writing strategies in light of various assignments and expectations" (82). Although undergraduate research in first-year composition is too new for clear data on transfer to have emerged, there is at least complementarity, then, between what would be required to teach for generalization beyond first-year composition and what first-year composition as undergraduate research does.

We imagine an undergraduate research experience that sees first-year composition as the entry point and researched theses in the major as final exit points. In first-year composition, students learn how to read and use scholarly texts, how to ask meaningful questions, how to seek out answers to those questions, and how to share their findings with others. These are practices and habits of mind that can set the stage for deeper research in their chosen fields. The exact methods used in first-year composition are less important than an understanding of what methods are; that the research projects are perfectly designed and carried out is less important than an understanding that research projects should have an intentional design (along with at least a plausible possibility of dissemination, though most projects may not ultimately reach that stage). Universities that want a rich undergraduate experience should look carefully at the possibilities of first-year composition as the place where expectations are set and appropriate habits of mind are taught. English departments (which usually house first-year composition programs) should thus consider how the first-year general-education courses they host and staff fit with other undergraduate research efforts in English studies and across the university.

Impediments to Contributive First-Year Research

If teaching research as genuine contribution in first-year composition were easy, it would already be common. Teachers' own attitudes (for example, as embodied by Fish) can be a clear impediment to large-scale implementation, particularly in a course like first-year composition that is taught by such a wide variety of instructors with various levels of knowledge and preparation. Other impediments include views on how writing should be assessed (that is, whether researched writing can be as "error free" as shorter, more polished papers), problems gaining human subjects' approval, views of writing that might see collaboration as plagiarism, and the limited time available for large-scale research projects.

Teacher Attitudes and Training

Solving many, if not most, teaching problems is often a matter of attitudes, expectations, and ways of thinking. We find this to be true of building undergraduate research into first-year composition courses. Perhaps the most important attitude is respect for and belief in students themselves—what they know and what they're capable of achieving. One way of demonstrating this respect is by believing that students can exceed our expectations. Very often, they will. Such respect must also be demonstrated in our willingness to mentor (not just teach). Faculty must be *present* to students who seek their guidance and perspective, just as in higher-level subject area courses. Undergraduate researcher Amber Watson's (2008) work on how undergraduates create contributive research suggests that mentors help students understand not just subject matter, but institutional and professional structures and opportunities that are otherwise invisible to undergraduates. Mentors show students aspects of conducting research that don't appear in the published results: how to get funding, how to find calls for papers, how to submit to conferences and prepare manuscripts for submission.

Writing teachers may also need to check their own conceptions of writing. They should be aware of the distinction between recitative and contributive research, as well as the difference between writing to learn and writing to contribute. They should also be aware of the many double standards entrenched in traditional research instruction that no longer work in contributive research. For example, in traditional research instruction, students often are not allowed to include opinion unsupported by sources; in contrast, researchers use research specifically in order to think and say things that others have not. Many writing teachers have simply never compared what they themselves were taught about research writing, and thus continue to teach, to what researchers actually do. Further, the nature of contingent labor in first-year composition instruction means that many writing teachers aren't themselves actively researching. Because most do have at least MA degrees (and some others are graduate students working toward them), they would need to rely on their own graduate experiences in order to guide students' processes. They might, however, want to research along with their students, and take research classes and institutional review board (IRB) training to supplement their previous training.

Standards for Evaluating Writing

One other necessary shift in instructor attitudes pertains to evaluation of writing. Since its inception, first-year composition has been understood by most stakeholders—university administrators and faculty, writing instructors, and students—as devoted to and measured by the creation of perfect *products*—shiny, flawless documents. Just as with today's SAT writing exam, *what a writer says* is of far less concern than the fluency and correctness with which it is said. This attitude is what made David Bartholomae's (1985) essay "Inventing the University" groundbreaking: he made writing instructors ask themselves which deserves the higher grade, a perfectly written piece of fluff, or a complex piece that takes risks and stretches the writer but winds up imperfect? This was a radical idea in 1985, and is unfortunately almost as radical now—but it's an idea that teachers of contributive research in first-year composition must embrace; to ask first-years to try their hand at contributive research entails big risks and reduces time available for proofing and polishing. Teachers need to look for the merit in students' work somewhere under the surface perfection, because even the best first-year research paper may feel rough and unfinished. Downs's experience editing submissions for the first-year feature in *Young Scholars in Writing* suggests that, more than upper-division students' submissions, first-year submissions require significant additional work. However, the published articles demonstrate what the results of that additional effort can be.

This approach to first-year composition demands that teachers carefully consider evaluation, collaboration, and research ethics. How does one evaluate "unfinished" work, or assignments that emphasize accomplishing particular thinking or research work rather than refining a perfect prose style? If evaluating refinement is important, can that evaluation be delayed—as through portfolio grading—while other evaluation, of engagement or progress, happens earlier in the semester? Ultimately, what needs deciding is, as always, (1) what is important to evaluate, and (2) how to evaluate it. The same analytical challenge applies to building community: finding points where students working on related but separate projects can contribute to one another's work; or using large-scale curricular moves, such as whole-class collaboration on a research problem by having small teams investigate particular aspects of it. The curricular question is, what assignments and uses of class time will allow students to assist and learn from each other and build on each other's work as research communities do? Expect such efforts to be met by lack of student understanding—after reading scholarship, collaboration is perhaps the biggest gap in students' grasp of how research works. Writing teachers must fight years of misconception in teaching students that professionals don't write alone.

Collaboration

Students aren't the only ones who falsely understand writing as a solitary activity; their teachers often set up course assignments that perpetuate this myth, even as those teachers do their own work with the help of others. Even in the humanities, which value "lone-genius" research, researchers form communities that share and develop their members' work. Such research communities directly refute the myth that brilliance happens in the absence of interaction. Yet first-year composition research instruction traditionally turns students into islands working on choose-your-own-adventure problems (usually personal positions on social issues) without reference to each other. This arrangement ignores the possibilities, both for teaching how research actually works and for getting it accomplished, created when a class works on related problems, as is easily arranged in writing-about-writing courses. Building first-year composition research communities has long been advocated—see Michael Kleine's (1987) work on inviting students to research as faculty do, and James Reither's (1985) critique of the isolationist "process" instruction. However, the field has largely ignored such calls.

Time

If assigning students to work alone is one way teachers expect their students to adhere to requirements that they themselves do not face, then requiring students to complete "research" in a very short time is another such double standard. Many semester-length first-year composition courses feature a five-to-eight-week library research paper as a culminating project—a window within which most academics would not be able to produce much. Wardle has piloted linking first- and second-semester first-year composition courses so that students conduct preliminary research on their question in the first semester and primary research in the second. This pilot enabled some exceptionally underprepared students to produce thoughtful, contributive research projects. Such a system may not be an option at many schools, but the principle holds: expect that students can conduct quality research in direct relation to the amount of time they have to do it.

We should make the most of whatever time is available by ensuring that most or all assignments contribute to the project. The assignments, while teaching important functions and skills, should also scaffold the project: exploratory writing leading to research questions, research proposals, source summaries, annotated bibliographies, reviews of literature, separate paper sections (such as Methods), abstracts and presentations—all build to a "main" written project. It is important to ensure that assignments are recognizable and teachable genres, and equally important that students can learn without perfecting such scaffolding projects. Teachers can worry less about what students can perfect than about which assignments will help them learn about writing and accomplish research.

IRB

Contributive research in first-year composition—particularly writing-about-writing classes—may present ethical challenges involving human subjects. At the least, classes need significant instruction about guidelines for ethical research. Beyond that, teachers at some institutions will need to consider arrangements for IRB approval of undergraduate, course-based human-subjects research. If a given IRB reserves to itself oversight of individual student research projects and lacks a system for turning review over to the course instructor, large-scale undergraduate research may not be feasible. But the undergraduate research movement is giving more and more IRBs cause to create systems that do let instructors oversee their students' research rather than requiring IRB review of projects. (It helps that most writing-about-writing research is relatively low risk.) In any event, teachers do need to consider how students' primary research is conducted safely and ethically.

Conclusion

Ultimately, we are arguing for undergraduate research as a vertical, comprehensive experience beginning in the first year. Our notion of first-year composition as a site of truly contributive undergraduate research makes such verticality feasible. What is required is a first-year composition class that seeks to instill scholarly habits of mind by encouraging students to ask and answer, via primary research, genuine questions that stem from their own experiences and their reading of published scholarship. Such a course, while unable to teach the methods and body of knowledge of all disciplines, can, by engaging students in its own scholarly field and research, teach them about the concept of methods, about the necessity of research design, and about the rewards of sharing genuine research with others—from classmates all the way to a national professional audience. Students who have completed such first-year composition courses will move on to their other classes viewing research as the norm. The burden is then on those other courses to provide further research and mentoring opportunities.

References

Augino, Lauren. 2008. Classic Is as Classic Does. *Young Scholars in Writing: Undergraduate Research in Writing and Rhetoric* 5: 123–30.

Bartholomae, David. 1985. Inventing the University. In *When a Writer Can't Write: Studies in Writer's Block and Other Composing-Process Problems*, ed. Mike Rose, 134–65. New York: Guilford Press.

Boyer Commission on Educating Undergraduates in the Research University, Shirley Strum Kenny (chair). 1998. *Reinventing Undergraduate Education: A Blueprint for America's Research Universities*. Stony Brook: State University of New York.

Downs, Douglas, Heidi Estrem, and Susan Thomas, with Ruth Johnson, Claire O'Leary, Emily Strasser, and Anita Varma. n.d. Learning with Students: Young Scholars Making Writing Visible in the Writing Classroom. In *Teaching with Student Texts*, ed. Charles Paine, Joseph Harris, and John Miles. Unpublished manuscript.

Downs, Douglas, and Elizabeth Wardle. 2007. Teaching about Writing, Righting Misconceptions: (Re)Envisioning "First-Year Composition" as "Introduction to Writing Studies." *College Composition and Communication* 58 (4): 552–84.

Fish, Stanley. 2002. Say It Ain't So. *Chronicle of Higher Education*, June 21. http://chronicle.com/article/Say-It-Aint-So/46137.

Graff, Gerald, and Andrew Hoberek. 1999. Opinion: Hiding It from the Kids (with Apologies to Simon and Garfunkel). *College English* 62 (2): 242–54.

Haas, Christina, and Linda Flower. 1988. Rhetorical Reading Strategies and the Construction of Meaning. *College Composition and Communication* 39 (2): 167–83.

Hyland, Ken. 2002. *Disciplinary Discourses: Social Interactions in Academic Writing*. Ann Arbor: University of Michigan Press.

Jackson, Erika. 2008. Past Experiences and Future Attitudes in Literacy. *Young Scholars in Writing: Undergraduate Research in Writing and Rhetoric* 5: 131–36.

Jenkins, Alan A., and Mick Healey. 2007. Critiquing Excellence: Undergraduate Research for All Students. In *International Perspectives on Teaching Excellence in Higher Education: Improving Knowledge and Practice*, ed. Alan Skelton, 117–32. London: Routledge.

Karukstis, Kerry K., and Timothy E. Elgren, eds. 2007. *Developing and Sustaining a Research-Supportive Curriculum: A Compendium of Successful Practices*. Washington, DC: Council on Undergraduate Research.

Kinkead, Joyce. 2007. How Writing Programs Support Undergraduate Research. In Karukstis and Elgren 2007, 195–208.

Kleine, Michael. 1987. What Is It We Do When We Write Articles Like This One—and How Can We Get Students to Join Us? *Writing Instructor* 6 (Spring–Summer): 151–61.

Perl, Sondra. 1979. The Composing Processes of Unskilled College Writers. *Research in the Teaching of English* 13 (4): 317–36.

Petraglia, Joseph, ed. 1995a. *Reconceiving Writing, Rethinking Writing Instruction*. Mahwah, NJ: Lawrence Erlbaum.

Pleasant, Eric. 2008. Literacy Sponsors and Learning: An Ethnography of Punk Literacy in Mid-1980s Waco. *Young Scholars in Writing: Undergraduate Research in Writing and Rhetoric* 5: 137–45.

Reither, James A. 1985. Writing and Knowing: Toward Redefining the Writing Process. *College English* 47 (6): 620–28.

Rijlaarsdam, Gert. 2008. The Yummy Yummy Case: Learning to Write—Observing Readers and Writers. Presentation, Writing Research across Borders: 3rd International Santa Barbara Conference on Writing Research. Santa Barbara, CA.

Russell, David R. 1995. Activity Theory and Its Implications for Writing Instruction. In Petraglia 1995a, 51–77.

———. 2002. *Writing in the Academic Disciplines: A Curricular History*. 2nd ed. Carbondale, IL: Southern Illinois Univ. Press.

Sommers, Nancy. 1980. Revision Strategies of Student Writers and Experienced Adult Writers. *College Composition and Communication* 31 (4): 378–88.

Strasser, Emily. 2008. Writing What Matters: A Student's Struggle to Bridge the Academic/Personal Divide. *Young Scholars in Writing: Undergraduate Research in Writing and Rhetoric* 5: 146–50.

Swales, John M. 1990. *Genre Analysis: English in Academic and Research Settings*. Cambridge: Cambridge University Press.

Wardle, Elizabeth. 2007. Understanding "Transfer" from FYC: Preliminary Results of a Longitudinal Study. *WPA: Writing Program Administration* 31 (1/2): 65–85.

Watson, Amber. 2008. Motivation through Mentorship: Making Publishable Research Available for Novices. Paper presented at the annual meeting of the Council of Writing Program Administrators, Denver.

Wyatt, Sarah. 2005. Extending Inquiry-Based Learning to Include Original Experimentation. *Journal of General Education* 54 (2): 83–89.

CHAPTER TWELVE

The Writing Center as a Space for Undergraduate Research

DOMINIC DELLICARPINI AND CYNTHIA CRIMMINS
York College of Pennsylvania

> *The difference that appears when occupations are made the articulating centers of school life is not easy to describe in words; it is a difference in motive, of spirit and atmosphere. As one enters a busy kitchen in which a group of children are actively engaged in the preparation of food, the psychological difference, the change from more or less passive and inert recipiency and restraint to one of buoyant outgoing energy, is so obvious to fairly strike one in the face. [. . .] The occupation supplies the child with a genuine motive; it gives him experience first hand; it brings him into contact with realities. It does all this, but in addition it is liberalized throughout by translation into its historic and social values and scientific equivalencies.*
>
> —JOHN DEWEY, *The School and Society* (1943, 15, 22)

The Writing Center as Dewey's Kitchen

Experiential education, at least within the humanities, is sometimes treated as a concession that liberal arts curricula (which espouse "learning for learning's sake") make to material realities —to the need to prepare students for the workplace. But neglecting the research opportunities that arise from these forms of learning neglects the richer version of pragmatism that John Dewey (1977) suggested could renew our schools. In this enlightened pragmatism, the impulse to learn comes "out of the struggles of organic beings to secure a successful exercise of their functions" (178). Dewey differentiated the traditional roots of the liberal arts in "schools aiming to produce 'gentlemen' in the English conventional sense" (182) from the liberal arts within our American, democratic educational system. In such a system, occupational impulses—that is, material work—need not be at odds with the undergraduate research conducted in humanities departments.

After all, the impulse to inquiry that underlies motivated student research usually springs from what Dewey characterized as "something inherently significant, and of such a nature that the pupil appreciates for himself its importance enough to take a vital interest in it." And this "vital interest" moves the student toward the goal of liberal learning at the heart of humanities-based research; this seems to be what Dewey had in mind when he noted that the inquiry is "liberalized throughout by translation into its historic and social values and scientific equivalencies." That is, *experience* becomes the subject of reflective impulses that drive students to ask wider questions about the practices of the field, and so to engage in disciplinary research. Dewey consistently articulated this connection between students' experiential motives and participation in the wider questions of a field of knowledge, noting that "occupations bring people naturally together in groups, develop a group consciousness and power to divide and yet cooperate harmoniously" (1977, 191).

The growth of research projects arising from students' work in our writing center, chronicled in the case studies in this chapter, demonstrates how occupational experience has begun to create this type of "group consciousness" among our undergraduate peer fellows within this new disciplinary space. This growth in undergraduate research, at least until we started to notice it, was not part of the plan. Originally, we had more narrowly pragmatic motives. When in 2002 we developed a course titled Teaching and Tutoring Writing (WRT 290), our major goal was to train undergraduate peer tutors for our writing center at York College of Pennsylvania. But that narrow pragmatism became something more akin to Deweyan "liberalization" as motivated students, rather than merely finishing the course and taking on paid positions as tutors in our writing center, began to approach us with ideas for their own undergraduate research. They sought information on how to research topics that would help them in their careers as teachers or move them toward graduate study in rhetoric and composition; they called on us to mentor them in research projects involving writing pedagogy conducted through independent study and internship experiences; and they asked us to advise them in developing research projects in our discipline as honors program theses. These cocurricular attempts by students to enrich their own education and provide themselves with occasions for undergraduate research have led us to consider how we might better nurture these research impulses *within* our formal curriculum. What follows, then, is the story of what we learned when we started paying attention to what was going on not only in our physical space, but in the disciplinary space that our writing center was rapidly becoming—a space where fully realized undergraduate research could widen the scope of what is traditionally considered undergraduate English studies.

Part of the reason for this expansion of undergraduate research areas can be attributed to the nature of the disciplines associated with writing studies.[1] Unlike the research in many other areas of English studies, research in composition studies and in writing centers grew from each field's struggle for respect within English departments and professional organizations, as well as within the liberal arts more generally. Much as the delivery of what Sharon Crowley (1998) called "the universal requirement" bred the discipline of composition studies,[2] writing centers research also grew, simply stated, from work that needed to be done, from actual labor—labor that doesn't fit comfortably within the ethos of the liberal arts (14–15 passim). From that labor grew a disciplinary literature driven by early scholars like Muriel Harris and Stephen North, who constructed theory *after the fact* from the practices of the people who inhabited and sustained these places.

Into that mix come undergraduate peer tutors, who have taken on the work of writing centers in ways that are no less real than the methods of "professional" tutors, and who have begun to develop the potential that Michael Pemberton (2003) saw for disseminating that research in venues like *Writing Lab Newsletter* (*WLN*), which, he noted, "has welcomed the newest discoveries of the least experienced tutors. In fact, the *Newsletter*, through its 'Tutors Column' has provided a publication outlet for undergraduate and graduate students, allowing them to become active members of the writing center community" (34). As we will demonstrate in this chapter, the participation in real disciplinary work has helped these undergraduates toward equally real research impulses—research impulses that, like our own field's scholarship, moved from *praxis* to *gnosis*, from experience to research. Not all students, of course, reach that point; but many do, and many more might do so with our encouragement—now that we are paying attention.

This work, in a place that greatly resembles Dewey's kitchen in its motivated and sometimes frenetic activity, has offered a new type of undergraduate research to the repertoire of that done in "English" departments—research that grows from, as Dewey's comments mentioned earlier suggest, the "struggles of organic beings to secure a successful exercise of their functions" (1977, 178), and which invites them into the "group consciousness" of the disciplines of writing pedagogy.

An Emerging Pattern: The Growth of Undergraduate Research Impulses

Several institutional factors have influenced the growth of undergraduate research within our writing center. Perhaps the two most crucial factors are (1) the development of a major in professional writing, which brings into the program students who treat writing studies as a discipline, and (2) the movement from conventional use of peer tutors toward a writing fellows program that creates deeper interactions between the fellows and the classroom instructors, fostering more collegial relationships. Undergraduate peer writing tutors are assigned to instructors of required first-year writing classes and developmental writing classes.

Involving students who treat writing pedagogy as an area of study as well as a set of practices has bred a pattern of growth toward the types of inquiry that we might consider "real" research—research that has not only attempted to answer questions that students themselves needed to answer to do their work, but also research meant to contribute to the shared work of the discipline of writing studies. Like most research impulses, those felt by students as they first experience the scholarship of writing studies are based in a certain level of dissatisfaction with what they find has been done before them. In fact, in their search for trade secrets that can help them become engaged in this work, they find instead that there *are no secrets* and that professionals in this field seem to (1) disagree a great deal about how to teach writing and (2) try awfully hard to answer some pretty simple questions. Or so it seems to them. After all, don't we know what good writing is?

Even after becoming peer tutors or peer fellows, undergraduates continued some resistance to the idea that the tutoring "theory" they had learned about was somehow more than good common sense—though the resistance, interestingly, was characterized in terms that drew liberally upon their reading and classroom discussions from the course on tutoring writing. Their experiences merged with disciplinary knowledge, illustrating something like Dewey's argument that experience is the prime mover of education.[3] That is, students who had spent time working as peer tutors were beginning to "liberalize" their experience, recognizing how the literature of the field ran parallel to their own practices.

What is most significant, even in this resistance, is that despite the privileging of experience, students' ability to articulate their experience in discipline-specific ways was clearly informed by the knowledge of various theories—Kenneth Bruffee's (1984) influential writings (and a presentation they attended at the National Peer Tutoring Conference), which moved collaborative learning into the mainstream of composition studies; essays on cognitive writing theory; and readings on establishing rapport and relationships in tutoring sessions. These readings took on the aura of "common sense" as long as students treated them as narrowly pragmatic how-to readings. However, we have begun to realize that this apparent resistance was creating a rather seamless merging of praxis and gnosis, of experience and disciplinary knowledge.

Part of the reason students seem to believe that their reading in the course is merely an articulation of common sense seems to come from liberal arts students' inexperience with research based in experiential or pedagogical purposes. (Education majors in the course seem somewhat more in tune with this type of research, because they are more experienced with the social sciences, and, as is noted in the case study of Jenny [Case 4 in this chapter], because they have more specific occupational goals.) But the resistance dissipates most significantly when students start to imagine research that they themselves might do—because they have unanswered questions arising from their experiences in the writing center. This process of formulating research questions begins as students move from the classroom to their roles as peer tutors.

Comments by new peer tutors collected in questionnaires, interviews, and focus groups show how that work had begun to move them toward research questions that are more closely allied with social sciences fieldwork than with the text-based research of traditional English studies. Students who had recently become peer tutors were asked to consider the types of research that they found most important for the discipline to pursue. One student suggested studying "why people are so defensive about their writing and how to address that" and the resistance that students display toward nondirective tutoring methods. New tutors also raised disciplinary questions about the value of nondirective tutoring as they tested out Jeff Brooks's (1991) advice on *minimalist tutoring*, in which he suggests coping with resistant students by simply refusing to do the student's work. They began to recognize the importance of John Trimbur's (1987) "Peer Tutoring: A Contradiction in Terms?" as they themselves felt torn between their roles as a student and an authority figure on writing—precisely the argument made by Trimbur in this piece. And they felt concerns about whether teaching the "standard paper" was in fact "preparing students for the writing they'll do after they're done school." These questions, which are very much like the ones veterans in the discipline continuously ask, arose naturally from students' work in the writing center. But what becomes increasingly apparent in this process is that students situate their work within the literature of the field only as they begin to situate *themselves* within the field through their experiences. This disciplinary engagement—and the primary research that follows from it—starts to gain real value only after field-based experience, as has become increasingly apparent in the reflective portfolios they create at the end of the course.[4]

In Dewey's understanding of pragmatism and experiential education, experience is not the end, but the means of education. It is the process of liberalization that provides the final stage—for those who attain it—in this developmental progression toward finding their experiences of teaching and tutoring writing a site for their own research. This is illustrated clearly in the fully realized undergraduate research chronicled in the case studies in this chapter.

Case 1—Cate: How Constructive Eavesdropping Opened the Road to a PhD

When Cate, a brilliant student of science who chose literary studies as her major, was given the chance to enroll in an early version of WRT 290 during our first attempts to construct a peer tutoring program, she jumped at it and soon became one of the early leaders of the program. But just the coursework wasn't enough. In fact, Cate found that her presence in the writing center, a place that she describes in ways that strikingly parallel Dewey's kitchen metaphor, drove her to a desire for research:

> It was the constructive eavesdropping I loved. Conversations that represented a world of learning surrounded me. Running above, below, and through it all, were the conversations with writers. Students came with their papers—freshmen who marched through research papers and personal narratives and persuasive essays, sophomores describing "dyadic encounters" for Human Communication, junior business students working collaboratively to profile a local company, seniors with seminar papers and cover letters, ESL students. [. . .] The writing conversations seemed to vary the most—while the econ tutor would help students who were at the same point in their classes and answer similar questions for an hour, the writing tutors responded to what the student brought, and to what the student said he or she wanted.

From her experience within this active "kitchen," Cate reported coming to the conclusion that she was not only a *practitioner*, to use North's (1987) terminology from *The Making of Knowledge in Composition*. The primary way that Cate began to distinguish herself as more than a practitioner was to see herself as a *participant* in disciplinary research. This is the watershed moment for true undergraduate research. In changing roles, she also changed her attitude toward what writing center work meant to her; no longer viewing herself as simply a consumer of materials written by "experts" to guide her practices, she now wished to be a producer of expert discourse herself. Since that change in roles was not fully available in our fledgling curriculum, Cate found another way into the disciplinary discourse: she began to do her own primary research through "constructive eavesdropping," that is, analysis of what she saw and heard in her experiences as a tutor. As Cate put it, "I could not seem to let go of WRT 290—I did two independent studies in the writing center. I observed tutoring sessions to try to figure out if writing tutors really did things differently than math and science tutors."

One of Cate's research projects involved "figuring out how tutors and tutees were using pronouns to relate to one another. I found patterns in ways that tutors and tutees construct." In that study, Cate found that tutoring methods across various disciplines could be captured in the use of first, second, or third person pronouns: "For example, tutors who said 'what are we working on today' tended to collaborate more than tutors who greeted tutees with, 'what have you brought today?'" And as she noted, not only the project, but its eventual dissemination to participants in disciplinary conversations, was the measure of her full participation in undergraduate research: "I got a lot of mileage out of that research and paper—I used it for grad school applications (it won me a fellowship to Ohio State), my honors program senior project, for conference presentations (MAWCA [Mid-Atlantic Writing Centers Association], Student Scholar's Day, CCCCs [Conference on College Composition and Communication]), and my first peer-reviewed scholarly publication (*Young Scholars in Writing*)."

No one can take credit for Cate's success but Cate. However, her experiences as a tutor provided her with opportunities for research in which she enriched and liberalized experiences in just the way envisioned by Dewey. She herself noted,

> I'm not overstating the case when I tell you that this class changed my life. It got me interested in composition and grad school and the profession of teaching writing. I may have come to these things without the class, but I didn't; this was my entry point. The course opened my eyes to the degree that teachers think about writing: how do we compose, how can we get other people to do this well and with pleasure?

That is perhaps as articulate an understanding of the overall project of the discipline of composition as there could be.

Cate, now a graduate student in rhetoric and composition at The Ohio State University, looks back on the influence of WRT 290 in ways that validate our own findings about student research methods. From her vantage point as a professional in the field, Cate was able to note that in her past experiences as an undergraduate, "theory and practice mutually reinforced one another" and that in writing studies research, "the value of practice and participant-observer research should not be underestimated." She also traced her current research interests to questions developed in her undergraduate experiences in our writing center.

Case 2—Molly: How Working with a Co-Dependent Student and Grammar-Lust Led to Graduate School in Rhetoric and Composition

A talented writer and a professional writing major, Molly's motivation for academic research really took hold once she completed the tutoring course and became a peer tutor in our Learning Resources Center. In class, we had discussed the demise of the "correctness" approach to the teaching of writing, reading essays such as Joseph Williams's (1981) "The Phenomenology of Error." But Molly's belief in the importance of teaching grammar led her to question the effects of what David Mulroy (2003) has called *the war against grammar*.[5] To address this question, she posited a historical study based on the hypothesis that the growth of writing centers was driven partially by needs created when formal grammar instruction lost its place in the classroom curriculum. This research impulse led Molly to enroll in a graduate course at the University of Maryland, where she continued to explore this hypothesis.

But it was a lived experience that led her into her first foray into undergraduate research. As a peer tutor, Molly worked with an English language learner (ELL) who quickly became dependent not only on her, but also on the services of our writing center more generally. After struggling with how to handle this situation, Molly completed a research project titled "A Case Study on the Dependent ESL Writer: The Perspective of the Writing Center, the Peer Tutor, and the Tutee." This study, like the bulk of undergraduate research generated in our writing center, had its genesis in Molly's own reflective experiences with this ELL. At first, Molly reported, she felt quite satisfied with her work with this student, especially because it allowed her to work with this student's special needs in English grammar—Molly's first love. As she noted in her essay, Molly was also able to draw on published research to support her approach:

> I had been taught in Teaching and Tutoring Writing to use a nondirective approach when tutoring. But, as the experts reconfirmed, this method is simply not effective when used with ESL students. I knew that non-native speakers needed a more direct approach because leading questions would lead to very little. The collaborative approach that is nondirective is used to draw the answer out of the student. With ESL writers, the answer is simply not in them.

But Molly's knowledge of disciplinary conversations, a crucial facet of undergraduate research, also led her to notice, "Something changed in the relationship; a new component had joined us in our sessions—dependency." It was this experience, and her "increasing frustration" and "ethical questions" about whether she was actually serving the student's long-term needs, that led Molly full circle, back into theory and research. She turned to research on ESL students, learning that "[n]ative-speaking writers have had the advantage of English integration." From this, she was able to develop what she considered ethically and theoretically sound practices: "All things being equal, my response to his ethical question of standards is to provide the ESL writer with as many resources as possible—the writing center being a key resource—and then hold them to the same standards as native-speaking writers."

Molly also turned back to the disciplinary conversation that we had introduced in WRT 290, blending gnosis and praxis. She developed what she described as a "combination of Current Traditional Rhetoric and expressivism that would be most effective" in addressing the problem. Drawing on these very different approaches, Molly was able to address the growing dependency, knowing that "if I were to allow the student to direct the session, we would spend a majority of our time correcting errors"; but by adding expressivist theory, she could "get the student to think, and so write, in English."

Having combined what at first seemed to her as competing methodologies, and having had some success with that recombining in her occupational role, Molly then took the next step toward true research, situating herself within the wider discourse on this topic. Her essay's conclusion directly addresses that disciplinary audience: "[T]he role of the writing center when working with a dependent ESL writer is to balance expectations by negotiating goals to most effectively help build a better writer. Tutors must strive to use collaboration and be fluid in approaches when dealing with the student, and consider the reality that dependent ESL writers face when they leave the center." Molly also moved toward dissemination of her work through a presentation at our annual Student Scholar's Day (our celebration of undergraduate research), and through her decision to pursue graduate studies. Thus, once again, an area of research that began in an experiential or, to use Dewey's term, an *occupational* need reached fruition through a combination of reflection and study.

Case 3—Jaclyn: My Praxis Trumps Your Gnosis: Questioning Directive and Nondirective Tutoring and the Development of a Research Impulse

Over the years, we often heard students reflect on nondirective tutoring methods, in class discussions, on our class discussion board, or in staff meetings. The especially apt students began to question whether our disciplinary assumptions about the value of nondirective tutoring were indeed well founded. After completing the tutoring seminar, Jaclyn, an undergraduate professional writing major, went on to use her learning to set up a peer tutoring center in a K–12 private day school. Though this work began as an internship project, Jaclyn developed what were originally narrow, pragmatic goals into more Deweyan ones, making her workplace a site for serious undergraduate research. The work did begin with occupational motives: she set up policies, trained tutors, worked with faculty, and developed schedules for during- and after-school tutoring. Drawing on her learning from the course and her observations from working with our writing center director, she developed a well-functioning program, including a procedures manual and a wealth of materials to be used in the writing center.

But in the process, Jaclyn continued to question the orthodoxy of nondirective tutoring methods that we had stressed in our course. In order to examine this question, she set up a systematic study of directive versus nondirective tutoring, which, though limited in scope, featured a well-constructed methodology. In the end, Jaclyn concluded that nondirective methods, while helpful to experienced and competent writers, were not nearly as effective for ELLs or inexperienced students. She delivered this research as part of our department's offerings during Student Scholar's Day, and it will likely become her writing sample for graduate school applications.

Jaclyn's study framed the disciplinary problem this way: "It is essential to explore how effective the language being used during tutoring sessions is, because it is important to writing centers for students to not only have a positive learning experience while they are being tutored, but also to feel like they have learned and accomplished something during their tutoring sessions." Jaclyn further contextualized her study by turning to the available scholarship on the topic, building on Bruffee's contention that "the heart of what we do in our writing centers is in the conversation, the talk about writing, rather than in the writing itself. [. . . T]he words we use are central to the tutoring process and to the relationships built between tutor and client" (qtd. in Blau, Hall, and Strauss 1998, 20–21). Beginning from Bruffee's work, Jaclyn found space for her own study within the disciplinary conversation by developing a strong declaration exigency statement—not just for her own writing center, but for writing center studies more widely: "The value of nondirective and collaborative versus directive language use in tutoring situations must be examined in order to try to evaluate which communication methods may be more beneficial to students, and for what reasons."

Jaclyn also grounded her analysis in the methodology of other researchers. In particular, she drew on a study by Susan Blau, John Hall, and Tracy Strauss (1998), which, she noted, "shows that by using lead questions, the tutor creates an environment where the student is prompted to think and correct the problem identified in their writing on their own, or with little direction from the tutor." Beginning from this previous research, Jaclyn was able to systematically create from her writing center a laboratory for her own primary research, analyzing the "common linguistic qualities" of the sessions she observed. She painstakingly transcribed interchanges between tutors and tutees, and noted the pattern of sessions that became more directive in nature. Then, using the methodology of the previous study, she was able to add discussion of observations from her own primary research and critique the adequacy of that study (and so perform a key function of primary research—replication testing). For example, after presenting a conversation she had transcribed, Jaclyn noted,

> In this instance, unlike the conversation seen earlier from Blau, Hall, and Strauss's study, the student was not cooperative, did not demonstrate a high level of maturity, and did not demonstrate that he recognized a problem in his writing. Therefore, the student was unable to correct his mistake and benefit from nondirective tutoring methods. Notice that at first the tutor in this situation uses language very similarly to the tutoring situation in Blau, Hall, and Strauss's study by asking, "what do you think," and "do you" type questions. The student in this situation, however, replies with the words, "I don't know," which puts the tutor in the position to have to try again to get the student to recognize the problem.

Jaclyn also learned to situate her own work within the work of other experts who had reported similar findings, using Alice Gillam's (1994) work to substantiate her own contention that orthodoxies can be problematic: "As Alice M. Gillam points out, the nondirective and collaborative method's 'theoretical formulations of practice tend to be idealized, unproblematic, and a-contextual' (39)."

Jaclyn concluded that though nondirective and collaborative methods represent the preferred and ideal type of verbal communication in writing centers, directive methods can, in many cases, be equally or more effective forms of linguistic communication for tutoring sessions. This argument, like Molly's, had multiple audiences. First, both students' work was meant to influence disciplinary work in situating itself amid previous scholarship—as is evidenced by its willingness to offer critique. And because their work was presented to the full college as part of our Student Scholar's Day, it helped to open the work of rhetoric and composition to an undergraduate community that has only recently started to acknowledge such work as true scholarship. Further, both Molly's and Jaclyn's work was meant to influence policies and practices in our own writing center—and it has. And finally, their work not only demonstrates the potential for undergraduate research in writing pedagogy, but suggests the potential for undergraduates to do work in writing program and writing center administration. In fact, not only was Jaclyn tasked with administration of a writing center, but Molly was also later hired to develop a writing center in a public school, based largely on what she accomplished in her undergraduate work and research. And both are now seeking to become members of the disciplinary community through graduate education.

Case 4—Jenny: So, How Does This All Play Out in the Real World? or A Secondary School Teacher's Tale

Because Jenny was a secondary education English major, her occupational goals and her research goals were more specific. The artifacts of her research share a clear purpose: to assemble what she needed to become an effective high school English teacher, especially in the teaching of writing. Jenny characterized her goals as "creating a portfolio which will include my independent research, teaching philosophy, lesson plans, and journal pieces that reflect upon my experiences teaching and tutoring." Her further research was focused on developing materials that would continue to serve her occupational needs, which were more imminent than those of Cate, Molly, or Jaclyn. In fact, Jenny's final portfolio for her honors program senior project was a conglomeration of materials showing the results of her interviews with students, and she took the next step toward turning what she studied into pedagogically useful lesson plans and assignments.

Jenny's project was designed to study changes in students' attitudes toward writing that resulted from their work in a developmental course for which she was the peer writing fellow. Her methodology was based in learning from primary (and largely affective) research with the students she encountered in the developmental course. She noted that she would "record the students feelings and thoughts towards writing and college at the beginning of the semester and then again at the end." She also rooted her research in her own occupational goals, declaring that "I will also ask students to help me develop as a teacher by evaluating my teaching and tutoring."

Using methodologies from previous studies of affective factors on student writing (including a similar study we had performed in local high schools and presented at CCCC), Jenny developed primary research materials to trace changes in student attitudes from those brought from high school to those held after the students' first semester in college. As a secondary education English major, her real concern was in bridging the gap between high school and college composition—an area of research that has become increasingly important to the National Council of Teachers of English (NCTE) and CCCC.[6] And though Jenny's work used methods of primary research, including questionnaires and interviews, its end result was more practical than theoretical. The extensive portfolio she created did develop an argument about the changes in student attitude; but the conclusion she drew closed the feedback loop, as she used her new knowledge of student attitudes and her consideration of the high school to college transition to develop usable lesson plans, activities, and assignments that responded to the exigencies of those attitudes.

Thus Jenny's case illustrates another important impetus for undergraduate research in writing studies, and another population of students who can benefit from this research. Her work illustrates how undergraduate research in English that is based in primary, experiential learning can help future secondary teachers to be more reflective about their work. Rather than merely accept a predetermined curriculum, Jenny became more sensitive to the attitudes and predilections of her potential students by seeing them from the other side—in a college writing course. As a result, Jenny is more apt to influence the writing curriculum in her future occupation, and to continue to think about the high school classroom as a site of ongoing study. It is hard to overstate how important such reflection and study could be to improving the writing instruction in our high schools, as well as to the ongoing work of NCTE. Rather than being a "trained" teacher, Jenny has left us as an educated and reflective teacher-researcher.

Rethinking the Writing Center as a Home for Undergraduate Research in English Studies

Though we still have much more to learn from our students, we can summarize our conclusion thus far in one clear assertion: our writing center and peer fellows program has demonstrated the potential of writing centers to act as a site for new types of undergraduate research in English departments. Now that we have started to pay attention, we have come to view our work as more than "training" teachers and tutors, and we are increasingly making efforts to include them as active participants in the scholarly discourse of the discipline. As we see it, the writing center is rapidly becoming a true *lab*, a place that can be a center not only for students seeking assistance, but for students in our language arts programs (professional writing, literary studies, and secondary education English) to perform experiments, test hypotheses, and contribute to the pool of knowledge in our discipline. This space offers new possibilities to English departments in which writing majors are increasingly popular, and in which the scholarship of rhetoric and composition that was previously limited to graduate study is finding a foothold in the undergraduate curriculum and imagination. And, unlike most research in undergraduate English departments, the work being done has its roots in primary research and methodologies akin to the social sciences, thus opening up a whole new world for our students—and new teaching opportunities for faculty.

Both our course and our expectations of the peer fellows have begun to change as we consider how to spend the riches we have somehow inherited. Those changes include a more explicit attempt to have students bring together their experiential learning with research in the field. Our goal in asking them to read the literature of the discipline is no longer primarily to guide their practices; we now strive to allow their practices to help them question the adequacy of the scholarship they read. And few attitudes can spur real undergraduate research more than the sense that published research may need to be revised by a student's own experience-based findings. Toward that end, we have reconceived some facets of the course in ways that not only more consciously support undergraduate research, but also support its dissemination in available venues like those we will describe in this section.

One consistent question we have had about the course design has involved sequencing. We have gone back and forth on whether it is best to begin with theory and move toward practical experiences in the writing center and classroom, or whether we should allow early experiences to drive the need for the course readings. What we have discovered is that the sequence is not linear but recursive. That is, students need to read scholarly work with two purposes: first, to inform their own observations and experience; and second, with an eye toward responding to it with their own critique and their own (often primary and replication) studies. One recent revision to the course, for example, involves the reading of disciplinary articles. Originally, we asked students to simply summarize assignments they had read. Now, we ask each student to read two articles over the course of the semester. Each student writes a précis of the article and posts it to our class website. The student then provides an oral summary of the article for the class and leads a discussion of the article's validity, based on students' own experiences. Then, after the class discussion, each student writes a response to the article that gives both the class and the individual presenters impetus to reflect upon and critique the adequacy and validity of published research. This assignment, along with discussions and other opportunities for reflection, has helped students approach each piece of reading as potential participants in an ongoing disciplinary discussion. We hope and expect that this method will breed an even greater number of research projects in the future. But, of course, this will require humanities students—and their teachers—to learn a whole new lexicon of what it means to "do research," including reliable methods for primary research. That task will have its own challenges.

We also provide students with opportunities for going public with their work. Student Scholar's Day, regional writing center conferences such as MAWCA (where our students regularly present), and publication venues such as *Young Scholars in Writing* and *Writing Lab Newsletter* have all been offered to students as ways to disseminate their work. For the highly motivated and accomplished, national conferences like NCTE and CCCC are potential venues; in fact, Cate was able to present the results of her undergraduate research study at CCCC.

The innovative work of the students whose efforts we have chronicled in this chapter has prompted us to think more seriously about extending the work they begin in WRT 290 into future semesters.[7] As the most successful students from the course move on to positions as peer fellows, we have begun to encourage them to consider the Learning Resource Center (the interdisciplinary space that houses our writing center) as a rich site for their ongoing research. Recently we have added a second course that will serve as both a practicum for peer fellows and a course in undergraduate research in writing theory. The course will include a required research project that draws on the students' experiences in the Learning Resource Center as well as published research. We will also require students to seek outlets for their research among available conference presentation or publication venues; one likely assignment will be writing a conference proposal. The course will, of necessity, include a unit on performing field research to help students to broaden their understanding of research. This unit can draw from the growing body of literature on quantitative research in composition studies, and respond to Chris Anson's (2006) challenge to writing program administrators to return to quantifiable and reliable research methods, including replication studies of past research. Asking students to replicate and test past assumptions through their own primary research can be an excellent introduction to the research methods of our field.

Our students' work and our own plans have led us to consider how the writing center can continue to widen the field of English studies to include primary and pedagogical research. Considering the growth of undergraduate writing studies majors (including our own), the movements toward undergraduate teacher-student research (which has flourished more in the sciences than in the humanities), and an increasing attention to writing instruction in secondary schools, the time is ripe to rethink what an "English major" is and does. Mirroring the rapid growth of rhetoric and composition at the graduate level, this new student interest and participation makes it probable that attention to the research potential in the discipline of writing studies can, as we have argued elsewhere, rewrite what we mean by research in the humanities in ways described in this chapter.[8] In this process, it is likely that the writing center will continue to act as a crucial space in the growth of undergraduate research in English studies.

Notes

1. We use the somewhat amorphous term *writing studies* to include the largely pedagogy-based fields of rhetoric, composition, and writing centers (though it can also include, of course, creative writing).

2. Sharon Crowley's *Composition in the University* (1998) traces the pragmatic roots of a field that began its research mainly from a single but "universal" requirement, first-year composition, and the separate but certainly unequal status of composition within English departments.

3. Dewey notes in *The School and Society* (1943) that work "gives the point of departure" from which liberal learning can begin (20).

4. This portfolio assignment asks students to develop a teaching philosophy statement, to contextualize that statement within various writing theories, and to use their experiences in the course and in the Learning Resource Center as support for their teaching philosophy. It is at this moment that most students begin to recognize the intersection of theory and practice, revising their earlier reactions to readings based on their experiences in the writing center.

5. Mulroy (2003) argues that the loss of formal grammar instruction was in part the result of misrepresentations of Dewey's work as it played out in "progressive education," and suggests a return to productive versions of grammar instruction.

6. For example, CCCC offers a $25,000 grant for research related to the intersection of writing in high school and writing in college.

7. As is evident from the words and work that inform this piece, we owe all of our students a great debt of gratitude. We thank especially Cate Sacchi, Molly Scanlon, Jaclyn Keys, Jenny Freudenberg, T. J. Bickert, Josh Olewiler, and Erin Collins.

8. See Dominic DelliCarpini (2007) for further discussion of the effect of writing studies on the tradition.

References

Anson, Chris M. 2006. The Intelligent Design of Writing Programs: Reliance on Belief or a Future of Evidence? Paper presented at the annual meeting of the Council of Writing Program Administrators, Chattanooga, TN.

Blau, Susan R., John Hall, and Tracy Strauss. 1998. Exploring the Tutor/Client Conversation: A Linguistic Analysis. *Writing Center Journal* 19 (1): 19–48.

Brooks, Jeff. 1991. Minimalist Tutoring: Making the Students Do All the Work. *Writing Lab Newsletter* 15 (6): 1–4.

Bruffee, Kenneth A. 1984. Collaborative Learning and the "Conversation of Mankind." *College English* 46 (7): 635–52.

Crowley, Sharon. 1998. *Composition in the University: Historical and Polemical Essays.* Pittsburgh: University of Pittsburgh Press.

DelliCarpini, Dominic. 2007. Re-writing the Humanities: The Writing Major's Effect upon Undergraduate Studies in English Departments. *Composition Studies* 35 (1): 15–36.

Dewey, John. 1943. *The School and Society.* Chicago: University of Chicago Press.

———. 1977. The Bearings of Pragmatism upon Education. In *John Dewey: The Middle Works,* Vol. 4, ed. Jo Ann Boydston, 178–91. Carbondale: Southern Illinois University Press.

Gillam, Alice M. 1994. Collaborative Learning Theory and Peer Tutoring Practice. In *Intersections: Theory-Practice in the Writing Center*, ed. Joan A. Mullin and Ray Wallace, 39–53. Urbana, IL: National Council of Teachers of English.

Mulroy, David. *The War against Grammar*. 2003. Portsmouth, NH: Boynton/Cook.

North, Stephen M. 1987. *The Making of Knowledge in Composition: Portrait of an Emerging Field*. Portsmouth, NH: Boynton/Cook.

Pemberton, Michael A. 2003. The *Writing Lab Newsletter* as History: Tracing the Growth of a Scholarly Community. In *The Center Will Hold: Critical Perspectives on Writing Center Scholarship*, ed. Michael A. Pemberton and Joyce Kinkead, 21–40. Logan: Utah State University Press.

Trimbur, John. 1987. Peer Tutoring: A Contradiction in Terms? *Writing Center Journal* 7 (2): 21–28.

Williams, Joseph M. 1981. The Phenomenology of Error. *College Composition and Communication* 32 (2): 152–68.

CHAPTER THIRTEEN

Rhetorics and Undergraduate Research: A Journey into the Genre of Memoir

LAURA GRAY-ROSENDALE
Northern Arizona University

Since 2004, I have taught a senior seminar course at Northern Arizona University (NAU) in which my students and I examine rhetorical history and theory and how they might be usefully applied to contemporary memoirs. Memoirs and their iRhetorics (rhetorical constructions of the self) raise critical issues that have personal relevance for many advanced undergraduate students in the English major or minor at an institution that includes many first-generation students from lower-middle income backgrounds in the Southwest—issues associated with identity, race, class, ethnicity, sexual preference, gender, region, environment, and religion. These concerns also echo some of the questions most central to our students as they contemplate their future careers and schooling: Which key moments or exigencies might I point to in my life as important to who I am, what I do, and how others view me? What sorts of varied and sometimes conflicted identities or ethos do I inhabit in my interactions with others—and what are the potential effects of adopting them? What sort of emotional and logical appeals as well as narrative tactics do I employ to represent my various "selves" within my writing and speech, and in what contexts are they persuasive?

As with any course that takes undergraduate research seriously, this class asks students to consider certain premises that encourage in-depth knowledge within the discipline of rhetoric: understanding of the methodological and ethical considerations inherent in disciplinary research, improving of communication skills through writing and speaking, learning how to cope with intellectual uncertainties, and discovering the importance of teamwork. As a group, my students and I study the ways in which our contemporary cultural moment has ushered in a "culture of confession" that includes examples ranging from reality television, talk radio, and websites to blogs, MySpace, and memoirs. Moreover, I encourage my students to bear in mind the widely accepted view in writing studies that not only is the self always socially constituted, but also experience is itself discursive. As Joan Scott (1992) contends in her landmark essay "Experience," experience is best understood as a "process [. . .] by which subjectivity is constructed" (27).

In large part, this course grows out of the perspectives of the Council on Undergraduate Research (CUR) and National Conferences on Undergraduate Research (NCUR) concerning undergraduate research and scholarship: the best undergraduate research is an inquiry or investigation that yields an original intellectual or creative contribution to the discipline. Further, Ernest Boyer (1990) reveals the vital ways in which teaching can also give rise to critical scholarly activity: "The arrow of causality can, and frequently does, point in both directions. Theory surely leads to practice. But practice also leads to theory. Teaching, at its best, shapes both research and practice" (16). Boyer's four essential, interconnected aspects of scholarship are

1. Discovery: scholarship as investigative, in search of new information yet to be known or found;
2. Integration: scholarship that draws connections and interpretations across interdisciplinary contexts to create comprehensive understandings;
3. Application: scholarship that seeks ways that knowledge can solve problems for community and campus; and
4. Teaching: scholarship that masters knowledge as well as transforms and extends it to others so that they might learn.

My students employ all four elements simultaneously as they compose and share short argumentative responses to the books;

construct dialogic, ongoing journals in which they explore their experiences and identity constructions as jumping-off points for class discussion and project development; and generate original research projects that rhetorically analyze how identities are constructed within a series of texts (books, collected letters, webpages, artwork and poetry, multimedia installations). This scholarship is shared with all members of the class and with the larger university and local communities. Throughout the course, students form small research teams around their mutual intellectual interests. As students' research develops, they often decide to move within and between research groups to offer and obtain additional feedback and tips for locating research relevant to each other's projects.

In this chapter, I provide case studies of two remarkable undergraduate students in this course, Dania Allen and Robert Finch,[1] tracing how their projects fulfill and extend Boyer's models for scholarship. These students' experiences and reflections reveal how we can foster a view of undergraduate research that incorporates teaching and scholarship as parts of one overlapping, shared process; how we can utilize undergraduate research to replace old archetypes of teacher and student with a collaborative, investigative model; how we can dispense with competitive modes of inquiry in favor of collective, community-building ones; and how we can help students learn through the process of doing. Though we have encountered problems along the way, my students have engaged directly in practicing and creating new work for our discipline. They have worked hard to foster internal networks to support their interdisciplinary and collaborative learning efforts. Each of my students has set out a concrete investigative problem, carried out a project, and shared new scholarly discoveries with peers and beyond the class walls. Likewise, the students have gained specific skills, such as making use of primary literature, formulating research hypotheses, interpreting data, communicating research results, reflecting on their work, gaining independence and self-confidence, and becoming more focused on career preparation. As Bob Pletka (2007) affirms in *Educating the Net Generation*, such approaches foster enjoyment, creativity, and engagement, and are essential to providing technological, visual, informational, and multicultural literacies for today's students (47).

I have my own reasons, both personal and professional, for teaching this class. Over the course of my own career as a rhetoric scholar, one of my key areas of research and publication has been autobiography and personal writing. For the first time, however, I am attempting to write a nonfiction memoir manuscript of my own. While this new work retains connections to my past research, it is still unfamiliar territory: I am very much like a student as I work within it. Teaching this course has afforded my students and me a wonderful opportunity to be co-inquirers, co-learners, and co-investigators of the genre and its rhetorical tactics, despite my expertise in the history and theory of rhetoric. As Ronald Smith (2001) articulates, in such teaching the "focus of deliberation becomes an act of scholarship itself" (73). As my own students engage in their research, I continually disclose my own scholarly processes within this genre—the various interconnections between my own discoveries, integrations, applications, and teaching. As a result, more than ever I find myself part guide, part facilitator, part fellow-traveler, actually "replacing competitive modes of inquiry with ones more focused on collective and collaborative work" (Dotterer 2002, 82). I am also learning how far our rhetoric courses focused on undergraduate research have come and how far they still need to go.

The Memoir Course

The memoir course is constructed to foster critical inquiry into how experience and identity are constituted. My students and I pose complicated questions about whether the processes of experience not only produce certain kinds of identities, but are also themselves rhetorical and situated in nature. As Sidonie Smith and Julia Watson (2001) argue, experience is always "embedded in the languages of everyday life and the knowledges produced at everyday sites" (25). While these everyday sites are subject to and shaped by real cultural, social, and political pressures, quite often they are represented as transparent and seamless (Gilmore 2001, 24). As a result, in order to understand more fully the complex languages of experience, we need critical tools to decipher them. So I assign my students a series of rhetorical theory and history texts, from Aristotle to Foucault, as a way to gain such tools.

Together, my students and I observe several central concerns within contemporary confessional, in particular that memoir and other autobiographical texts invoke thorny questions, such as what indeed constitutes "selfhood" and "truth." These issues are frequently challenged and considered open to interpretation. Consider, for example, the scandals around James Frey's *A Million Little Pieces* (2005) and Margaret B. Jones's *Love and Consequences: A Memoir of Hope and Survival* (2008). Moreover, autobiographical texts raise significant questions about the reliability of memory itself because the "remembering subject actively creates the meaning of the past in the act of remembering" rather than during the time that the real events took place (Rose 1993, 16). In this way, the creator of autobiographical texts is always already at a remove from the autobiographical events. And, as Maureen Murdock (2003) puts it in her book that is part memoir and part theory about memoir, the "deliberate act of remembering is always a form of willed creation—an intentional creating of identity" (30).

Beyond this, my students and I come to acknowledge that culture, historical context, politics, and community often actively shape the ways in which selfhood, truth, and memory can be defined. We apply these concepts and theoretical and rhetorical tools to the task of reading contemporary memoirs such as *Jarhead* (Swofford 2005), *Goat* (Land 2004), *Name All the Animals* (Smith 2005), *Another Bullshit Night in Suck City* (Flynn 2004), *A Heartbreaking Work of Staggering Genius* (Eggers 2001), *A Piece of Cake* (Brown 2007), and *Running with Scissors* (Burroughs 2006). This work culminates in students' creation of projects that make meaningful, oftentimes original, contributions to the rhetoric discipline.

Dania's Research: Investigating PostSecret

Dania's project, "Your Secret Is Safe with Me," draws on both rhetorical theory and psychology to analyze how identity operates within a unique online community, PostSecret, in which she engages regularly. Through PostSecret, members mail or post secrets to the Web in an anonymous forum and then receive anonymous responses from others. Through the research process, Dania moves back and forth between discovering new ideas, integrating the views of others across disciplinary boundaries, applying theories she has learned to her own new disciplinary research, and teaching what she has uncovered about the rhetoric of PostSecret to her rhetoric and psychology student peers and faculty.

Dania engages in genuine inquiry, investigation, and discovery. While reading all of the research in the discipline of rhetoric that she can find about digital rhetorics, Dania realizes that established scholars have yet to examine the very recent cultural phenomenon of PostSecret. After I confirm this gap in the available research, Dania initially decides to address this research question: How does PostSecret operate rhetorically, and what are its similarities and differences from the traditional memoir genre? Narrowing her focus further, Dania decides that she is fascinated by how identities are constructed in this environment—both individually and collectively—and how the culture of confession is shaping this particular Internet community.

Dania soon realizes that her knowledge of psychology can be useful for the project as well. Her research team and I urge Dania not to draw demarcations between disciplines as she immerses herself in the project, but rather to integrate them, and she agrees. In framing her research problem for her readers, Dania learns that she must adopt the voice of a rhetoric scholar herself, effectively teaching her readers something about which they know little, and tracing the history of PostSecret before she builds to a detailed analysis. Dania explains that PostSecret began in November 2004 when small business owner Frank Warren began a simple art project while attending the University of California–Berkeley. Warren printed 3,000 self-addressed postcards inviting people to mail in their secrets anonymously with these instructions: "Share your secret in as few words as possible, decorate the postcard creatively and send it in—no strings attached." Initially, Warren left the cards in public places and also handed them out to strangers. To date, more than 200,000 secrets have been submitted. Four books have been published, and the blog posts updates every week. However, not until 2005 did the project gain mass appeal, when the band All-American Rejects made a music video for their hit single "Dirty Little Secret" featuring many PostSecret cards. The blog has spawned the PostSecret Community, an active Internet space where people gather to discuss the secrets posted.

Dania's research team partners and I next recommend that Dania continue with her plan to jump to a close analysis of the initial postcard, narrowing her focus yet further to scrutinize one key theme related to identity within many postcards: family. Using rhetorical readings of both the written and visual elements within various postcards, Dania exposes how issues related to paternity, in-laws, and humor among relatives recur repeatedly. Dania also charts examples of PostSecret cards that focus on more serious confessional issues, such as child abuse, violence in the home, and molestation. Dania wonders if it is appropriate to contend that this is a subgenre within the genre of memoir. Her research team encourages her to do this. As a result, Dania argues that PostSecret is one key example of a new and rapidly growing form of personal writing and confession—the collective memoir. Dania thus makes a discovery that has even wider-reaching implications. The collective memoir subgenre has much in common with the traditional memoir genre. Just as the memoir genre has increasingly had to grapple with issues of "truth," within PostSecret communities there may be no way to distinguish the authentic secrets from the fake. This is perhaps even more the case, Dania asserts, because PostSecret itself relies on and requires anonymity.

Once she has drafted her history section and close rhetorical readings, Dania realizes that she may need to incorporate different research methodologies and switch to a case study approach. In an effort to ascertain why people send in these secrets, Dania resolves to become an investigator from within the community itself, posting a discussion thread to the blog: "Why send them in?" We discuss the ethical import of this approach, and Dania determines that, because she has been an active member of the community itself, she should take what Jaqueline McLeod Rogers terms a *netnographic* approach (see her chapter in this collection). Although "ethical issues are still under review and changing," as Rogers states, Dania elects to acknowledge her role to the others with whom she is interacting in the community. Based on her primary research, Dania receives a set of intriguing responses, including the following:

> It can be like getting a weight off your shoulders. It can be like opening the windows in your heart. It can be like getting a 2,000 pound screaming rabid gorilla off your back. I think the point is it's freeing, cathartic, and cheaper than therapy. It helps to know that I'm not the only one holding the secret anymore, that there are others out there who feel it as well.

Others respond with statements such as "Well, Frank said he reads every single postcard that comes in . . . so even if you know you won't get published, at least you can be sure that someone out there in this big, unsympathetic world knows and is willing to listen. It's a bit therapeutic if you ask me" and "I send mine in because someone else reads them—& to me that means the world, Frank may not know it but he knows more things about me than anyone else in this world does [. . .] my secrets are constant ups & downs—it's just wonderful knowing that someone will take the time out of their day to read & understand & just love how wonderful/ horrible/ funny/ scary your secret is."

Dania realizes that she needs to learn more about the history of confession itself, particularly the role of the Catholic church. Once more, a new discovery through the research process leads Dania to integrate others' knowledge. Dania concludes that, located as we are within a historical context in which many are disillusioned with religious confession and the role of priest as expert mediator, PostSecret, and other forums like it, have become new, safe spaces for confession.

Once Dania completes her creative piece that incorporates both visuals and written text, cites widely from rhetorical and psychological theories, and includes multiple investigative and methodological modes (disciplinary research, interdisciplinary studies, close reading, rhetorical analysis and interpretation, as well as case study), she takes the next step: dissemination. Our class presentations are open to peers from our class and to other invited students and faculty from across the university community; students choose their guests and are responsible for extending these invitations. Here, Dania shares her research alongside other members of the class. Her poster presentation features her main ideas for the project, along with colorful visuals and written text from PostSecret postcards. Dania encourages active learning from her audience members by posing questions and asking them to offer their own interpretations. Dania chose this form of dissemination largely because, like oral presentations, posters of this kind honor the scholarly nature of our students' inquiry while also supplying additional points for discussion, reminding us all that research is itself always in process—not a finished product, but a living, dynamic entity. Dania teaches us all about her research as she leads us into the Web community of PostSecret. She uses the multimedia capabilities of our wired classroom, and we are able to experience her research process more effectively, from the inside out. We are also able to offer good feedback to Dania, who plans to pursue her research in her advanced psychology capstone courses in upcoming semesters and in a graduate program in psychology.

Robert's Research: Interrogating the Memoir Genre

Robert's project, "The Rhetoric of Memoir: The Dangerous Gap between Perception and Reality," offers a new, meta-rhetorical reading of the memoir genre itself, which he considers problematic and self-contradictory. Robert, too, moves between discovery of a neglected problem within the discipline, integration of the history of memoir across disciplinary boundaries, application of theories to create new knowledge and meanings, and teaching others in class and within the discipline about one of its blind spots.

Robert and I meet frequently in the beginning of the course to chat about his project ideas. He asks me whether it would be appropriate for him to undertake an unconventional project. Could he fill a gap in the literature by creating a meta-analysis, one that centers on advancing a careful, critical examination of the rhetorical contradictions within memoir itself, exposing specific problems he sees at the heart of the genre? I encourage him to pursue this project because, to my knowledge, no rhetoric scholars have yet fully addressed the ways in which the language used in the memoir genre undermines the genre's own claims to validity based on truthfulness and authenticity.

Much like Dania's, Robert's first strategy is a process of inquiry and discovery, as he immerses himself in the history of the memoir genre. His research question is this: Why does memoir have certain rhetorical tactics, and what are their potential effects on the genre itself? As he reads numerous theoretical and historical texts, as well as primary texts in the genre of memoir, Robert perceives his project in new ways. During his discovery process, Robert ascertains that, in fact, the memoir genre has undergone significant historical shifts over time. Initially memoirs centered on military leaders and important political figures, endeavoring to clarify and justify their actions during a particular time period or set of events. These early memoirs may employ very different rhetorical approaches than do today's memoirs, Robert begins to believe. He perceives that now memoir has also adopted many of the stylistic and rhetorical tactics previously reserved solely for fiction—the very tactics that, years earlier, would have called the veracity of such memoir accounts into question. Robert considers why this change may have happened and why it could be significant.

Robert and I meet again to confer about his desire to contemplate more fully the problem of fiction in memoir. Because Robert is fascinated by military history, I ask him to consider analyzing primary texts. What might happen if he juxtaposed the memoirs of historical figures, such as Ulysses S. Grant's *The Civil War Memoirs of Ulysses S. Grant* (2002) and George Armstrong Custer's *My Life on the Plains* (1962), with contemporary examples? Robert readily takes up this experiment in an effort to see what he can uncover, and makes use of his journal entries and discussions with his research team to move toward close analyses of the primary texts and application. Through this move toward application, Robert recognizes that between contemporary memoirs and earlier memoirs, the differences go deeper still. Reading multiple examples of today's memoirs, Robert establishes that they rely heavily on rhetorical forms never used in the past, such as synecdoche and dialogue. Instead, modern memoirs are what Robert terms *memoir-novel hybrids*, no longer simply endeavors to craft nonfiction accounts, as in the groundbreaking *In Cold Blood* (1965) by Truman Capote, but rather blends of equal parts fiction and nonfiction. Robert indicates that this poses an enormous problem for the genre. Working with his research team and me, Robert raises crucial concerns about the genre's dependence on truth for its mark of authenticity, yet its reliance on fiction in order to capture an ever-shrinking book audience.

Very quickly, Robert gathers his research team members' suggestions about whether any receptions of contemporary memoirs have exposed this problem. Several of his team members advocate that he scrutinize the audience responses to Frey's book because its public reception exposed the issue of truth in memoir. Responding in large part to these conversations, Robert uses Frey's book as a key text in his argument.

However, as Robert continues to integrate and apply what he has discovered, it is significant that he refuses to propose that the whole genre is compromised, because doing so would oversimplify the case. Citing autobiography theorist Leigh Gilmore (2001), Robert argues that the fact that the voices of women, people of color, gay men and lesbians, the disabled, and survivors of violence have come to the fore is very positive. In the end, Robert comes to believe that as the genre grows and progresses, increasingly subtle changes will also inevitably result—always balancing the need to garner an audience with the genre's dependence on truth. Moving toward teaching, however, Robert concludes that without careful self-reflection, the description of the memoir genre may cease to have any real meaning, let alone to adequately represent the texts under its purview.

When Robert shares his research, he brings in examples from many different memoirs, only some of which he wrote about in his project. Robert invites active learning from his audience as they offer their own thoughts about the similarities and differences between memoirs of today and those of the past. Robert teaches us about the existing scholarship around the rhetoric of memoir, situating himself as a contributor to new knowledge in this area. Once his presentation in the class is complete, other class participants, Robert's research team, and others from the university community extend their suggestions, furnishing additional ideas for expanding the project. Robert hopes to attend graduate school in English and to continue work on this project.

The Problems and Possibilities of Undergraduate Research

I include reflection in my course because I believe that without such reflection, it is hard to move one's inquiry to the next level. These reflections are often shared with the larger class group. The following statements by Dania and Robert strike me as significant in that both students revel in their complex processes of discovery, integration, application, and teaching, but struggle with the tough responsibilities that accompany a researcher within a larger scholarly community. These responsibilities are hard to negotiate and must be constantly reassessed and altered within disciplinary scholarship itself. As Dania puts it,

> I was incredibly excited to write about PostSecret, something near and dear to my heart. However, searching through the sheer volume of PostSecret information took a long time. Even when I finally finished my paper, I still felt as if there were 10 more pages worth of information I could have included. I find myself disappointed that I wasn't able to contribute more, that I couldn't think of more ways to include information.

Dania had to confront the problems caused by the artificial limits of course length—the page restrictions and time crunches. She had to combat her own disappointment at seeing the problems in her research that she wanted to address, while knowing that she wouldn't be able to take them up as fully as she hoped. Similarly, Robert notes that "time constraints threatened to damage the overall effectiveness of my arguments," yet "I still feel that I succeeded. Keeping in mind that this is only the beginning of something much larger, I am pretty happy with it." Robert recognizes that the best projects do not depend necessarily on the final written products but rather the discoveries along the way. He appreciates that he has presented a well-organized argument, that his claims are sound, and that the evidence he supplies does in fact support his claims.

Dania's further commentary concerns both the problems and possibilities posed by a greater focus on undergraduate research itself. What Dania indicates is perhaps surprising and instructive for those concerned about how to best teach rhetoric and research to undergraduates:

> This memoir class is one of two English classes in which I've written anything like a research paper. The other was my freshmen English class. I much prefer my memoir class. Although this was the most difficult assignment I have ever taken on, it was also the most rewarding. I picked a topic I was passionate about, that made an impact on my life. While the journey to completion was long, it was very rewarding as well. My paper is a work in progress, and will continue to be for some time. I picked a fascinating topic, one that means a great deal to me—and my motivation to write tripled.

Throughout her undergraduate career, Dania has written very few research papers and has never engaged in inquiry-based undergraduate research. Dania's experience signifies that communication within and between disciplines about the importance of undergraduate research is happening too slowly.

Robert, too, takes on the question of undergraduate research more directly:

> Undergraduate research can be frustrating because of built-in limitations. We are not only limited by our lack of experience but also by the boundaries the academic hierarchy places upon us. Though this system may be difficult to cope with at times, these limitations also force writers to be more creative about how they approach synthesizing arguments as well as more cognizant of other, preexisting views.

Robert's reflections illustrate that his own inexperience and the structures of universities themselves seem to undermine his ability to be perceived as a researcher. Although Robert hopes to be able to engage in inquiry-based research projects, he is aware that institutions of higher learning, and the disciplines they represent, still depend on power structures in which advanced degrees are valued more, in which undergraduates' voices are likely to be seen as less credible. And, though the undergraduate research movement has tried hard to bring undergraduates into our discussions, Robert acknowledges that a hierarchy of learning still very much exists, one that he values but sometimes struggles with.

Implications and Future Directions

Each time I teach this course, I continue to ponder exactly how much we can accomplish by making undergraduate research more central to our curricula, and what we must modify in our academic environments for it to truly be effective. I also become more aware of what my students are going through. As a novice in the world of memoir writing, I, too, am prone to feel overwhelmed by the task, to have trouble seeing what my contributions might offer, to have difficulty synthesizing what others have written before. Like my students, I lose confidence in my ability to make an original contribution, habitually question my own project's significance, and have the nagging sense that my project will never really be finished. I am also constantly bumping up against the hierarchies that exist within our discipline—hierarchies that imply that certain sorts of research are appropriate for rhetoric scholars, while others might not be. And when I write in the creative, nonfiction mode, I am stepping into an arena in which I have to tentatively take on the mantle of an expert, even though at times I feel ill-equipped to assume that role.

Since I am experiencing much of what my own students undergo and sharing this with them along the way, I am ever surer that how I integrate undergraduate research into my course will need to adjust and grow more as well. Just as Dania and Robert have come to recognize the importance of the progressive, inquiry focus of writing undergraduate research papers in rhetoric, as their teacher and co-inquirer, I have come to understand how the memoir course—and how I incorporate undergraduate research itself—is still truly in process.

My experiences, and Dania's and Robert's reflections, lead me to reflect on and suggest important future directions for undergraduate research. First, undergraduate rhetoric courses need to use prompts and questions that are open-ended, to better encourage creativity and self-expression. Providing freedom and flexibility in approach and topic selection is one crucial way to connect with our students. Along with this exciting freedom to produce original research and craft significant contributions to the discipline, though, come genuine anxieties and fears.

Second, undergraduate students need to realize that their struggles do not reveal them to be inadequate as researchers. Still, undergraduate researchers must have more support as experts-in-training. This may entail inviting students from previous classes to work in teams with our current students, helping them work through these difficulties. We need additional, larger cross-disciplinary events that have energizing social and intellectual components, drawing together student researchers from across universities. And we need more conferences run by students themselves that examine the real problems and possibilities posed by undergraduate research— to help our students deal with the real pressures of conducting original research, not just in one class, but throughout the structure of our curricula across the disciplines. As teachers, placing ourselves in situations that force us to be novices can be a powerful way to appreciate what our students are experiencing, to get an even better sense of their needs.

Third, our curricula need to be frequently assessed and, as necessary, changed. Sustaining this new model from first-year courses through senior capstones is imperative if we want to adequately prepare our undergraduate students for the sorts of research they will do throughout their continuing education and careers. This is also essential if we want to enable today's researchers to affect, foster, and support the research of the future.

Finally, dissemination must be made more central. Students need the chance not only to discover, integrate, and apply their original ideas but also to share them. We must give our students opportunities to teach—to share their work with their peers in small and large groups, with others from both inside and outside the university community. Giving students more and more avenues and opportunities to circulate their work among those in other disciplines, as well as outside the university community, will also be crucial if undergraduate research in rhetoric classes is to have lasting effects on both our curricula and our discipline.

Note

1. I would like to thank Dania Allen and Robert Finch for permission to cite their work in this chapter.

References

Boyer, Ernest L. 1990. *Scholarship Reconsidered: Priorities of the Professoriate*. Carnegie Foundation for the Advancement of Teaching. Princeton, NJ: Princeton University Press.

Brown, Cupcake. 2007. *A Piece of Cake*. New York: Three Rivers Press.

Burroughs, Augusten. 2006. *Running with Scissors*. New York: St. Martin's.

Capote, Truman. 1965. *In Cold Blood*. New York: Random House.

Custer, George Armstrong. 1962. *My Life on the Plains; Or, Personal Experiences with Indians*. Introd. Edgar I. Stewart. Norman: University of Oklahoma Press.

Dotterer, Ronald L. 2002. Student-Faculty Collaborations, Undergraduate Research, and Collaboration as an Administrative Model. *New Directions for Teaching and Learning*, 90 (Summer): 81–89.

Eggers, Dave. 2001. *A Heartbreaking Work of Staggering Genius*. New York: Vintage.

Flynn, Nick. 2004. *Another Bullshit Night in Suck City: A Memoir*. New York: Norton.

Frey, James. 2005. *A Million Little Pieces*. New York: Anchor Books.

Gilmore, Leigh. 2001. *The Limits of Autobiography: Trauma and Testimony*. London: Cornell University Press.

Grant, Ulysses S. 2002. *The Civil War Memoirs of Ulysses S. Grant*. Ed. Brian M. Thomsen. New York: Forge.

Jones, Margaret B. 2008. *Love and Consequences: A Memoir of Hope and Survival*. New York: Riverhead Books.

Land, Brad. 2004. *Goat: A Memoir*. New York: Random House.

Murdock, Maureen. 2003. *Unreliable Truth: On Memoir and Memory*. New York: Seal Press.

Pletka, Bob. 2007. *Educating the Net Generation: How to Engage Students in the 21st Century*. Santa Monica, CA: Santa Monica Press.

Rose, Steven. 1993. *The Making of Memory: From Molecules to Mind*. New York: Anchor Books.

Scott, Joan W. 1992. Experience. In *Feminists Theorize the Political*, ed. Judith Butler and Joan W. Scott, 22–40. New York: Routledge.

Smith, Alison. 2005. *Name All the Animals*. New York: Scribner.

Smith, Ronald. 2001. Expertise and the Scholarship of Teaching. *Scholarship Revisited: Perspectives on the Scholarship of Teaching. New Directions in Teaching and Learning*, 86 (Summer): 69–78.

Smith, Sidonie, and Julia Watson. 2001. *Reading Autobiography: A Guide for Interpreting Life Narratives*. Minneapolis: University of Minnesota Press.

Swofford, Anthony. 2005. *Jarhead: A Marine's Chronicle of the Gulf War and Other Battles*. New York: Simon and Schuster, Pocket Books.

Chapter Fourteen

Cultivating Rhetorical Dispositions through Curricular Change in Technical and Professional Communication

Brian J. McNely
Ball State University

During the summer of 2007, while visiting family in the San Francisco Bay area, I made a brief visit to the University of California–Berkeley, a campus where I had spent more than a little time as a teenager, attending Cal football games with my father. Passing through Sather Gate, I noticed a striking blue-and-gold banner draped above the doors of Dwinelle Hall:

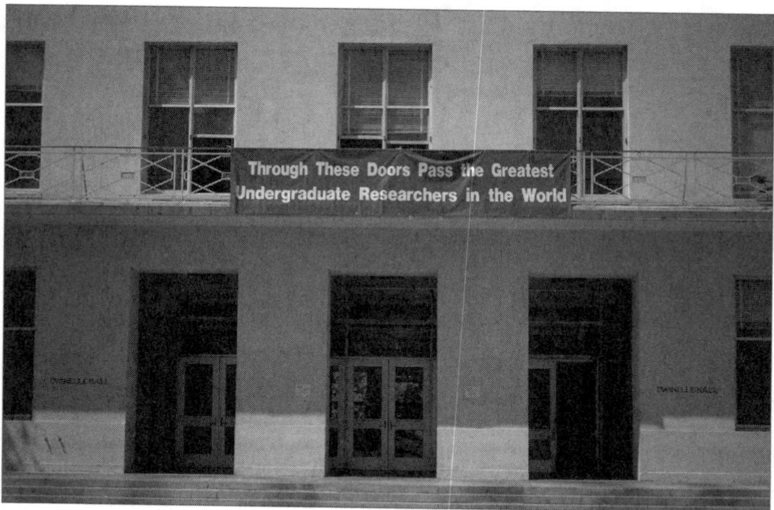

Figure 14.1. *UC–Berkeley undergraduate research banner.*

"Through These Doors Pass the Greatest Undergraduate Researchers in the World." The simple yet profound expectation that this establishes for students at UC–Berkeley struck me as terribly important, especially given the fact that I had recently been discussing with colleagues the viability of inquiry-based methods of undergraduate research in the rhetoric and writing studies program of my own institution at that time, the University of Texas at El Paso (UTEP).[1] This chapter explores the redesign of technical and professional writing courses within the UTEP program, focusing on the curricular change that helped transform a traditional workplace writing course into a viable site for fomenting undergraduate research.

The UC–Berkeley banner effectively encapsulates a complex of kairotic moments that converged during the summer of 2007. These moments included the publication of Douglas Downs and Elizabeth Wardle's (2007) tremendously influential article, which sought to reenvision first-year composition as an "Introduction to Writing Studies" (see also Downs and Wardle's chapter in this collection) and the invigorating discussions the article engendered among faculty and doctoral students in our program. At this time, we were also developing an undergraduate major in rhetoric and writing studies, and redesigning courses in professional and technical writing to better align with both the forthcoming major and the realities of communicating in the contemporary workplace. Using this complex of kairotic moments as a touchstone, and drawing on recent work in undergraduate research as a curricular movement, this chapter argues that programs and departments of rhetoric, writing, technical communication, and related fields should focus first and foremost on curricular change as a method of fostering meaningful udergraduate research—change that is inculcated at UTEP by the development of rhetoric and writing courses that *study rhetoric and writing itself*.

At the center of this curricular philosophy for our[2] redesign of the professional writing course is the concept of *rhetorical dispositions*, a method of heuristic thinking and doing cobbled together from several sources, including the idea of *learning dispositions* that originated in educational research, the "durable, transposable dispositions" of Pierre Bourdieu (1977, 72), and the "rhetorical aptitudes" of Brenton Faber (2002, 136). The impetus for exploring rhetorical dispositions and undergraduate research was the planned redesign of both professional and technical writing courses that serve a significant cross section of undergraduate students from a variety of majors, from sophomores to seniors. Properly realized, the concept of rhetorical dispositions is simultaneously a curricular and pedagogical approach that promotes metacognition and complex rhetorical thinking, and gives our undergraduate students both a grounding in theories of rhetoric essential to effective communication in the contemporary workplace and the opportunity to become participant *researchers* in our field.

In the remainder of this chapter, I describe the importance of drawing on our field's own disciplinary content, its relationship to the concept of rhetorical dispositions, and the programmatic curricular change that grew out of such an approach. Most important, I describe the impact that such curricular change has on our undergraduate students as researchers and knowledge workers: how fostering meaningful undergraduate inquiry in technical and professional communication can contribute to our disciplinary knowledge. Finally, I describe the dissemination of such undergraduate inquiry, drawing on the research of my own students, who presented remarkable original work in professional and organizational communication at a large regional conference.

Disciplinary Content and the "Workplace Writing" Course

Prior to 2007, the majority of workplace writing sections offered at UTEP contained very little disciplinary content. Other than what might be available in a typical professional writing textbook (such as Locker [2006], for example) students would study little (if any) primary, seminal works in rhetoric and writing theory. Yet from the early work of William Hart-Davidson (2001) to the more recent work of Downs and Wardle (2007) and that of Libby Miles and colleagues (2008), there has been an increasing emphasis on incorporating disciplinary content in undergraduate rhetoric and writing courses, and using such content to likewise germinate and promote new, original research. As we continued to develop the vertical curriculum that will comprise our forthcoming undergraduate major in rhetoric and writing studies, a curriculum that includes both professional and technical writing courses, we felt that what should drive meaningful undergraduate inquiry is a grounding in our own disciplinary theory, practice, and research methods. Charged with the task of heading up the redesign of the undergraduate workplace writing curriculum, I argued to our program's faculty that the professional writing classroom represents a unique space in which to explore both landmark and contemporary theories of writing, rhetoric, and organizational communication. Hence, the first order of business was to revisit the politics of naming, by changing the course title to better reflect the complexity of the contemporary, sociotechnical, networked workplace: the pilot course was known as Workplace Writing and Organizational Communication, a change that underscores a greater breadth of research and supports a key philosophical approach to organizations as discursive formations.

Like many undergraduate courses, our redesigned Workplace Writing and Organizational Communication course serves multiple stakeholders at our institution. While there is a growing contingent of students from fields such as computer and information science and sociology, the majority of the students come from the College of Business Administration. Instead of tempering the amount and complexity of disciplinary content for this audience, we viewed these students as especially suited to exploring theories of writing and rhetoric, mainly by following Clay Spinuzzi (2006), who draws on research in activity theory, management, sociology, and technical communication to describe organizations as polycontextual and distributed. Spinuzzi argues that knowledge workers—those whose primary workplace currency is "information that is continually interpreted and circulated across organizational boundaries"—must become "*strong rhetors*" (1, 3) in order to succeed in the complex, technology-saturated workplaces of tomorrow. It followed, therefore, that in order to become strong rhetors, our students needed a broader, more effective grounding in rhetorical theory. Similarly, they needed practice in document design that responds to the agile realities of digital communication. Finally, a grounding in disciplinary knowledge would give every student, regardless of major, the opportunity to conduct meaningful research in the field.

The changes to our workplace writing curriculum were also driven by disciplinary content that has impacted our philosophical approach. For example, the influential scholarship of James Porter and others (2000) in describing a methodology of institutional critique has certainly been germane to our efforts at effecting programmatic curricular change. More recently, the work of Jeffrey Grabill (2003, 2008), W. Michele Simmons and Grabill (2007), and Stuart Blythe, Grabill, and Kirk Riley (2008) all provide trenchant precedents for exploring the confluence of disciplinary knowledge, organizational structures, and professional writing and rhetoric. These studies reflect the kinds of methodologies that are extremely useful for undergraduate inquiry, as they combine research in rhetoric and writing with real-world organizational experiences and implications. Because many students at UTEP are employed, and because many more business students seek and perform summer internships, a grounding in important rhetorical theory and a view of workplaces as discursive formations provides students with a rich, built-in terrain for performing their own research.

Cultivating Rhetorical Dispositions

In an article published just over twenty years ago, Peter Drucker (1988) turned the focus of management theory toward the concept of knowledge work, primarily in response to the growing demands of the nascent information economy. In both empirical and theoretical explorations of knowledge work, an area of research is found where the intersections of rhetoric and writing studies and business administration are especially prevalent. Spinuzzi (2006) argues that knowledge work "tends to be organized in distributed, heterogeneous networks rather than in modular hierarchies" (1); both business professionals and academics work with information sources that are varied across geographies, cultures, and disciplinary or professional domains. Spinuzzi further argues that "knowledge work demands different *sorts* of texts, and it also demands different ways of *thinking* about how those texts are produced, received, and managed." He thus emphasizes rhetoric, indicating that future professionals need to "understand how to make arguments, how to persuade, how to build trust and stable alliances, how to negotiate and bargain across boundaries" (3). Similarly, in describing the information-based organization, Drucker (1988) argues that knowledge will be made and disseminated by "specialists who do different work and direct themselves" (45). The question becomes, how do we foster self-direction in our students? An answer, I argue, is found in the form of rhetorical dispositions and a proclivity toward inquiry-based research.

The scenarios described by Drucker and Spinuzzi, and the skills they argue are necessary for dealing with the complexities of the distributed, information-based economy, have at least one thing in common: they position the knowledge worker, sometimes explicitly, sometimes tacitly, as a *researcher*. In order to direct oneself, in order to communicate effectively across organizational boundaries, students need not only to become strong rhetors, to develop what Faber (2002) calls "rhetorical aptitudes" (136), but also to develop dispositions and inquiry paradigms (Emig 1982) that demonstrate a proclivity toward research and self-directed inquiry that continually recognizes and negotiates the role of rhetoric in knowledge-making and interpretation. In short, they need to think and act rhetorically.

Shari Tishman, Eileen Jay, and D. N. Perkins (1993) argue that "what sets good thinkers apart [. . .] is their abiding tendencies to explore, to inquire, to seek clarity, to take intellectual risks, to think critically and imaginatively" (148), tendencies that they term *thinking dispositions*. The authors offer several interrelated thinking dispositions that should be cultivated in students, one of which receives particular attention in the concept of rhetorical dispositions that drives our curricular change: the ability to be metacognitive. They note that metacognition is characterized by the "tendency to be aware of and monitor the flow of one's own thinking; alertness to complex thinking situations; [and] the ability to exercise control of mental processes and to be reflective" (150). Ultimately, the authors suggest a model of pedagogical "enculturation" that "asks teachers to create a culture of thinking in the classroom" (154). This is consistent with Bourdieu's (1977) concept of the *habitus*, the environmental and material conditions that potentially structure student agency and inquiry in the classroom (and beyond). The challenge for curriculum development is inculcating such inclinations toward *rhetorical inquiry*.

Our redesign of the workplace writing course seeks to create a culture of *rhetorical thinking* in the classroom (and beyond). To think rhetorically, metacognitively, and with a rhetorical disposition, students must understand, at even a basic level, theories of rhetoric as epistemic, of the role of language in knowledge-making and ontology. Rhetorical thinking encourages students to view organizations and institutions as discursive formations, to explore the ways in which discourse produces organizational image and identity. At the same time, thinking rhetorically provides ample opportunity for student-led inquiry. Equipped with a basic knowledge of disciplinary content and methods, students can explore workplaces and other contexts of language-in-use as sites of research. Following the recent work of Grabill (2008), who explores problems of assembly, infrastructure, and indicators in studying public rhetorics, I offer this definition of a rhetorical disposition: a continual metacognitive approach to communicative practices that assembles relevant stakeholders, displays an acute awareness of organizational infrastructures and agency/structure dynamics, and seeks real-time indicators of workplace performance and rhetorical effectiveness. Ultimately, a rhetorical disposition, as both a curricular and pedagogical philosophy, positions students as knowledge workers, a dynamic that presupposes and fosters undergraduate research.

Curricular Change

Given the range of students who enroll in the UTEP course, we have found that the concept of knowledge work has been especially productive, as it allows students to digest disciplinary content along a broad continuum of approaches and skill sets. Students range from those who will use such knowledge to more effectively communicate in the workplace to those who will actually seek out opportunities to study rhetoric and writing beyond the classroom. The syllabus helps establish the habitus for the course, the rhetorical thinking environment that positions students as knowledge workers:

> In this course we will examine the role that language plays in our lives and organizations, from our ways of acquiring and expressing knowledge, to the ways that we perceive the world, ourselves, and others. More specifically, we will examine workplaces as *discursive formations*, taking a rhetorical approach to workplace writing and communication, and seeing organizations as complex, polycontextual, and distributed. The first half of the course takes a broad theoretical approach, introducing influential readings from researchers in Professional/Technical Communication and Rhetoric and Writing Studies. The second half of the course applies these theories to common workplace writing contexts through case analyses and developmental projects.

The course objectives bring the expectations to the forefront. Students will

- investigate and implement theories of language, rhetoric, and analysis;
- explore and practice methods of rhetorical thinking and metacognition;
- explore and practice the common conventions of workplace writing and organizational communication;
- explore and practice writing research in the workplace; and
- investigate and practice writing as a way of thinking, knowing, and being, using their writing to negotiate their world.

Finally, many of the ideas that support the theory of rhetorical dispositions (and the theory itself) are explicitly delineated as a component of the course: an approach that, more than any other, directly positions students as *contributors* and fellow travelers in the exploration of new knowledge. In this sense, the theoretical foundation for the curricular change is not something that is furtively discussed by faculty and administration, only to be foisted on an unwitting student populace. Instead, such theories are central to the course, and are reflected in the "key terms and phrases" section that follows the course objectives:

> *Rhetoric—Discourse/Discursive—Metacognitive—Distributed Work—Epistemology —Ontology—Organizational Identity —Agency—Invention—Rhetorical Thinking—Rhetorical Dispositions—Polycontextual—Multilingual—Recursion—Aggregation—Inquiry—Structure—Power—Image—Subjectivity —Assembly—Indicators—Effectiveness—Knowledge Work*

In order to cover such a broad and complex range of topics, students spend the first half of the semester (eight weeks) exploring seminal primary research in rhetoric and writing studies. They read early articles by Barry Brummett (1979) and Janet Emig (1982) alongside contemporary articles by Spinuzzi (2006, 2007). They read Drucker (1988) and compare his early ideas about the "new organization" with the contemporary distributed work environments described by Spinuzzi. They also read real-world studies of professional writers, like those of Dorothy Winsor (2006) and Hart-Davidson and colleagues (2008). Most important, they read Faber's (2002) *Community Action and Organizational Change*, an accessible and important work that covers ideas ranging from Aristotle to Foucault. Finally, during the first half of the course, students examine these theories by working in teams, and *by writing*.

The second half of the course seeks to build on this theoretical knowledge by giving students opportunities to practice rhetorical dispositions. At first, there is an emphasis on using the case method, on asking students to explore real-world scenarios that demand complex rhetorical thinking and metacognition. From there, students examine research in the field on their own, selecting a current theoretical or empirical study and reporting on methods and outcomes for their fellow knowledge workers, effectively broadening the base of disciplinary knowledge for everyone in the class. Finally, students position themselves as either internal or external consultants for a real organization, responding to a real-world problem and creating a recommendation report that can help effect change.[3]

Student Research and Dissemination

To our pleasant surprise, the course has received overwhelming approval from the students who have taken it thus far, and not simply because the ideas it fosters are perceived as helpful to eventual career success.[4] More important, several students have developed rhetorical dispositions leading to meaningful disciplinary research beyond the course.

Although the undergraduate research that grew out of two separate sections of the course was ultimately student directed, as the instructor, I helped inform my students of the various opportunities that existed for the dissemination of such research. For example, I used class time to describe several different opportunities for conferences and writing contests that I had encountered in the course of my own professional work. I also informed students of ways in which they could seek out their own research opportunities by examining the University of Pennsylvania Calls for Papers archives, and those of H-Net. I showed my students *Young Scholars in Writing*, and discussed the prestige associated with publication in an academic journal. I considered the Southwest Texas Popular Culture and American Culture Association (SWTX PCA/ACA) annual conference a strong option for students who wanted to pursue writing research beyond the classroom: the conference is well attended, has several content areas for which student work could be situated, and is held in Albuquerque, within a comfortable travel range—about 250 miles from El Paso. In order to facilitate research beyond the classroom, I made our program's conference room available at certain times so that students interested in pursuing writing research beyond the class could meet and discuss ideas. Eventually, six students from two different sections approached me about forming one or two panels for the SWTX PCA/ACA conference. I agreed to help them organize their proposal and to vet ideas for their collective and individual abstracts.

Perhaps the most difficult work, my students soon discovered, was building on the foundational theories we discussed in class in a way that was contextualized for the technical communication area of a popular culture conference (the area to which they submitted). Because the panel of five (one decided early in the process not to participate) consisted of one communications and four business majors, the students decided to organize their research around NBC's sitcom *The Office*. The title of the panel, "Rhetoric at Dunder Mifflin: *The Office*, Business Communication, and Undergraduate Research," and the following panel abstract give the tenor of their collective research:

> Is Michael Scott sensitive to variant channels of discourse? Is he capable of negotiating both the formal (Jan and newly corporate Ryan) and informal (Dwight, Pam, Jim, et al.) networks of communication at Dunder Mifflin's Scranton branch? Perhaps more importantly, does he have any cognizance of the differing governing gazes employed (sometimes tactically, sometimes tacitly) by his team both in the office and in the warehouse? Is Michael Scott an effective rhetor, the type of person capable of managing knowledge workers in a distributed workplace?
>
> Given Steve Carell's portrayal of the bumbling, insensitive, and ineffectual Michael in NBC's *The Office*, the answers to these questions appear to be a resounding "no." Nonetheless, the popular portrayal of a professional workplace in *The Office* provides an interesting opportunity for the exploration of professional communication mores. Our panel, comprised of undergraduate students in Business and Communication at the University of Texas at El Paso, will approach *The Office* as both the source and jumping off point for our discussion of Accounting as a discursive practice, behavioral subjectivity, power, image, and technology, interpersonal communication, and the entrepreneurial gaze [. . .]
>
> [D]rawing from and moving beyond the core theoretical research from two separate sections of Workplace Writing and Organizational Communication, this panel will offer a coordinated and coherent investigation of the intersections between rhetoric, professional communication, and popular culture.

I agreed to serve as panel chair for the session, and I helped the students prepare for the process of submitting and presenting at a professional academic conference. We met to discuss and compose both collective and individual abstracts, and once our panel was accepted, we applied for, and received, travel funding from the College of Liberal Arts. These experiences, to say nothing of the conference itself, gave students a valuable opportunity to pursue and disseminate research and to learn some of the ins and outs of doing academic scholarship.

The real work of scholarship began after the panel proposal was accepted. Students had to take the ideas from their respective abstracts and craft them into academically rigorous, well-researched presentations. For the purposes of this chapter, I focus on the work of two students who developed compelling research that can truly add to our disciplinary knowledge. Wendy, a sophomore accounting major, developed a theory of "behavioral subjectivity" as a means to understanding the character Dwight from *The Office*. Her abstract details this concept:

> In today's corporate world, a complex adaptive strategy is key in the ascension to the top of an organization's competitive hierarchy. One such strategy is employing a malleable identity, where getting in the boss's good graces might be facilitated through one's willingness to assume a variety of subject positions. A particularly apt example is Dwight Schrute from *The Office*; he can be seen enacting warrior-like behavior to capture an intrusive vampire bat, or taking on the task of cutting employee medical benefits in response to the merest suggestion from his manager, Michael.
>
> Although this "behavior" might seem silly to some, it can be pragmatically impressive within corporate culture because it reflects not only a young professional's ability to adapt, but also the high regard in which the individual holds the organization's identity. By being flexible enough to mold an existing mentality and genuinely adapt to an organizational identity, professionals are that much more prepared than those who maintain a positivistic worldview and are unable (or unwilling) to assume different subject positions.

In her presentation, Wendy extended the knowledge of subject formation that she learned in the course by drawing on theories from Louis Althusser (1971), Michel Foucault (1972), and Helen Foster (2007), and in the process coining the phrase *behavioral subjectivity*, a concept that I have continued to use with my students.

Similarly, Ricky combined his own experiences as a young business owner with the theories of rhetoric and writing that we explored in class to produce a theory of the "entrepreneurial gaze," building upon Emig's (1982) notion of the *governing gaze*. His abstract follows:

> This presentation views the culture of young professionals that approach their corporate agency with an entrepreneurial gaze. I'll consider the benefits and pitfalls of how today's professionals play the corporate game differently in order to move through the structure of a corporation. In addition, I will address how these effects are mediated through different channels of communication and how expectations have changed in light of new work environments.
>
> I will also explore the different identities formed in these environments by interrogating the agency of young professionals in distributed workplaces. What worked twenty years ago in terms of structure, ideals, beliefs, and expectations will not work in the same way today. This is primarily attributed to the postmodern corporation's approach to organizational identity and the young professional's role within that structure.
>
> Now more than ever, corporate organizational structures have flattened and discourse communities have changed. This plays a significant role in the young professional's identity. They assume an entrepreneurial gaze, one that is fundamentally and inescapably rhetorical; as Spinuzzi has noted, young professionals above all need to be good rhetors. In *The Office*, newly corporate Ryan embodies the entrepreneurial gaze; he's the former temp, looking to advance his career while using Dunder Mifflin as his stepping stone to bigger and better things.

Ricky's work represents a potentially significant contribution to disciplinary knowledge. For example, his theory of the *entrepreneurial gaze* effectively updates Drucker's (1988) contention that knowledge workers must thrive in the absence of management, directing themselves and communicating with other specialists. Ricky's work positions this concept as inherently rhetorical, and indicative of an entrepreneurial ethos.

The research examples of Wendy and Ricky offer the promise of both rhetorical dispositions and undergraduate research. The panel presentation was extremely well received, and our audience was composed entirely of faculty in first-year writing, technical, or professional communication. The research produced by these students also indicates the deep changes that can be brought about and developed by rethinking curriculum design and our expectations of student research. Four more students presented research at the same conference in 2009, and programmatic adoption of the curriculum continues to foment undergraduate research. Certainly, our experience has not been free of problems or resistance (from either students or faculty). In each section, several students have voiced displeasure with reading theory, and expressed cognitive dissonance at navigating a course that didn't meet their initial expectations. Yet it is informed curricular change that can act as the philosophical framework for changing such expectations of professional and technical writing as viable and worthwhile objects of study. Moreover, *our* expectations of students as researchers and knowledge workers drive a broader culture of inquiry within our program, our department, and our institutional standing across campus. Our experiences at UTEP illustrate how a curriculum built on inquiry and the cultivation of rhetorical dispositions can foster undergraduate contributions to rhetoric and writing studies.

Notes

1. The University of Texas–El Paso, located on the United States–Mexican border, is the only doctoral research-intensive university in the United States with a student body that is predominantly Mexican-American. With an undergraduate enrollment of just more than 20,000, UTEP's student population is 72.5 percent Hispanic, primarily serving students from the El Paso region. UTEP offers eighty-one bachelor's degree options, more than seventy master's degree options, and fourteen doctoral options.

2. Though the redesign of the workplace writing curriculum was largely my own project, I certainly didn't create such changes in a vacuum. In the remainder of this chapter, references to "we" or "our" indicate my reliance on the feedback and ideas of colleagues, in particular Helen Foster, director of the rhetoric and writing studies program.

3. Sometimes students will create a report that can be used in a real organization, but more often than not, they'll address real issues from within the context of the course. For example, a typical scenario might have an accounting student offering financial recommendations to a subprime lender for negotiating the current mortgage crisis.

4. Initially piloted to two sections of twenty-five students each, the course has since been taught to another five sections, with similarly positive results. We planned an even larger offering for the spring semester of 2009, and the success of the course also has led to meaningful collaboration with the College of Business to incorporate more of the kinds of writing experiences described here into the core College of Business curriculum.

References

Althusser, Louis. 1971. *Lenin and Philosophy and Other Essays*. Trans. Ben Brewster. New York: Monthly Review Press.

Blythe, Stuart, Jeffrey T. Grabill, and Kirk Riley. 2008. Action Research and Wicked Environmental Problems: Exploring Appropriate Roles for Researchers in Professional Communication. *Journal of Business and Technical Communication* 22 (3): 272–298.

Bourdieu, Pierre. 1977. *Outline of a Theory of Practice*. Cambridge: Cambridge University Press.

Brummett, Barry. 1979. Three Meanings of Epistemic Rhetoric. Paper presented at the annual meeting of the Speech Communication Association, San Antonio, TX.

Downs, Douglas, and Elizabeth Wardle. 2007. Teaching about Writing, Righting Misconceptions: (Re)Envisioning "First-Year Composition" as "Introduction to Writing Studies." *College Composition and Communication* 58 (4): 552–584.

Drucker, Peter F. 1988. The Coming of the New Organization. *Harvard Business Review* 66 (1): 43–53.

Emig, Janet. 1982. Inquiry Paradigms and Writing. *College Composition and Communication* 33 (1): 64–75.

Faber, Brenton D. 2002. *Community Action and Organizational Change: Image, Narrative, and Identity*. Carbondale: Southern Illinois University Press.

Foster, Helen. 2007. *Networked Process: Dissolving Boundaries of Process and Post-Process*. West Lafayette, IN: Parlor Press.

Foucault, Michel. 1972. *The Archaeology of Knowledge*. New York: Harper.

Grabill, Jeffrey T. 2003. Community Computing and Citizen Productivity. *Computers and Composition* 20 (2): 131–50.

———. 2008. Problems with Researching and Assembling Public Rhetorics. Paper presented at the annual meeting of the Conference on College Composition and Communication, New Orleans.

Hart-Davidson, William. 2001. Reviewing and Rebuilding Technical Communication Theory: Considering the Value of Theory for Informing Change in Practice and Curriculum. *Proceedings of the Society for Technical Communication Convention*: 1–6. Chicago: STC.

Hart-Davidson, William, Grace Bernhardt, Michael McLeod, Martine Rife, and Jeffrey T. Grabill. 2008. Coming to Content Management: Inventing Infrastructure for Organizational Knowledge Work. *Technical Communication Quarterly* 17 (1): 10–34.

Locker, Kitty O. 2006. *Business and Administrative Communication*. 7th ed. Boston: McGraw-Hill/Irwin.

Miles, Libby, Michael Pennell, Kim Hensley Owens, Jeremiah Dyehouse, Helen O'Grady, Nedra Reynolds, Robert Schwegler, and Linda Shamoon. 2008. Interchanges: Commenting on Douglas Downs and Elizabeth Wardle's "Teaching about Writing, Righting Misconceptions." *College Composition and Communication* 59 (3): 503–11.

Porter, James E., Patricia Sullivan, Stuart Blythe, Jeffrey T. Grabill, and Libby Miles. 2000. Institutional Critique: A Rhetorical Methodology for Change. *College Composition and Communication* 51 (4): 610–42.

Simmons, W. Michele, and Jeffrey T. Grabill. 2007. Toward a Civic Rhetoric for Technologically and Scientifically Complex Places: Invention, Performance, and Participation. *College Composition and Communication* 58 (3): 419–48.

Spinuzzi, Clay. 2006. What Do We Need to Teach about Knowledge Work? Computer Writing and Research Lab White Paper. Austin: University of Texas.

———. 2007. Guest Editor's Introduction: Technical Communication in the Age of Distributed Work. *Technical Communication Quarterly* 16 (3): 265–77.

Wardle, Elizabeth. 2007. Understanding "Transfer" from FYC: Preliminary Results of a Longitudinal Study. *WPA: Writing Program Administration* 31 (1/2): 65–85.

Winsor, Dorothy. 2006. Using Writing to Structure Agency: An Examination of Engineers' Practice. *Technical Communication Quarterly* 15 (4): 411–30.

Afterword

KATHLEEN BLAKE YANCEY
Florida State University

Mentorship is the first of four characteristics that Toufic Hakim (1998) uses to distinguish undergraduate research projects from more conventional assignments that require students to do research. Originality, acceptability of research methods and techniques, and dissemination are the other three characteristics (190).

To begin, a bit of musing about how undergraduate education has changed.

As an undergraduate, I saw my professors as *professors*: teachers, yes, but more—scholars. On their best days, these men and women of all shapes and sizes specializing in fields ranging from Geoffrey Chaucer to Carson McCullers seemed more than smart, although they were that. They seemed *knowledgeable*, both about the knowledge already made that they were sharing with us and about the knowledge they were themselves making. *Knowledge they were making*: I'm not sure that anything else in the world was as exciting to me, in part because I knew that I was following their path, not in classes where I wrote predictable answers to faux questions, but in my undergraduate thesis, where I plotted a reading of William Faulkner that no scholar had mapped. Still, I didn't think of it as *research* nor of myself as a scholar. I didn't visit a library; we weren't explicit about the processes I used; neither we nor I reflected on those processes. The processes—a contradiction in terms—were decidedly a-social. I saw an interesting pattern; I applied for permission to pursue it; I composed the paper; and I submitted it to a single person. I'm pretty sure that was the extent of the circulation. In sum, although the project satisfied the undergraduate thesis requirement, I did not find it satisfying.

Some thirty years later, students are identified as scholars; they do conduct research; it is distributed; and we all reflect on those processes. And that research: it's diverse in topic, materials, and methodologies; rich in insight and contribution; provocative and interesting intellectually; and perhaps best of all, just plain alive. Whether students are documenting new learning in writing center spaces, or contributing to a wiki, or uncovering through archival work the lives of previously "silent" women, their research makes visible what we mean when we say that in higher education, we make knowledge. What's new is the *we*, and what's also new is how these efforts seem to revise rhetoric and composition scholar David Bartholomae's construction of the university and its students. In 1985, Bartholomae coined the expression "Inventing the University" to explain the basic task of the postsecondary student aspiring to success: "He must learn to speak our language" (134). In connecting *our* language and students' invention of the university, of course, Bartholomae highlighted a need for students to accommodate to and assimilate into *us*, into *our* institutions. But today's institution, seen through the lens of undergraduate research, seems much more dialogic by design and in practice, engaging both faculty and students in a making of knowledge that is an ever-widening engagement. In the postsecondary institutions hosting these research efforts, we work with students to invent a new identity, literally a new student, one who raises provocative questions; pursues them in various modes—alone, collaboratively, and in mentorships; synthesizes what has been learned; and shares the learning locally, nationally, and internationally.

Read together, these projects share four common features.

A first characteristic is the extracurricular location or site of the research. Ordinarily, school takes place inside of the school walls and the course "box," although increasingly, school includes other, often off-campus sites, like those associated with service-learning, internships, and co-ops. As presented here, undergraduate research in English studies takes place in another set of *new* learning spaces, which are typically spaces not designed either for schools or for undergraduates: online spaces like databases, blogs and wikis; library spaces; conference spaces; archival spaces; and travel spaces. In the model of learning represented here, then, it's not that learning in the course box is left behind—although necessary, it's not sufficient. Because to do research, one needs the multiple spaces supporting that endeavor, these projects have taken on a migratory aspect. Rather than replicate in school the spaces of research, undergraduate researchers *go* to the multiple spaces where research is made. Moreover, these extracurricular spaces are continuous in a way the typical college course is not: that is, they exist outside of the academic structure and the term-based calendar. Such spaces aren't designed for undergraduate researchers per se, of course, but instead are designed to support research and researchers of whatever variety. Built into the model of learning these spaces support is a concept of time radically different from that in school. Because these sites can be accessed year-round, they can support projects that require more than a term to complete. And a benefit of such multi-site–based projects is that students develop a new kind of independence, one that emerges from practices of research like the design of one's own project and the management of it.

A second factor characterizing undergraduate research in English studies is the set of processes and materials that constitute undergraduate research. Dating from at least the 1980s, as undergraduate education has shifted from a sage-on-the-stage model of lecture and test to student-centered projects, an accompanying emphasis has included helping students understand how knowledge is made. Unfortunately, recent research suggests that we in higher education aren't as successful as we'd like. Rose Marra and Betsy Palmer (2008), for example, find that even by the junior and senior years, college students all too often understand humanities as a collection of facts as opposed to a construction based on multiple sources of evidence. In their sample of students, for instance,

> there was a sizable proportion [. . .] (thirty-one of eighty-two ratable students) who espoused a simple "knowledge is facts" orientation. [. . .] Given that both samples were drawn from junior and senior students at respectable universities, we find it somewhat distressing that students are not developing an

> understanding of knowledge that allows them to acknowledge, let alone evaluate, competing knowledge claims. (108)

More specifically in the field of history, Sam Wineburg (2001) makes a similar claim, finding that students majoring in history neither work with the materials of history nor learn historical processes—like corroboration and sourcing—that would allow them to understand how history is made and to make history themselves.

In the projects described in this volume, however, both materials and processes are central to each project—whether those materials are primary and secondary documents, or transcripts of interviews, or annotated bibliographies; and whether those processes are completing source analysis worksheets or presenting to campus members at a local conference. In other words, both the materials of research—which can be messy and unbounded—and the processes of conducting research—which frequently take multiple circuitous routes decidedly at odds with the clean narrative line presented to students in courses and textbooks[1]—seem inherently to raise the kinds of questions that put what we know under erasure, yet still encourage us to ask new questions. It's a quest located in an understanding of knowledge as incomplete and contingent, as one undergraduate researcher explains:

> I began to understand why professional researchers know so many things: because the learning process is addictive. The more I read, the more I wanted to know. I uncovered one fact only to be confronted with the need for other facts. One question led to another. In an effort to discover Gower's sensibility and manner of composition, I discovered medieval nominalism and hunting techniques and began to understand how professors learn to anticipate the question, how do you know that?

A third factor characterizing undergraduate research in English studies is the focus on writing and sharing as distinctive and fundamental practices. Several scholars in rhetoric and composition have noted that students learn to write well when they experience two kinds of apprenticeships: (1) a cognitive apprenticeship, which is typically classroom-based, structured, and formal; and (2) a social apprenticeship, which is laboratory or studio-like, collaborative, and informal. For example, Huiling Ding (2008) traces the ways that the social apprenticeship of writing grants—a recursive process involving many genres and also, ultimately, a very specific task with real-world consequences—fosters both disciplinary and writing expertise for advanced undergraduates and graduate students. Similarly, the students engaged in undergraduate English studies research are writing continually and in multiple genres keyed to task—notes, analyses, interviews, bibliographies, posters, and published papers. In these processes focused on completing a research task important to them and others, they learn to write themselves into the discipline as a "natural" outcome. And it's important not to overlook audience in these projects. Here, there are typically *several* authentic audiences: the student writer, of course; the peers who may be involved; the faculty who are part of the project (and in various capacities, from mentor to collaborator); campus audiences; and disciplinary audiences. All these audiences, taken together, mean that the students are writing for others, creating real texts for others to read and learn from. The undergraduate research experience in English studies, as exemplified here, thus functions as a social apprenticeship for students, encouraging both compositional and disciplinary expertise.

A fourth factor characterizing undergraduate research in English studies is twofold: the engagement and satisfaction that faculty express as a consequence of working with undergraduates, and a sense that for these projects to be sustainable, new structures may need to be invented. The faculty reporting on their efforts in this volume are unanimous in their response: they not only see education and students anew, but they also come away with an increased appreciation of their own research practices. At the same time, most of these projects, especially at the upper levels of the undergraduate experience, are small scale. Even for those small projects to be sustainable, structures supporting them need to be designed and implemented.

As a genre, an *afterword* is not quite accurately named: it tends to look back and synthesize, but it also often extends a handshake into the future. In that spirit, reading across the collection, I'll identify seven questions that those of us who care about undergraduate research need to address.

1. *Seen from 30,000 feet, what are the purposes of undergraduate research? Can we take this good work and create a taxonomy of undergraduate research in English studies?* Such a categorization, especially if it were visualized electronically, would perform several functions, among them two that are particularly important. First, we could use it as a mechanism for introducing the universe of projects to others, whether administrators or colleagues. Second, we could use it to plot our local efforts across a national landscape, and also to plot new projects; it could be updated. With such a base, we would be better able to contextualize our efforts, to write grants collaboratively and inter-institutionally, and to locate our own work relative to that of others, especially others in the humanities.

2. *How is undergraduate research like graduate research, and how might or should it differ?* Put differently, how do we see the relationship between the two? Historically, undergraduate education has been seen as the time for the learning of material and processes. Graduate study, by way of contrast, has provided the opportunity for both specialization and research activity. In fact, the doctor of philosophy is regarded as a research degree, as distinct from a doctor of arts, for example, which is closer to a clinical degree. The argument in this volume, at least implicitly, is that research in higher education should be less stage-bound—learn context in one moment and do research in another—and more continuum-like—engage in research throughout one's intellectual career. In fact, one might argue that these projects collectively redefine education as intellectual career. If this observation is accurate, what else might we say about the continuum? Are there differences in types of questions, methods, or outcomes at different moments in the career? If so, are these differences more in kind or degree? If not, how so?

3. *Where is the best place to begin undergraduate research?* Is it in the first year? Is it in an introductory course in the major? Is it in the junior year? If it's in lower-division courses, what is the relationship of those efforts to efforts located in the discipline? And as important, if the lower division is where we should begin, shouldn't we expect to see a parallel set of models develop in community college contexts?

4. *How might undergraduate research be assessed?* As someone who worked in 2008 with two students on undergraduate research projects, of whom one is now completing an honors thesis that grew out of her program, I know firsthand how difficult it is to assess such projects. In my review of our collaboration, I lamented the fact that I couldn't tell if we'd completed the experience correctly. In this context, what does *correct* look like? Is the purpose to acquire assistance for my project? Is the purpose to provide an opportunity for student research independent of any project of mine? Is it some hybrid of these, perhaps a project paralleling one of mine? And whichever model we choose, what are the criteria? Can someone fail an undergraduate research experience? Somehow that seems a contradiction in terms, especially given the project descriptions in this volume, but I sense that failure is possible. More interesting to me is how we describe success and how we scaffold that into the curricular model.

5. *How are these efforts supported and built into the faculty model?* One question, of course, pertains to the institutional structures governing teaching assignments, release time, and rewards. How can we align these to support approaches that are systematic? And a related question: What is ideal capacity? Would we wish for every English major to experience some version of undergraduate research? A percentage of majors? What's the rationale for each? Another query has to do with sustainability when such projects are linked to a national program, and in this case, the Research Experiences for Undergraduates (REU) program sponsored by the

National Science Foundation is one we might want to examine. Its purpose is specific: to encourage undergraduates to think of themselves as researchers, which they do during special summer institutes that bring them together with accomplished faculty from a wide region; the students' goal is to complete a project that is disseminated. Another possibility is to create a hall specifically for undergraduate research in English studies inside the National Gallery of Writing (www.galleryofwriting.org) sponsored by the National Council of Teachers of English (NCTE). There, undergraduate research could be archived for current researchers and used by future scholars. If we could create a model like this, what impact might it have on undergraduate English studies programs?

6. *How might we document the efficacy of these efforts for students?* Thus far, given the nascent quality of undergraduate research in English studies, we have limited results. But more generally and more systematically, as these projects move from pilots to regular extracurricular parts of the curriculum, what are the results? Do students graduate at a higher rate? Do they go on to graduate school at a higher rate? What might they tell us five years after graduating from college about the contribution these projects made to their lives, their professions, their sense of self?

7. *And in a parallel move, we need to consider, how might we conduct our own research on the efficacy of this new intellectual and educational endeavor for faculty?* It would be good to know, for example, what difference it makes, or doesn't, when a faculty member chooses to engage in such projects over a period of years. Would the projects change? How might the development of individual projects change course or approach? Would we see more collaborative authorship?

Undergraduate research in English studies offers all of us new ways of seeing, new ways of making knowledge, and new ways of sharing that knowledge. Because it is situated at the heart of what we do, it offers what few educational reforms do: the possibility of transformation.

Note

1. Wineburg also discusses the relationship of textbooks to students' epistemological understanding, noting that when given primary texts and textbooks as sources, undergraduates tend to defer to textbooks, believing that the most authoritative account resides there.

References

Bartholomae, David. 1985. Inventing the University. In *When a Writer Can't Write: Studies in Writer's Block and Other Composing-Process Problems*, ed. Mike Rose, 134–65. New York: Guilford Press.

Ding, Huiling. 2008. The Use of Cognitive and Social Apprenticeship to Teach a Disciplinary Genre: Initiation of Graduate Students into NIH Grant Writing. *Written Communication* 25 (1): 3–52.

Hakim, Toufic. 1998. Soft Assessment of Undergraduate Research: Reactions and Student Perspectives. *CUR Quarterly* 18 (4): 189–92.

Marra, Rose M., and Betsy Palmer. 2008. Epistemologies of the Sciences, Humanities, and Social Sciences: Liberal Arts Students' Perceptions. *Journal of General Education* 57 (2): 100–18.

Wineburg, Sam. 2001. *Historical Thinking and Other Unnatural Acts: Charting the Future of Teaching the Past.* Philadelphia: Temple University Press.

Index

Editors

Laurie Grobman is professor of English and women's studies at Pennsylvania State University, Berks. Her articles on undergraduate research include "Affirming the Independent Researcher Model: Undergraduate Research in the Humanities" in *Council on Undergraduate Research Quarterly* (*CURQ*) in 2007 and "The Student Scholar: (Re)Negotiating Authorship and Authority" in *College Composition and Communication* (CCC) in 2009. In 2003 Grobman co-founded *Young Scholars in Writing: Undergraduate Research in Writing and Rhetoric*, a peer-reviewed international journal for undergraduates, now in its seventh year. She has published two monographs and a coedited collection, which received the International Writing Centers Association Outstanding Scholarship in a Book award for 2005. Grobman's work has been published in several journals, including *College English*, *Profession*, *JAC*, *MELUS*, *College Literature*, and *Journal of Basic Writing*.

Joyce Kinkead, associate vice president for research and professor of English at Utah State University, is among the national leaders in undergraduate research. Although her edited volume *Valuing and Supporting Undergraduate Research* is written for a general university audience, "How Writing Programs Support Undergraduate Research," in *Developing and Supporting a Research-Supportive Curriculum,* addresses ways in which composition courses could provide a foundation for research-based learning. An essay in the forthcoming twenty-five-year retrospective on Stephen North's *The Making of Knowledge in Composition* (edited by Gebhardt and Massey) focuses on undergraduate research in the new writing studies major. Kinkead's publications include *The Center Will Hold: Critical Perspectives on Writing Center Scholarship*; *Writing Centers in Context*; *A Schoolmarm All My Life: Narratives from Early Utah*; and the four-volume *Houghton Mifflin English*. The undergraduate research program that she oversees has received acclaim for its commitment to access in undergraduate research for all students. Kinkead is a councilor in the Undergraduate Research Program Directors Division of the Council on Undergraduate Research (CUR).

Contributors

D. Heyward Brock has published in all the areas of his interest: the Renaissance, Ben Jonson, comparative drama, American literature, Australian/New Zealand short fiction, science and culture, and literature and medicine. He is also the author of an autofictional novel. A former dean in arts and sciences, Brock has taught at the University of Delaware for more than forty years and has been an exchange professor at the University of Essex in Colchester, UK. He regularly directs undergraduates in research projects in a variety of fields and in the university's nationally acclaimed McNair Scholars Program.

Christine F. Cooper-Rompato is assistant professor of English at Utah State University and coeditor of the *Journal of Medieval Religious Cultures*. Her specialties include medieval hagiography and fourteenth- and fifteenth-century English literature, and her articles have appeared in venues including *Studies in Philology* and the *Yearbook of English Studies*. She has a book forthcoming from Pennsylvania State University Press on the miracle of xenoglossia in later medieval religious literature. Cooper-Rompato directs the Medieval and Early Modern Studies program at Utah State, and she enjoys teaching a variety of classes including Chaucer, medieval drama, and medieval women's writings.

Cynthia Crimmins began her career teaching high school English, then tutored and taught college writing courses for fifteen years. She is currently director of the Learning Resource Center and Writing Center at York College of Pennsylvania, a position she has held for twelve years. As director, Crimmins developed a successful peer writing fellows program and has been instrumental in many community and college outreach programs. Crimmins presents regularly at the Conference on College Composition and Communication (CCCC) and The Mid-Atlantic Writing Centers Association (MAWCA) on composition and tutoring pedagogy, highlighting collaborations between writing programs and writing center initiatives. She has been published in the *Writing Lab Newletter* on that topic as well.

James M. Dean, professor of English and medieval studies, has taught at the University of Delaware since 1986. He is the author of *The World Grown Old in Later Medieval Literature*, coeditor of *The Idea of Medieval Literature*, and editor or coeditor of five student texts: two on Chaucer's poetry for New American Library, and three on Middle English writings for the Medieval Institute. Dean has published articles in *PMLA*, *ELH*, *Speculum*, *Philological Quarterly*, the *Chaucer Review*, and elsewhere. He has coauthored articles in scholarly journals with undergraduates.

Dominic DelliCarpini, associate professor of English, is the writing program administrator at York College of Pennsylvania, where he directs the first-year writing program and professional writing major. He also has served as an executive board member of the Council of Writing Program Administrators. His research focuses on the intersection of writing and civic engagement, concerns that inform his books *Composing a Life's Work* and *Conversations* (with Jack Selzer). Recent articles explore topics such as the effect of the growth of writing majors on college English departments, and the role of information literacy initiatives toward preparing active citizens. DelliCarpini has forthcoming book chapters on the often-neglected "middle sisters" of the rhetorical canons—style and memory—and on the role of academic research in developing a deliberative citizenry. He presents regularly at the Council of Writing Program Administrators (WPA) and the Conference on College Composition and Communication (CCCC), and at the National Council of Teachers of English (NCTE), the National Writing Project, and the Modern Language Association (MLA).

Douglas Downs is assistant professor of rhetoric and composition in the Department of English at Montana State University. His research centers on conceptions of writing: how writers' and teachers' understandings of writing influence their writing and teaching of writing. Currently Downs is launching research on ways that undergraduate research shapes students' conceptions of writing. He regularly mentors students on conference presentations (National Conferences on Undergraduate Research [NCUR], Conference on College Composition and Communication [CCCC], PCA/ACA) and serves as a faculty advising editor for *Young Scholars in Writing*, also coediting its first-year writing feature. He authored the CD-ROM tutorial *i-Cite* and is writing a textbook on inquiry-based writing. With Elizabeth Wardle, Downs is coauthoring a reader for writing-about-writing approaches to first-year composition.

David Elder is a doctoral candidate in rhetoric and composition at Texas Christian University. He published as an undergraduate in *Young Scholars in Writing* and now serves on the editorial board of the journal. He is a coeditor of *The Rhetoric of Saint Augustine of Hippo: De Doctrina Christiana and the Search for a Distinctly Christian Rhetoric*. David is trying to be a full-time father while writing his dissertation about the intersections between critical pedagogies and epideictic rhetoric. His teaching and research interests include first-year composition, popular culture, epideictic rhetoric, and war rhetoric and propaganda.

Marta Figlerowicz graduated with a BA in English and American literature and language from Harvard University. A native of Poland, she spent part of her childhood in Illinois and pursued her secondary education in a francophone program cosponsored by the French government. Her critical and creative work has appeared in *New Literary History*, *Prooftexts*, the *Harvard Advocate*, and the *Harvard Book Review*. Figlerowicz wrote an honors senior thesis on sound and vision in the novels of Thomas Hardy. She is currently a graduate student at UC Berkeley.

Christie Fox is honors program director and teaches in honors and the Department of English at Utah State University. Her book, *Breaking Forms: The Shift to Performance in Late Twentieth-Century Irish Drama*, was recently published. She is coediting a collection of essays investigating the intersection of sports and performance. She teaches and researches dramatic literature, Irish studies, and issues facing honors education.

Scarlet Fronk is an undergraduate at Utah State University majoring in creative writing. Her interests in writing encompass fiction, poetry, creative nonfiction, and playwriting.

Evelyn Funda is associate professor of American studies at Utah State University, where she specializes in western American literature, especially literature written by women from a rural background. Funda has published numerous works on Willa Cather (including essays in *Western American Literature, Narrative,* and *Religion and Literature*, and a monograph on Cather's *The Song of the Lark*). She also has published a critical biography of Montana memoirist Mary Clearman Blew, and several creative nonfiction essays about her own family's history in agriculture in such journals as *Prairie Schooner* and *ISLE: Interdisciplinary Studies in Literature and Environment*.

Laura Gray-Rosendale is professor of English at Northern Arizona University (NAU) and recipient of the President's Distinguished Teaching Fellow Award. She specializes in rhetoric and composition, visual literacies, discourses of autobiography, and cultural studies. For twelve years Gray-Rosendale has been director of NAU's Multicultural Summer Writing Program for S.T.A.R. (Successful

Transition and Academic Retention). In addition, she served as chair of the NAU President's Commission on the Status of Women. Gray-Rosendale has published more than forty articles and book chapters. In addition, she has authored books including *Rethinking Basic Writing*, *Alternative Rhetorics*, *Fractured Feminisms*, *Radical Relevance*, and *Pop Perspectives*. Her current research centers on rhetoric and creative nonfiction.

Jane Greer is associate professor of English and Women's & Gender Studies at the University of Missouri, Kansas City, where she teaches courses on the literacy practices and rhetorical performances of girls and women, as well as composition classes. Her research on the history of rhetorical education has been published in *College Composition and Communication* (CCCC), *College English*, and numerous edited collections. Greer is the editor of *Girls and Literacy in America: Historical Perspectives to the Present*, and she is currently serving as guest editor for *Young Scholars in Writing: Undergraduate Research in Writing and Rhetoric*.

Matthew Henningsen earned his BA in English from the University of Denver in 2008. He is a graduate student at Clark University in Worcester, Massachusetts, and the recipient of a teaching assistantship in the Department of English.

Ted Hovet is professor of English and directs the interdisciplinary minor in film studies at Western Kentucky University. He has been the principal organizer of the English department's Undergraduate Conference on Literature, Language, and Culture since 2001. His publications include "The Teacher as Exhibitor: Pedagogical Lessons from Early Film Exhibition," in *Pedagogy: Critical Approaches to Teaching Literature, Language, Composition, and Culture*.

McKay Jenkins is Cornelius A. Tilghman Professor of English at the University of Delaware. He is a journalist, nonfiction writer, and scholar of American studies, specializing in environmental studies and the history, journalism, and literature of race relations and social justice. He has a BA in English from Amherst College (1985), a master's in journalism from Columbia University (1987), and a PhD in English from Princeton (1996). A former staff writer for the *Atlanta Constitution*, Jenkins is the author of *The South in Black and White: Race, Sex, and Literature in the 1940s*; *The White Death: Tragedy and Heroism in an Avalanche Zone*; *The Last Ridge: The Epic Story of the U.S. Army's 10th Mountain Division and the Assault on Hitler's Europe*; and *Bloody Falls of the Coppermine: Madness, Murder, and the Collision of Cultures in the Arctic, 1913*. He is also the editor of the *Peter Matthiessen Reader*, and is currently at work on a book about toxic chemicals. Jenkins teaches classes in nonfiction writing, nature writing, the journalism of genocide, the journalism of terrorism, and twentieth-century American literature.

Kevin Kerrane, professor of English at the University of Delaware, teaches courses in journalism, film studies, drama, and Irish literature. He is coeditor, with Ben Yagoda, of *The Art of Fact: A Historical Anthology of Literary Journalism*, and author of the award-winning book *Dollar Sign on the Muscle: The World of Baseball Scouting*. Kerrane's articles have appeared in *Sports Illustrated*, *Irish Studies Review*, and the online magazine *Salon*.

Matthew Kinservik has taught at the University of Delaware since 1997. He teaches courses in literature and theater, with emphasis on eighteenth-century Britain. His most recent book, *Sex, Scandal, and Celebrity in Late Eighteenth-Century England*, was published by Palgrave MacMillan in 2007. Kinservik has published articles on drama, literature, and theater history in journals including *Theatre Survey*, *British Journal of Eighteenth-Century Studies*, *Huntington Library Quarterly*, and *Harvard Library Bulletin*, and in the ProQuest database. He is currently director of graduate studies in the Department of English.

Amanda Marinello earned a BS from Utah State University in 2007. Her undergraduate honors thesis explored the genre of Victorian confession albums. She has presented at the 2007 National Conferences on Undergraduate Research (NCUR).

Brian J. McNely is currently assistant professor of English, rhetoric, and composition at Ball State University, and a fellow with the Center for Media Design. His recent dissertation, *Un/Commonplaces: Redirecting Research and Curricula in Rhetoric and Writing Studies*, situates undergraduate research and the development of the undergraduate major in rhetoric, writing studies, and professional and technical communication as central to the future disciplinary identity and viability of English studies. In concert with this focus on undergraduate research, NcNely's work explores writing on small-screen devices and rhetorics of social and ubiquitous computing platforms.

Christopher Penna is associate professor of English and composition at the University of Delaware. He has a BA from West Chester University, an AM from Syracuse University, and a PhD from the University of Delaware. His areas of interest include modern poetry and twentieth-century literature, the intersection of literature and composition, and technology-enhanced instruction. Penna has written about Seamus Heaney, Michael Longley, and other contemporary poets. Recently he has received grants to develop hybrid approaches to teaching composition that incorporate technology with traditional face-to-face instruction, and he has presented his findings at several conferences. Penna currently teaches courses in composition, survey courses in British and American literature, and Shakespeare. In addition to classroom teaching, he teaches both composition and literature courses online to distance-education students.

Jaqueline McLeod Rogers is associate professor in the Department of Writing, Rhetoric and Communication at the University of Winnipeg, an institution specializing in teaching undergraduate students and that has recently developed a writing major. She is fascinated by the origins and implications of narrative research, and currently considering—in her teaching, writing and research—how it is connected to the popular genre of creative nonfiction and to the art of fiction.

Joonna Smitherman Trapp is associate professor of English and chair of English and foreign language at Waynesburg University in Pennsylvania. She is editor of the *Journal of the Assembly for Expanded Perspectives on Learning* (*JAEPL*). Trapp has published her nonfiction in *New Texas* and *JAEPL*, and has book chapters and articles in publications such as *Dialogue: A Journal for Writing Specialists* and *Journal of Advanced Composition*. For the last decade, she has been at work recovering popular oratory on the lyceum circuit in the antebellum South. Trapp teaches courses in spiritual writing, debate, persuasion, Gothic literature, film studies, and rhetorical history.

Deaver Traywick earned an MFA in creative writing at the University of South Carolina. He currently lives in Spearfish, South Dakota, where he directs the writing center and teaches English at Black Hills State University. In addition to short fiction and writing center studies, his interests include long-distance walking and cotton farming.

Elizabeth Wardle is associate professor and director of writing programs at the University of Central Florida in Orlando, Florida. She has published in journals including *College Composition and Communication* (*CCC*), *Technical Communication Quarterly*, *Enculturation*, and *Across the Disciplines*. Wardle recently completed a four-year longitudinal study of writing-related knowledge transfer; and with Douglas Downs, she is co-writing a textbook for teaching composition as a writing-about-writing class.

Margaret Earley Whitt retired from the University of Denver in 2008, where she was professor of English. She has published books on Flannery O'Connor and Gloria Naylor. Most recently, Whitt's books include a composition textbook, *The Civil Mind*, and an edited collection of stories, *Short Stories of the Civil Rights Movement*. She now lives in western North Carolina, where she is at work on a collection of coming-of-age short stories.

Kathleen Blake Yancey, Kellogg W. Hunt Professor of English at Florida State University (FSU), directs the FSU graduate program in rhetoric and composition. Immediate past president of the National Council of Teachers of English (NCTE), she has served as president of the Council of Writing Program Administrators and as chair of the Conference on College Composition and Communication (CCCC). Yancey also co-founded and co-directs the International Coalition on Electronic Portfolio Research. Author of more than sixty chapters and refereed articles, Yancey has written, edited, or coedited eleven scholarly books, including the award-winning *Delivering College Composition: The Fifth Canon*. Co-founder and coeditor of the journal *Assessing Writing* (1994–2001), she is the editor of *College Composition and Communication* (CCC).

This book was typeset in Sabon by Barbara Frazier.
The typefaces used on the cover are Neuzeit Grotesk Bold Condensed and Versailles Roman and Black.
The book was printed on 50-lb. Williamsburg Offset paper by Versa Press, Inc.